AF529177

Election Politics in Assam: Issues, Trends and People's Mandate

Election Politics in Assam: Issues, Trends and People's Mandate

ABU NASAR SAIED AHMED
JOYDEEP BARUAH
RATNA BHUYAN

AKANSHA PUBLISHING HOUSE
NEW DELHI-110002

AKANSHA PUBLISHING HOUSE
4649-B/21, Ansari Road
Darya Ganj, New Delhi - 110 002
Email: ektabooks@yahoo.com
Ph.: 23263193/9811582579
Fax: 011-23263193

Election Politics in Assam: Issues, Trends and People's Mandate

© Authors

First Published 2006
ISBN 81-8370-057-8

All rights reserved. No part of this publication may be reproduced or transmitted, in any form or by any means, without prior permission of the authors. Any person who does any unauthorized act in relation to this publication may be liable to criminal prosecution and civil claims for damages.

[The responsibility for the facts stated, conclusions reached etc., is entirely that of the Authors. The publisher is not responsible for them, whatsoever.]

PRINTED IN INDIA

Published by M.P. Misra for Akansha Publishing House, New Delhi and Printed at Tarun Offset Press, Delhi

To

L. C. JAIN

The First Chairman of the Institute

A friend, philosopher and guide . . .

Preface

The present book is the product of a study sponsored by the Indian Council of Social Science Research (ICSSR), New Delhi. There has been a great deal of studies on elections in India essentially covering the voting pattern and behaviour. However, the Institute felt that there has been a vacuum in the study of election as only a few attempts have been made to cover the socio-economic and political setting under which elections generally take place in India. In the case of Assam, except a few unpublished doctoral theses, no major study has been so far done covering the aforementioned environment. It is also felt that to understand the complex matrix of election politics, one needs to examine the various societal contours which lay impact on the final act of elections. Further, a study conducted on the basis of random opinion on a few hundred voters is least likely to project a vivid picture of election politics. The present attempt, therefore, is a deviation from the traditional approach to election study.

The Institute owes its gratitude to the ICSSR for funding the present study, without which it would not have been possible to accomplish this arduous task. The authors gratefully acknowledge the help and cooperation of Dr. Namita Dutta Baruah of North Lakhimpur College and Ms. Sewali Kurmi, a Ph.D Research Fellow at Dibrugarh University. They also appreciate Mr. M.P. Misra of Akansha Publication for promptly bringing out this volume and making it available to the readers.

Authors

CONTENTS

List of Tables

Abbreviations

Party Type	Abbreviation	Party
National Parties		
	1. BJP	Bharatiya Janata Party
	2. CPI	Communist Party of India
	3. CPM	Communist Party of India (Marxist)
	4. ICS	Indian Congress (Socialist)
	5. INC	Indian National Congress
	6. JNP	Janata Party
	7. LKD	Lok Dal
	8. AICC (T)	All India Indira Congress (Tiwari)
	9. JD	Janata Dal
	10. SAP	Samata Party
	11. ICS (SCS)	Indian Congress Socialist (Sarat Chandra Sinha)
	12. NCP	National Congress Party
State Parties		
	1. PTC/PTCA	Plains Tribal Council of Assam

(Contd...)

Party Type	Abbreviation	Party
	2. RSP	Revolutionary Socialist Party
	3. AGP	Asom Gana Parishad
	4. ASDC	Autonomous State Demand Committee
	5. NAGP	Natun Asom Gana Parishad
	6. FBL	All India Forward Block
	7. AITC	All India Trinamool Congress
	8. ASDC (P)	Autonomous State Demand Committee (Progressive)
	9. ASDC (U)	Autonomous State Demand Committee (United)
	10. JD (S)	Janata Dal (Secular)
	11. JD (U)	Janata Dal (United)
Registered (Unrecognised) Parties		
	1. AMB	Amra Bangalee
	2. CPI (ML)	Communist Party of India (Marxist-Lennist)
	3. ICS	Indian Congress (Socialist)
	4. RCPI (R)/RCI	Revolutionary Communist Party of India (Rasik Bhatt)

(Contd...)

Party Type	Abbreviation	Party
	5. SHS	Shivsena
	6. SP	Samajwadi Party
	7. UMFA	United Minorities Front, Assam
	8. URMCA	United Reservation Movement Council of Assam
	9. ADC	Autonomous State Demand Committee
	10. AJD	Asom Jatiyatabadi Dal
	11. AJP	Asom Jatiya Parishad
	12. DDP	DoorDasthi Party
	13. GGS	Ganatantric Gana Sammelan
	14. IPF	Indian Peoples Front
	15. RCPI	Real Communist Party of India
	16. SLP	Sanjukta Loka Parishad
	17. UPCA	United Peoples Congress of Assam
	18. IGL	All India Gorkha League
	19. SUCI	Socialist Unity Centre of India
Independents		
	1. IND	Independent

A few more abbreviations

NA - Data not available	**NE** - Does not exist	**N** - National Party
NC - Not contested	**UC** – Uncontested	**S** - State Party

FD - Forfeited Deposits

CHAPTER 1
The Environment

I
THE POLITICAL SCENARIO

Introduction

In a discourse on the democratic theory focusing on the centrality of its subsistence, elections figure prominently. The reason is simple. Viewed from the perspective of social contract theory as propounded by John Locke, elections set the conditions of the social contract between the political sovereign (the people), and the rulers. The contract stands on a rational basis as the people who go to cast vote on the day of elections have with them the rational basis for casting vote in favour of a candidate or a party. Although the rationality paradigm may not be always drawn on the line of what John Stuart Mill has prescribed[1], educated voters too sometimes behave irrationally[2]. Rather illiterates

[1] John Stuart Mill writes that it is wholly inadmissible that an illiterate person, who has no rational thinking capacity, could participate in elections. See his *Considerations on Representative Government* (Chicago: Henry Regnery Company, 1962), p. 170.

[2] There are strong views against the conservative perception of Mill which holds that despite lack of information, lack of knowledge and interests in public life, the electorate can demonstrate rational thinking while casting vote on the day of election. See David Apter (ed), *Ideology and Discontent* (New York: Free Press, 1964) and Angus Campbell *et.al.*, *Elections and the Political Order* (New York: John Wiley and Sons, 1968).

sometimes act more rationally than the elites. At any rate, the elections, for their decisive role in the formation of government play the most politically charged part of the democratic process in a country.

Elections in India have always been the cornerstone of the political system of the country. Each election, whether parliamentary or assembly, stands unique because of the shifting political climate of the country or the states where the Assembly elections are to be held. Accordingly, the attention, involvement and choice of the individual voters tend to change[3]. There are transitional issues which some times overtake perennial and national issues, and thus, transcend regional issues. At the same time, there are regional issues which spread wings across regional boundaries. There are occasions, as in the case of 1977 Lok Sabha election[4], when one single issue dominates the entire election scenario. It becomes quite interesting to see how social forces play their roles differently at different times. The people who rejected Indira Gandhi in 1977 Lok Sabha poll brought her back to power in less than three years time.

In the context of varied and experiment-hungry Indian pattern, the 2004 Lok Sabha poll became academically interesting. The Bharatiya Janata Party (BJP) led National

[3] This is a universally acknowledged phenomena which makes elections so interesting and worth noticing. Almost half a century back what two American scholars, Herbert McClosky and Harold Dahlgren, asserted still holds valid. See their article "Primary Group Influence on Party Loyalty", *American Political Science Review*, 53 (1959), pp. 757-76.

[4] It was internal emergency clamped in June 1975 by the Union Government headed by Mrs. Indira Gandhi which became the main election issue of 1977 Lok Sabha Poll. All the opposition parties rallied under the banner of anti-emergency forces. The Congress Party was defeated in the election. Democracy returned with triumph. The Janata Party comprising four different parties formed the Government headed by Moraji Desai. It is also a matter of history that it did not take time to get the euphoria of instant victory evaporated. For details of this significant election see Myron Weiner, *India at the Polls: The Parliamentary Elections of 1977* (Washington: American Enterprise Institute, 1978).

Democratic Alliance (NDA), which was in power at the Centre for six continuous years, decided to go for early election with the expectation that it would sweep the 14th Lok Sabha poll. Their assessment of the situation was based an erroneous speculation of outright victory caused by a sense of jubilation aftermath of the Assembly elections held in five states in which it performed magnificently, even beyond their expectation. It captured power in three states, Madhya Pradesh, Rajasthan and Jharkhand. The outcome of the elections propelled the NDA to prepone the Lok Sabha elections assuming that the political climate was favourable for an early poll and the results would definitely be in its favour.

The 14th Lok Sabha poll was unique in a number of ways. It was time to assess the performance of the six year rule of the NDA and test the efficacy of the 'feel good factor' and 'India shinning' slogan. As Norman D. Palmer argues that during an election a political system is on display[5]. Therefore, arguably the Lok Sabha poll did offer an opportunity to put the political system in the country on display. Further, elections have been conceived as the end product of a political process determined by the political environment which includes party system, voters' political information, awareness and participation that establish the linkage between the citizens and the polity. While Norman D. Palmar considers elections as a dependent variable[6], James N. Rosenau, however, writes more eloquently about the role of multi-faceted variables:

> An election...might be viewed as an independent variable in a model explaining the strength of political parties, as an intervening variable in a hypothesis anticipating the nature of public

---

[5] Norman D. Palmer, *Election and Political Development: The South Asian Experience* (New Delhi: Vikas, 1976), p. 1.

[6] *Idem.*

> policies and as a dependent variable in a position predicting the consequences of political campaign. In a feedback model, moreover, the same attribute, attitude or behavior might be conceived to operate simultaneously as all three types of variables[7].

Rosenau's understanding of elections inspires one to find the drama and thrill in elections, which could be studied. In a methodical study taking aggregate data, it is possible to focus on the complicated political process that includes the totality of socio-economic and political environment of a country. That is why the present study has incorporated the socio-political climate of Assam in which the 14th Lok Sabha poll was held, the process of nomination, the campaign, the issues on which the elections had been fought, the role of mass media, and finally the voting behaviour in order to present the totality of the environment under which the last parliamentary elections were held in the State.

The result of the 14th Lok Sabha poll in the State was almost predictable. Its apparent predictability can be understood when one takes stock of the political scenario of the State for the last couple of years preceding the election.

The Political Scene

The results of the 1998 and 1999 Lok Sabha polls and the Assembly election of 2001 indicated the trend to be set once again in the 2004 election. Although the Congress lost the 1996 Assembly election, managing to capture only 34 out of 126 Assembly seats and the Asom Gana Parishad (AGP) returned to power for the second time with 59 seats, it did not take time to turn the table diagonally. The ruling AGP drew a blank in 1998 and 1999 Lok Sabha polls with the Congress capturing 10 out of 14 seats in both the elections (Table 1.1).

---

[7] James N. Rosenau, *The Dramas of Politics* (Boston: Little, Brown, 1973), p. 171.

Table 1.1
Results of Lok Sabha Polls in Assam (1998 & 1999)

Party	Seats Won (1998)	Seats Won (1999)
INC	10	10
BJP	1	2
CPI (ML)	-	1
AGP	-	-
ASDC	1	-
UMFA	1	-
IND	1	1
TOTAL	14	14

Source: www.eci.gov.in

The Congress staged a resurrection and came back to power in the State in the 2001 Assembly election. Table 1.2 shows the trend of this election.

Table 1.2
Percentage of Votes Polled by the Leading Parties in Assam

Parties	1998 Lok Sabha Poll	1999 Lok Sabha Poll	2001 Assembly Poll
AGP	12.7	11.92	20.02
BJP	24.47	29.84	9.35
Congress	38.97	38.42	39.75
Left Parties	1.46	1.53	1.02

Source: www.eci.gov.in

The trend undoubtedly confirms that the Congress would sustain its consolidation. The Congress having had a solid rural base in the State could not be totally wiped out even in its worst times of 1977 and 1985. It was defeated in the 1996 election mainly due to the sudden vacuum created by the death of Hiteswar Saikia, the then Chief Minister of Assam, only a few weeks before the election. The party, therefore, did not take time to get the scenario changed soon after the 1996 elections.

The BJP although made notable inroads in these elections, it was yet to emerge as a force to be counted in the formation of the State government. The party was yet to find enough space to even share power in the State where the social set up is not communally divided and where the Muslims constitute a significant factor by virtue of their demographic composition, constituting 30 per cent of the total population. The AGP, on the other hand, did not have a secured base, not even among the Assamese middle class[8]. The outcome of the State Assembly election of 2001 hence was an unassailable indicator to forecast the result of the 2004 parliamentary election, because even in an adverse situation in 2001, when both Dispur and Delhi were under anti-Congress rule, the Congress scored an emphatic victory capturing 65 seats.

The Congress Government in Assam soon after taking the reins of power held the elections for the panchayat bodies which had been withheld by the AGP Government since 1997. In the Panchayat elections too, held in December 2001, the Congress backed candidates captured about 80 per cent of the seats[9]. It, therefore, became even more difficult for other political parties to face the Congress decisively in 2004.

[8] Sandhya Goswami, "Mixed Verdict", *Economic and Political Weekly*, Vol. xxxix, No. 51, December 18-24, 2004.

[9] Official results did not reveal the party affiliations of the winning candidates. However, the newspaper reports suggested that the Congress Party was in winning spree in the last Panchayat elections held in December 2001.

In this context and perspective, the Lok Sabha poll held in May 2004 covering the 14 parliamentary constituencies in Assam, turned out to be politically exciting. The formal announcement of the election on February 29, 2004 was not unexpected, because, soon after the Assembly elections of 2003 in five states, the NDA Government had sounded that the Lok Sabha poll would be advanced. It was rather a culmination of political speculation marking the beginning of a tense, action-packed period of electioneering and finally making the stage ready for the final act of the drama, the polling day. At any rate, the preparation for the 14th Lok Sabha poll had been geared up in Assam by all the leading parties. While the Congress decided to go alone without forging electoral understanding with any party, as it was confident of its strength, there were speculations about the possibility of other parties going for alliances. There were reports that the AGP would try for an electoral alliance with the BJP. At the time of Assembly poll in 2001, there was a loose alliance between them, for, in some prestigious constituencies, despite their alliance, both the parties fielded their candidates in the same constituency proving thereby that the alliance was too loose and fragile to work. Being confident of their own strength, both the parties ultimately abandoned the idea of an alliance. Other parties too tried for alternative alliances. P.A. Sangma[10] took the initiative to build an anti-Congress platform and organised a conclave of small like-minded parties like the Nationalist Congress Party (NCP). The effort fizzled out, as various components could not work united under one umbrella. Thus, even with

---

[10] P.A. Sangma has a long political background. A former Chief Minister of Meghalaya, Sangma has been representing the Tura constituency in Meghalaya in the Lok Sabha and also has been the Speaker of the Lok Sabha from 1996 to 1998. He resigned from the Congress along with Sarad Pawar in 1998 on the issue of foreign origin of Sonia Gandhi and since then has occupied a key position in the newly formed Nationalist Congress Party (NCP). However, he snapped his relations with the party and joined the Trinamool Congress, from which he again has resigned recently.

the atmosphere of polls looming large on the State, the old phrase "politics makes strange bed-fellows" failed yet once again in Assam.

In earlier occasions too the alliance building syndrome did not work. Prior to the Assembly election of 2001, the ruling Asom Gana Parishad (AGP) led coalition alliance in Assam showed clear signs of cracks and strained relationships[11]. Abdul Muhib Mazumdar, leader of the United People's Party of Assam (UPPA) and a then State Cabinet Minister, voiced his dissatisfaction with the AGP over some differences long time back. Similarly, the CPI (M), another key partner in the government, served a virtual ultimatum on the AGP seeking clarification of its relationship with the BJP.

Just before the Assembly election of 2001, the CPI (M), which was trying to come up steadfastly as a 'third front' of political alternative at the national level, had made it clear about its one-point agenda in the State for the coming poll. Defeating the BJP and Congress at all costs by putting up all necessary efforts in Assam became the sole aim of the party. With this aim, Prakash Karat, the CPI (M) leader, who was in Guwahati for addressing a State-level rally of the party, literally asked the AGP for clarifying its stand over BJP. As the party doubted AGP's tacit overtures with the BJP just before the poll, and also for its failure in solving popular grievances of the State's masses, it decided to review its relationship with the AGP. Added to it, Karat later reiterated that AGP's action of voting in favour of the BJP-led NDA government in the Rajya Sabha over the

[11] The signal of an imminent crack in the relationship of the ruling coalition members was seen right from the time the Asom Yuba Parishad (AYP) - a front organisation of AGP held its annual convention. In this rally none of the Left allies were formally invited while the highly placed office-bearers of Shiv Sena from Mumbai were given a red carpet welcome. It was imminent that the two left allies, the CPI and CPM would show their dissatisfaction. This crack only developed further without there being any check initiatives.

Ayodhya issue did not go very well with the CPI (M). He, therefore, called on the AGP to come out with a convincing justification for the action. Karat later told the press. "Besides, further continuation of the alliance with AGP will actually depend upon AGP's agreeing or not to our line of 'defeat BJP and Congress' agenda in a straightforward manner without leaving any scope for duplicity later on"[12].

Significantly enough, the CPI (M) salvo was fired just on the eve of the AGP's convention at Nagaon that began on January 29, 2001. This convention was expected to discuss in detail, issues like poll alliance, manifesto for polls and the general poll strategy, among others. The idea of having alliance with the Left parties thus disappeared in no time.

The issue of insurgency has remained a vitally important political plank for all parties. Insurgency has become a part of life in most of the states in Northeast India. It is more so in Assam, which has been experiencing the wrath of insurgency-related violence since 1979 when the United Liberation Front, Assam (ULFA) was formed[13]. During the subsequent period of two decades since the formation of the ULFA, many more ethno-centric insurgent groups emerged. The Bodos formed the National Democratic Front of Bodoland (NDFB) on October 3, 1986, another parallel militant outfit called the Bodo Liberation Tigers (BLT) was born on June18, 1996. A section of the Muslims formed their own outfit called the Muslim United Liberation Tiger Force of Assam (MULTA) in 1993. Later on, the ethnic tribes, the Karbis, the Dimasas, the Hmars and the Kukis formed their own militant groups. The inter-ethnic conflicts, together with the position taken by the insurgent groups against the State

---

[12] "Assam: The Pre- Poll Panorama", A Freelance Peace, *Vedanti: Burning Assam*, Back Issues, http//www.vedanti.com.

[13] Samir Kumar Das, *ULFA (United Liberation Front of Assam): A Political Analysis* (Delhi: Ajanta Publications, 1994). Also see B. Pakem (ed), *Insurgency in Northeast India* (New Delhi: Omson Publication, 1997) and Chandra Bhushan, *Terrorism and Separation in North-East India* (Delhi: Kalpaz, 2004).

and the Central government, made the political situation terribly unstable. There were speculations about which group would take the side of which political party. In earlier occasions in 1991 and 1996, the Assembly elections in the State and the Lok Sabha election in 1998 were held under the shadow of the militants' guns, as pointed out by Wasbir Hussain[14], so was the case in 2001. The spectre of fear and uncertainty loomed large even at the time of the 2004 electioneering.

While analysing the burning problem of insurgency in the State, it was found that the State government claimed that a total of 823 militants belonging to different groups have been killed during counter-insurgency operations between January 21, 1997 and December 31, 2000. Added to it the Government also claimed that 5,827 militants had surrendered to the authorities during the same period[15]. Moreover, the alleged unholy relationship between the politicians and militant organisations made the political situation extremely volatile and uncertain. As such, no headway could be made on political fronts to settle the vexed insurgency problem with mounting operations of the United Liberation Front of Assam (ULFA), the National Democratic Front of Bodoland (NDFB), the Bodo Liberation Tiger (BLT), the Muslim United Liberation Tiger Force of Assam (MULTA) and the United People's Democratic Solidarity[16] (UPDS). The casualty in terms of loss of life and permanently

---

[14] Wasbir Hussain, "Elections under the Shadow of the Gun", *Economic and Political Weekly,* Vol xxxvi, no 5 & 6, February 3-10, 2001. Also see Girin Phukon, "Assam Elections 1998: A Phase of Assamese Regionalism" in his edited volume *Political Dynamics of North East India: Essays in Honour of Professor Barrister Pakem* (New Delhi: South Asian Publishers, 2000) pp.156-164.

[15] But the fact remains that the rebels had killed as many as 1,548 people, including 333 security personnel in Assam between 1997-2000. Appeared in *Vedanti-Burning Assam,* Back Issues http//www.vedanti.com.

[16] *Ibid.* UPDS gunned down eight Hindi-speaking people in Karbi-Anglong Hill district, supposedly with the support of Pakistan's Inter Service Intelligence (ISI).

maimed in an insurgent ridden political situation in the State is shown in Table 1.3(A) and 1.3(B)

Table 1.3(A)
Insurgency Related Casualties (1991-2004)
(A Summary of Counter Insurgency Operations)

Year	Insurgents Killed	Security Personnel Killed	Civilians Killed
1991	12	21	163
1992	15	41	72
1993	29	23	54
1994	40	38	88
1995	21	66	125
1996	44	80	261
1997	136	89	237
1998	165	77	387
1999	196	87	179
2000	328	80	412
2001	307	86	261
2002	322	36	218
2003	276	15	260
2004	135	25	202
Total	2026	764	2911

Source: Police Records, Government of Assam

Table 1.3(B)
Fatalities in Insurgencies and Terrorist Conflicts in Assam (1992-2001)

Year	Category	Fatalities
1992	C	80
	SF	34
	M	19
1993	C	74
	SF	24
	M	33
1994	C	173
	SF	35
	M	63
1995	C	170
	SF	73
	M	27
1996	C	302
	SF	87
	M	62
1997	C	285
	SF	85
	M	167
1998	C	531
	SF	72
	M	180
1999	C	214
	SF	77
	M	212
2000	C	366
	SF	65
	M	327
2001	C	264
	SF	59
	M	283
Total	C	2459
	SF	611
	M	1373
State Cummulative Total		4443

Source: "Survey of *Conflicts & Resolution* in India's Northeast", Ajai Sahni Faultlines: Writings on Volume 12. New Delhi: Bulwark Books May

Note: Cumulative Total (All Categories): M: Militants; SF: Security Force Personnel; C: Civilians

It is not out of context to mention that in the recent times there has been symptoms of graduated reduction of violence in the Bodo dominated areas of Assam after the Bodo Accord was signed in 2004[17], facilitating the formation of Bodoland Territorial Council (BTC) and holding the elections to form the elected Council in May 2005. But the gun factor yielded by the active insurgents, it is feared, will continue to play a dangerous role threatening the democratic process in the State for an indefinite period of time.

The Issues

It is only certain that the issues taken up by political parties just before the polls are something ornamental. In Assam some of the issues such as flood, insurgency and influx of foreign nationals, have always remained ornamental as parties take up these issues at the time of elections to be forgotten soon after the polling day. It remains only to be seen how the voters actually react to the political banter, which begins in right earnest. The politicians at times promise even the impossible to be fulfilled in about a month's time. The whole gamut of promises on the part of the party candidates are so weaved which can easily hoodwink the masses once again for another period of five years.

With 1.5 crore people enrolled in the updated voters' list out of a total population of 2.2 crores in the State, the parties before the 2001 Assembly election unfolded a red carpet of promises to woo the voters.

---

[17]In 1993, an accord was reached between the Bodos, and, the Central and State governments. The accord established the Bodoland Autonomous Council, which gave the Bodos limited political and administrative autonomy. This, however, could not root out the problem completely. Violence once again broke out in 1994. Members of the Bodo Security Force, in the wake of demands for a "liberated Bodoland" took to mass killings. Both local counterinsurgency forces and army units were sent in to engage the Bodo militants. The movement continued and was at its peak during the AGP's rule. Cleansing of the non-Bodo communities allegedly by the Bodo militants, through plunder, arson, massacre and persecution became the order of the day during the AGP tenure of 1996-2000. A large number of the non-Bodos were forced to take shelter in the relief camps in the BTC areas.

- In the poll plank, the parties promised to the population yet again to end insurgency and bring back peace.
- To usher in economic growth reducing unemployment was yet another promise.
- Flood control and better flood damage management seemed to be another area of concern for the parties. This was one of the popular issues taken up by the different political parties prior to the elections in the State.
- The parties also seemed eager to fulfill the promise of lifting of ban on State government jobs, appointments, etc.

However, a vital issue like the Illegal Migrants (Determination by Tribunals) (Act) [IMDT Act] passed by the Parliament in 1983 was left out. This was one of the key issues on which a candidate or party could see the light of a win or to that extent even lose the elections in the State. However, not to mention the repeal of the IMDT Act, the ruling party, AGP[18] declared only 219 persons in the State to be illegal migrants from January 1, 2000 to November 30, 2000. Out of these 219 persons detected, only 111 were served expulsion orders. Further, the irony was that out of these 111 persons, only 11 were actually expelled. It is rightly argued that not a single political party would like to raise the issue of scrapping the controversial Act because of the fear of losing the immigrant Muslim votes.

The common mass in the State was rather disenchanted. The AGP led government had failed miserably in the State.

[18] The AGP came about in 1985 with the very promise of freeing the state of the illegal Bangladeshi immigrants and scrapping the IMDT Act. That the same AGP even after being in power for almost two terms in the State has failed to fulfill its promise is another matter. The BJP too has been always vocal with the demand of reverting the IMDT. But it did not initiate any step to do so during its rule at the Centre for six years. Only recently on July 12, 2005 the Supreme Court in a historic judgment declared it as unconstitutional and thus void. For some details on IMDT, see Indrani Barpujari, "Illegal Migrants (Determination by Tribunals) Act and Assam–Promulgation and Repeal: A Contextual Analysis" (New Delhi: Akansha, Forthcoming).

Insurgency reached new heights. This only kept the potential investors away from the State. Almost all the development works in the State had been at a halt following the financial mismanagement of the State treasury[19]. Failure to pump in funds left the most sought after Gas Cracker project in the State in jeopardy. A severe fund crunch that almost stifled the development works in the State kept its economy within the confines of stagnation. Added to it, the unemployment figure rose to more than 16 lakhs in the State. All sorts of recruitments were stopped officially. Of course, the Government of Assam did come out with a draft paper on employment scheme on the eve of polls. The draft paper quoted:

> Live registers of employment exchange had 12.39 lakh job seekers in 1995, which increased to 14.96 lakh in 1997, 16.19 lakh in 1998 and 16.35 lakh in 1999. This indicates a growth of 31.96 per cent from 1995 to 1999. There is a strong tendency for the educated unemployed to seek government jobs. But the government sector itself has reached a saturation point. To arrest this situation some thrust areas has been identified for providing self-employment to the unemployed persons in the coming two years, i.e., the remaining period of the Ninth Five Year Plan (2000-2002). The areas are agriculture, fisheries, rural development industries and commerce, handloom and textile, sericulture, khadi and village industries, tourism, transport and public distribution system.

---

[19] Persisting fiscal deficits had emerged as one of the most significant weaknesses of the state economy, with public sector borrowing crowding out the private sector borrowing and thereby, increasing macroeconomic risks. The fiscal deficit in 1999-2000 of the State stood alarmingly high at 9.90 per cent. While net central loans contributed 0.89 per cent to cover the deficit, the market borrowings for the same stood at 1.39 per cent.

However, the State government failed to implement the draft plan. These factors laid an impact on the voters' choice. They at best preferred to choose the Congress party rather than a disunited and incompetent AGP, the regional party which was given two chances to rule the State. While Bhrigu Kumar Phukan, who once happened to be the Home Minister, and second in the power position in the AGP ruling echelon, left the party and joined the NCP. A few stalwarts named Atul Bora, the Minister for Public Works Department, Pulakesh Baruah, the former Speaker formed a new party called Trinamool Gana Parishad. The clash of personality between Prafulla Kumar Mahanta and Brindaban Goswami already surfaced prominently. The AGP turned out to be a divided house. Further, the AGP's share in coalition politics at the Centre was too small to be counted. This left the voters with a limited or to that extent even a negative choice and to elect the Congress to power.

The unrest among the tea-garden labourers in the State heightened. Their pathetic economic condition and the failure on the part of the government and the tea-garden owners to solve the long standing demands of the labour community for regular payment of wages and bonus led to a volatile burst of anger in many tea gardens of upper Assam. This, however, remained unresolved. This was one issue that the State government failed to bring to solution.

Rampant corruption ruled the State secretariat[20]. Tara Pada Das, the Chairman of the Assam Public Service Commission (APSC) was charged with mass corruption. Das did not resign from his office despite the fact that valuables, illegal assets and cash worth several lakhs were recovered from his residence. The AGP government did not initiate

[20] The then Chief Minister Mr. Prafulla Kumar Mahanta was himself not above corruption. The 'LOC' scandal associated with him was not over. Moreover, the faction ridden State government failed to come to grips with rampant corruption in its various departments. See *Vedanti-Burning Assam*, Various Issues.

any legal prosecution and the Income Tax Department too took excruciatingly long time in completing the investigation. This created the impression that Das would get a free go[21]. There was also dissatisfaction among the State government employees because of irregularities in payment of salaries. The State had to grapple under severe financial crunch. All these culminated into mass dissatisfaction with the ruling Asom Gana Parishad. The deteriorating and almost dying Assam State Transport Corporation (ASTC) was a case in point. The then ruling party failed to support and revive the dying ASTC. This created a sense of despair among the ASTC workers and the organisation was almost on the verge of closing down, laying at stake the lives of those involved with the organisation[22]. This only added to the woes of the AGP, the ruling party. The teaching community in the government schools was the most severe victims of the government's failure in payment of regular salaries[23]. With these flaws in AGP[24], the Congress once again appeared to be on a comeback trail when it won 10 of the 14 Lok Sabha seats in the 1999 poll. The AGP, despite being the ruling party drew a blank. This background not only had an enduring impact on the political scenario of the State till the 2001 Assembly election

---

[21] This incident made it more evident that the government does not exercise sufficient care while appointing an officer for a prestigious post whose probity is not beyond doubt.

[22] The ASTC employees went on a hunger strike for a month during the AGP tenure on non-payment of their salaries for nine months.

[23] A large number of the teachers could get their salaries for a month after a gap of three months period. In some cases, salaries remained unpaid for six months or more. Under the events, the AGP led coalition Government's monthly tug-of-war with the Reserve Bank of India at Guwahati for lifting the ban on taking overdrafts to meet the salary component of the State government employees every month spoke volume of the State's financial position.

[24] After ruling for five years, what the Mahanta Government achieved was a chronic financial crisis with no signs of improvement. Whatever little was done did not get recognition as unaccomplished promises and tasks weighed heavily against the little done. Consequently, almost all constituencies reeled in backwardness in the State.

but also went on to decide the outcome of the Lok Sabha poll held in 2004.

In the Lok Sabha poll of 2004, three major players were in the fray- the Asom Gana Parishad (AGP), the Congress and the Bharatiya Janata Party (BJP). As in the case of the rest of the country, a general impression was created by the media in the State that the NDA might be able to come back to power yet once again at the Centre. With Assam having only 14 seats in the Lok Sabha, it was felt tat if the AGP could improve its performance by capturing at least one or two seats it could have a role to play in the formation of the next NDA government. While even if the Congress retained its earlier position it would not have an impact if the NDA returned to power this time too. However, in democracy the number game matters, and it is more so in the era of coalition politics, in which each individual member, including the Independents matter. Further, where each individual candidate as well as each party would not like to be a loser, the election fever was destined to be strong.

II
THE ECONOMIC SCENARIO

Endowed with rich natural resources, the State once accounted for higher per-capita income than the all-India level in the early 1950s. However, since then the State has continuously slipped down in the process of economic growth compared to not only the all-India level, but to the other states in the country as well, including the states of Northeast[25]. Along with the other reasons, this slow growth in the economy also has been attributed to - (a) the two wars of 1962 and 1971 in the eastern front, and (b) influx of population (Table 1.4), mainly the large scale migration of people from erstwhile East Pakistan both immediately after

[25] Mohan Guruswamy, *Left Behind: A Case Study of Assam* (New Delhi: Centre for Policy Alternatives [CPA], 2005).

independence and after the creation of Bangladesh, while in the later decades – especially, the seventies and eighties, the growth process of the State was adversely affected by the socio-political movements in the State.

Table 1.4
Population Variation in India and Assam

Years	Assam	India
1901-11	16.99	5.75
1911-21	20.48	-0.31
1921-31	19.91	11.00
1931-41	20.41	14.22
1941-51	19.93	13.31
1951-61	***34.98***	***21.51***
1961-71	***34.95***	***24.80***
1971-81	23.36	24.69
1981-91	24.24	23.82
1991-01	18.85	21.34

Source: Census of India, Various Years

Inter alia, as there is an inter-relationship between the social and political factors on one hand, and the economic factors on the other, it was but natural that the State's economy suffered the most amidst the tensed socio-political environment.

Though, Assam had a lower incidence of poverty at 51 per cent in 1973-74 compared to the national average of 55 per cent, the fall in the poverty ratio since then has been slower in the State compared to the all-India level. Post reforms, 1991, the poverty scenario has not changed much. The State has been successful in reducing the extent of poverty only by about 5 per cent between 1993-1994 and 1999-2000 (to 41 per cent) as against about 10 per cent for the country as a whole (to 36 per cent) (Table 1.5). Despite the decline, its relative ranking among the major states in the country has dropped from 6 to 12[26], and compounded by the large-scale migration, this has aggravated the problem of unemployment as well.

Table 1.5
Percentage of Population Below Poverty Line (Official Estimates)

	Assam			All-India		
Years	**Rural**	**Urban**	**Total**	**Rural**	**Urban**	**Total**
1973-74	52.67	36.92	51.21	56.44	49.01	**54.88**
1993-94	45.01	7.73	40.86	37.27	32.36	**35.97**
1999-2000	40.04	7.47	36.09	27.09	23.62	**26.1**

Source: Assam Development Report, Planning Commission, Government of India, 2002

As the per-capita income growth reflects the movement of poverty ratio, it will be in fitness of things here to focus on the growth in the per-capita income as well in the State. In 1950-51, the per-capita income in Assam was 4 per cent above the national average. Five decades later, in 1998-99, it dropped to 41 per cent below the national average at current prices and 45 per cent below the national average at 1980-81 prices. There has been a constant rise in this gap and between 1980 and 1998, the per-capita income in Assam grew by 10 per cent compared with 39 per cent for all India (Table 1.6).

[26] Apart from Haryana, Assam saw the drastic worsening of its rank [Agarwal and Srinivasan (2000)], Assam Development Report, 2003.

Table 1.6
Per Capita Income (at constant 1980-81 prices)

Year	1950-51	1960-61	1970-71	1980-81	1990-91	1995-96	1996-97	1998-99
India	1127	1350	1520	1630	2222	2608	2761	3132
Assam	1173	1140	1221	1284	1524	1606	1628	1708
Difference	46(+)	210(-)	299(-)	346(-)	698(-)	1002(-)	1133(-)	1424(-)
Assam/India	1.04	0.84	0.80	0.79	0.69	0.62	0.59	0.55

Source: *Vision Assam 2025,* Government of Assam

Figure 1
Per Capita Income (at constant 1980-81 prices)

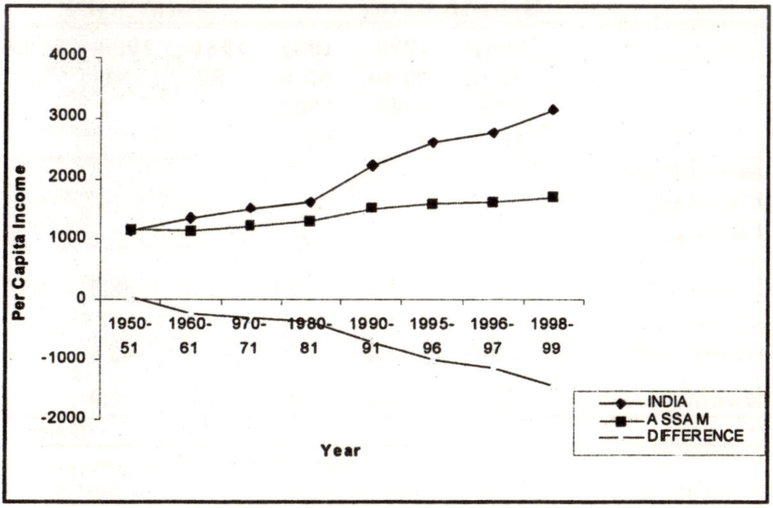

During 1951-79, Assam's economy grew more or less at the same rate as that of the rest of India. But as the Indian economy grew at 6 per cent over 1981 to 2000, the State GDP grew only at 3.3 per cent. In the post liberalization era, the State's economy decelerated instead of accelerating without any indication of change in the trend growth rate. Examining this trend growth rates by the three broad sectors - primary, secondary sand tertiary, it has been found that the primary sector has grown at around 2 per cent during the decades of 1980s and 1990s. The growth rates in the secondary and tertiary sectors too have remained the same around 4 and 4.5 per cent respectively[27] (Table 1.7 and 1.8). Thereby, it is not that Assam could make any compensatory progress in the sectors other than the primary, which too showed a slow growth. Therefore, notwithstanding a decade of relatively rapid economic growth rate in India following the sweeping economic reforms in 1991, the pace of growth in Assam, infact, has slowed down in recent years.

Table 1.7
State GDP at Factor Cost Industry of Origin at Constant (1980-81) prices

Sector	Acerage Annual Growth Rates			Per cent of Total SGDP		
	1981-82 to 1990-91	1990-91 to 1999-00	1981-82 to 1900-00	1981-82	1990-91	1999-00
Agriculture, Forestry, Fishing and Logging	2.6	1.6	2.1	41.6	38.3	33.5
Mining and Quarrying	0.1	2.0	1.0	5.2	3.8	3.4
Manufacturing	2.4	3.4	2.9	7.7	6.9	7.1

(Contd...)

[27] There has been a marginal fall in the growth rates of the primary and secondary sectors in the last decade but that has been compensated by a marginal rise in the service sector. Overall, the State projects a picture of stagnancy in growth rates for all the three sectors.

	1981-82 to 1990-91	1990-91 to 1999-00	1981-82 to 1900-00	1981-82	1990-91	1999-00
Construction	3.7	2.4	3.1	4.3	4.3	4.1
Electricity, Gas and water Supply	9.4	0.9	5.0	1.2	1.9	1.6
Trade, Transport, Banking and Other Services	4.9	4.5	4.7	40.1	44.7	50.3
Gross SDP	3.6	3.1	3.3	100.0	100.0	100.0

Source: Assam Development Report, Planning Commission, Government of India, 2002

Table 1.8
Growth in Real Gross State Domestic Product

(Per cent per annum)

Period	Primary	Secondary	Tertiary	GSDP
1980-1990	2.16	4.13	4.37	3.34
1991-2001	1.89	3.88	4.52	3.27
1980-2001	1.81	3.80	4.57	3.25

Source: Assam Development Report, Planning Commission, Government of India, 2002

Note: Estimates of growth rate for the period 1980-2001 made by fitting the equations of the type Ln (Y) = a+bT where Y is relevant income series and T is time trend.

For the sub-periods, growth rates are computed from the equation Ln (Y) =a+bT=c.D.T where D is a dummy variable with value 1 for 1991 onwards and 0 otherwise.

Above all, persisting fiscal deficits has emerged as one of the most significant weaknesses of the State economy, with public sector borrowing crowding out the private sector borrowing and thereby, increasing macroeconomic risks. The declining contribution of Central transfers to the total State spending in the last decade has led the State to rely increasingly on market borrowings[28] (Table 1.9, 1.10 and 1.11).

[28] The 'debt servicing costs' account for as much as 95 per cent of fresh debt contracted and the payment of principal and interest on Central loans exceed the receipts [GoA (1999)], *Assam Development Report*, 2002.

Table 1.9

Percentage Share of Expenditure in GSDP

Years	Development Expenditure			Non-Development Expenditure			Other Revenue Expenditure	Other Capital Expenditure				
	Revenue Expenditure	Capital Expenditure	Total	Revenue	Capital Expenditure	Total	Compensation and Assignment to Local Bodies	Discharge of Internal Debit	Repayment of Central Loans	Loans and Advances by State	Total	Total Expenditure
1990-91	12.40	2.28	14.685.61		0.05	5.66	0.46	0.01	3.18	1.72	4.91	25.70
1991-92	13.54	2.35	15.893.73		0.06	3.78	0.07	0.07	0.65	2.07	2.78	22.53
1992-93	12.10	1.76	13.866.63		0.06	6.69	0.05	0.12	2.24	1.07	3.44	24.04
1993-94	12.60	1.66	14.264.01		0.05	4.06	0.06	0.12	2.02	1.04	3.18	21.56
1994-95	12.43	1.62	14.057.35		0.06	7.41	0.04	0.01	0.79	0.78	1.58	23.07
1995-96	13.31	2.10	15.426.93		0.05	6.98	0.11	0.01	2.13	1.05	3.20	25.71
1996-97	11.84	1.25	13.086.92		0.03	6.95	0.06	0.09	1.64	0.65	2.38	22.48
1997-98	12.09	1.58	13.677.60		0.03	7.63	0.05	0.13	2.53	0.53	3.19	24.54
1998-99	12.82	1.64	14.467.26		0.02	7.28	0.05	0.17	1.41	0.35	1.93	23.72
1999-00 (RE)	19.02	2.88	21.9011.75		0.08	11.830.05		0.18	1.60	1.13	2.92	36.71
2000-01 (BE)	19.58	7.29	26.8610.42		0.07	10.480.05		0.19	1.48	1.28	2.95	40.35

Source: Assam Development Report, Planning Commission, Government of India, 2002

Table 1.10
Composition of Expenditure (Percentage of GSDP)

Years	Revenue Expenditure	Capital Expenditure	Total Observed Expenditure	NIPFP Projections (with state level reforms)
1990-91	18.46	7.24	25.70	
1991-92	17.34	5.19	22.53	
1992-93	18.78	5.25	24.04	
1993-94	16.68	4.88	21.56	
1994-95	19.81	3.26	23.07	
1995-96	20.36	5.34	25.71	
1996-97	18.82	3.66	22.48	
1997-98	19.75	4.80	24.54	26.25
1998-99	20.13	3.59	23.72	31.69
1999-00 (RE)	30.82	5.89	36.71	30.61
2000-01 (BE)	30.04	10.31	40.35	28.04

Source: Assam Development Report, Planning Commission, Government of India, 2002

Notes: GSDP figures from 1997-98 are projected based on past trends
The NIPFP trends incorporate increased salaries due to the 5th Pay Commission recommendations but with a downsizing of staff

Table 1.11
Fiscal Deficit as a Percentage of GSDP

Composition of Fiscal Deficit

Year	Fiscal Deficit	Revenue Deficit	Capital Outlay	Net Lending
1998-1999	1.54	-0.14	1.66	0.29
1999-2000(RE)	9.90	5.84	2.97	1.09
2000-2001(BE)	8.31	3.63	7.35	-2.68

Financing of Fiscal Deficit

Year	Fiscal Deficit	Net Central Loans	Net Market Borrowings	Net Lending
1998-1999	1.54	0.64	1.62	-0.72
1999-2000(RE)	9.90	1.12	1.44	7.33
2000-2001(BE)	8.31	0.89	1.39	6.03

Source: Assam Development Report, Planning Commission, Government of India, 2002

In addition to borrowings, government guarantees are growing and are being used extensively in mobilising funds for capital expenditure (Table 1.12 and 1.13). Diversion and inefficient utilisation of funds is not only aggravating the problem of fiscal deficit resulting from an unsustainable level of indebtedness, but is infact, blocking the channelising of funds for strengthening the foundations of economic growth.

Table 1.12
Gross Fiscal Deficits (1999-2000)
(Percentage of NSDP)

Assam	
1998-99	338.2 (1.6)
1999-00	1605.8 (6.4)
2000-01	1923.5 (7.1)

Source: CMIE, Public Finance 2002 and *Economic Survey* 2001

Table 1.13
Guarantees (contingent liabilities) given by Assam State Government (Rs Lakh)

Year	New	Outstanding Guarantees Total	% Given to ASEB
1991-92		102796	80
1992-93	11921	109399	76
1993-94	12462	122984	68
1994-95	32482	138382	64
1995-96	14214	124986	53
1996-97	500	114939	56
1997-98	850	143000	63
1998-99(RE)		143000	66

Source: Assam Development Report, Planning Commission, Government of India, 2002

Note: ASEB refers to Assam State Electricity Board

Overall growth is a product of many a factor, among which, infrastructure development and social advancement matters most. To add to the poor performance of Assam in almost all economic aspects compared to the national level, she fails in other indicators of development as well. The existing infrastructure and facilities of transport and communication are hardly adequate enough to meet the requirements of the State. Infact, Assam has the poorest infrastructure and social indicators[29]. The total road length in the State stood at 33,343 Km. in 1999-2000, of which only 26 per cent has been surfaced. The road density per sq.km hence stands at 0.425. The other modes of transport like the railways, airways, and water transport are also in a sorry state of affairs. However, the postal and telecom facilities have been growing steadily in the State in the recent years.

At various stages, the Central government has recognised the need to pay special attention to infrastructure development in Northeast. A number of initiatives were taken in the 1990s. A committee was constituted in February 1990 under the chairmanship of L.C. Jain, the then Member of the Planning Commission. A high level commission was set up under the chairmanship of S P Shukla yet again in 1997 to tackle the problem of backlog in basic minimum services and infrastructure needs of the Northeast. The recommendations of these committees were reflected in programmes announced by the various Prime Ministers. Thus, an economic package of Rs. 6,100 crore for specific projects in Northeast states as announced in October 1996 by the then Prime Minister, H.D. Deve Gowda, included fourth rail-cum-road bridge over the Brahmaputra at Bogibeel in Upper Assam, up gradation of Guwahati Airport and a few industrial growth centres in addition to some road projects, drinking water supply schemes and health care

[29] Its infrastructure development index is only 79 in comparison to the base level of 100 for the country [NIPFP (1998)].

programmes. He also introduced the Northeast sub-plans in all Central Ministries for which 10 per cent of their budgets would be earmarked. I. K. Gujaral, who followed Deve Gowda as the Prime Minister, also assured the implementation of the package in toto. In January 2000, Atal Behari Vajpayee further announced Rs. 10,271.66 crore package for the region.

Though the road network in Assam is extensive in terms of road density, that is, road length per thousand square km, in terms of density of surfaced road, Assam is way behind the country and the gap is increasing. However, the increasing length of highways in Assam in the recent years would only imply that the State government has invested on extending the road network rather than on improving the quality of roads. Though it was expected that the recent improvement and initiation of new projects would add even more national highways but unfortunately with emphasis on new roads, inadequate attention is being paid to the maintenance of the existing roads. Many roads are in poor state and all weather connectivity for many villages is limited (Table 1.14).

Table 1.14
Roads in Assam and India

	Road Length ('000 Km)			**Road Density (Km Per '000 Sq. Km)**		
Year	**Surfaced Road**	**Unsurfaced Road**	**Total**	**Surfaced Road**	**Unsurfaced Road**	**Total**
All India						
1970-71	398	520	918	121	158	279
1980-81	684	802	1486	208	244	452
1990-91	1025	977	2002	312	297	609
1996-97	1394	1072	2466	424	326	750

(Contd...)

Year	Surfaced Road	Unsurfaced Road	Total	Surfaced Road	Unsurfaced Road	Total
Assam						
1970-71						
1980-81						
1990-91	10	55.6	65.5	127	709	836
1996-97	11.6	56.8	68.4	148	724	872

Source: *CMIE,* Various Issues

For public transport, the Assam State Transport Corporation (ASTC) was set up. But it failed to put up the effort required with dearth of finance needed to meet the demands of the staff. ASTC had an annual deficit of Rs.22.55 crore and accumulated liability of Rs. 80 crore including 12 months of employee salaries of Rs. 28 crore. The bus staff ratio stood at 1:40[30]. Notwithstanding this failure, the implementations of the recommendations of the various committees are said to be in progress in the State (Table1.15).

Table 1.15

Roads: Recommendations of Different Committees

Recommended by	Recommendations	Status in April 2001
Jain Committee (April 1990)	1. Improve efficiency and economic viability of Assam State Road Transport Corporation (ASRTC)	No progress

(Contd...)

[30] However, the ASTC registered a spectacular resurgence in recent years mainly due to the efforts made by the Minister in charge of the Corporation. Now it is known as a vibrant sector.

Recommended by	Recommendations	Status in April 2001
S P Shukla Commission (March 1997)	2. Develop as National Highways a Daboka-Silchar Highway b Kohima-Amguri between Nagaland and Assam (241 km)	No objection for handing over land to Centre given by State on 9.3.99. Estimate was not sanctioned by GOI till 14.3.01.
Prime Minister Vajpayee's Announcement of January 22, 2000	3. Road Projects a Baithalangshu -Raha (48 km) b Naharkatiya-Khonsa (57 km) c Panchgram-Hailakandi (58 km) d Megherita-Changlang (43 km) e Zamuang-Durlavcherra (79 km) f Jotte-Balijan (58 km) g Fatikroy-Kailashwar (98 km)	Work initiated and is in various stages of completion
	4. New National Highways totaling 1962 km in the NE of which 433 km is in Assam.	Declared as National Highways and consultancy quotations invited.

Source: Assam Development Report, Planning Commission, Government of India, 2002

Similarly, the development of railways (Table 1.16) took a long time to reach a reasonable level. Things have changed in recent times as Dibrugarh is being connected by lines which are under construction. The recommendations of the Jain and the Shukla Committees (Table 1.17) thus seem to have had an impact.

Table 1.16
Development of Railways in Assam

Year	Route Length All India	Route Length Assam (Km)	Density India	Density Assam (Km/1000 Sq Km)
1990-91	62367	2467	19.0	31.4
1993-94	62462	3728		
1996-97	62725	2435		
1998-99	62809	2392	19.1	30.5

Source: CMIE, Various Issues

Table 1.17
Railways: Recommendations of Different Committees

Recommended by	Recommendations	Status in April 2001
Jain Committee (April 1990)	1. Speed up and complete a Rail-cum-Road Bridge at Jagighopa	1a Inaugurated in April 1998
	b BG line from Jagighopa to Guwahati which were taken up in 1983-84	1b. Completed Feb.2001

(Contd...)

Recommended by	Recommendations	Status in April 2001
	2. BG line from Guwahati to Dibrugarh	2. Most of it completed, rest expected by end 2001
	3. New BG line from Jalukbari to Panikheti	3. No proposal for survey work
	4. Extension of BG track from Lanka to Silchar	4. Conversion work sanctioned in 1996-97
	5. A rail-cum-road bridge at Bogibeel near Dibrugarh	5. Final location survey completed. Final clearance is awaited.
S P Shukla Commission (March 1997)	6. Expeditious completion of Bogibeel bridge	6. Final clearance is awaited.
	7. (a) Diphu-Karang and (b) Bairabi-Sareng lines be taken up in 9th plan	7.a. Survey completed by Mizoram has indicated preference for a new alignment. 7.b. Survey work awarded for a proposed line but facing local opposition

(Contd...)

Recommended by	Recommendations	Status in April 2001
	8.Overnight trains between Dimapur and Guwahati	
	9. Linkage with Bangladesh	9. Survey on Indian side completed, awaiting Bangladesh Report
	10. Linkage with Myanmar	10. No proposal
Jain Committee	11. Establish a railway training institute	

Source: Assam Development Report, Planning Commission, Government of India, 2002

Being one of the lowest ranked States in the country in terms of per capita electricity consumption, the per capita electricity supplied is mere 116 kwhr/person/year which is only one fourth of the all India per capita generation of 479 kwhr. Inspite of large resources in Assam and the Northeast, the abysmally low per capita consumption of electricity reflects both poor quality of life and low level of economic activities. The installed capacity remained the same at 574.4MW since 1997-98 to 2003. The power generation in the State gradually declined from 1996-97 and this downward trend continued till 2001-2002. In order to meet the domestic demand, the State continued to purchase power from other sources (Table 1.18). Therefore, since the past several years the overall power supply position in the State has not been much satisfactory.

Table 1.18
Power Supply Position in Assam

ITEMS	1998-99	1999-2000	2000-2001	2001-2002
1	2	3	4	5
Energy Requirement (Million unit)	3,073.00	3,077,00	3,323.16	3,415.32
Availability (Million unit)	2,832,78	2,985,21	2,984,97 (R)	3,301.59
Shortage (Percentage)	7.80	2.90	10.18 (R)	3.33

Source: Economic Survey, Assam 2002-2003
Note: (R) – Revised Estimate

Telecommunication is one area in which technological progress has overcome traditional bottlenecks and some relief is observable. Though the telephone density has grown fourfold in Assam, it is still only about 40 per cent of that in India.

Agriculture in Assam is also subject to various social and institutional constraints. The most obvious is the land holding pattern, which is dominated by the small holdings, i.e. the small operational size of the farms (Table 1.19). Nearly three-fourths of all operational holdings are either 'marginal' or 'small'. As a result, the average size of holdings in Assam is only about 1.27 hectares. These small and marginal farmers typically face severe financial constraint. Considering the importance of agriculture in the State's economy, the topmost priority of the government of Assam has been on development of this sector. Hence, in 1996-97, the government of Assam enthusiastically initiated the scheme of installation of shallow tubewells under Samriddha Krishak Yojana (SKY) with finance from NABARD and Assam Rural Infrastructure and Agricultural Service Project (ARIASP) financed by the World Bank to accelerate the pace of development of agriculture in the State. The government of Assam had aimed at and installed 1, 47,250 STWs by March 2001, and the primary objective of the scheme had been to increase the area under assured irrigation for increasing productivity and cropping intensity and thereby bridge the gap between production and requirement. Considering the technical and geo-hydrological parameters, 18 out of 23 districts had been brought under the scheme. Installation of the STWs in different parts of Assam had definite visible impacts on the agricultural sector of the State. The programme had been successful to create an additional potential to irrigate about 294 thousand hectares or approximately 13 per cent of the net area sown in the State. However, the programme failed to achieve the norm of self-sufficiency in food grain production in the State.

A Few Insights

Reasons for Low Growth Syndrome in the State

Wars of 1962 and 1971

Failure to implement the Green Revolution of the 1960s

Socio-political movements in the State

Population influx

Persisting problem of insurgency

Lack of infrastructural facilities

Lack of investments

Table 1.19
Number, Area and Average Size of Operational Holding in Assam, 1990-91 and 1995-96 (all social groups)

Size/Class	Number of Holding		Operational Area		Percentage to Total		Average Size of Holding	
Hectaress/Year	1995-96	1990-91	1995-96	1990-91	1995-96	1990-91	1995-96	1990-91
Marginal								
<0.05	1036853	914496	212834	208415	6.80	6.50	0.21	0.23
0.5-1.0	632399	606337	402073	398707	12.84	12.44	0.64	0.66
1.0-2.0	561078	559863	769698	784081	24.58	24.47	1.37	1.40
Small								
2.0-3.0	241615	237135	565823	566720	18.07	17.68	2.34	2.39
3,0-4.0	109630	105420	358435	351277	11.44	10.96	3.27	3.33
Semi-medium								
4.0-5.0	50482	49567	212436	210999	6.78	6.58	4.21	4.26
5.0-7.5	38914	38267	225145	224140	7.19	6.99	5.79	5.86
7.5-10.0	7022	6864	57077	56472	1.82	1.76	8.13	8.23
Medium								
10.0-20.0	3051	3051	39323	39503	1.26	1.23	12.89	12.95
Large								
>20.0	1953	2379	289144	364438	9.23	11.37	148.05	153.19
All sizes	**2682997**	**2523379**	**3131988**	**3204752**	**100.00**	**100.00**	**1.17**	**1.27**

Sources: *Statistical Handbook of Assam*, 1999 and 2004, Government of Assam

Are the reasons cited enough to justify the low growth syndrome in the State? Where does political will power stand amidst these reasons? The density of population figures in Assam has been pointing at the rapid rate of increase in population leading to reduction in the land: man ratio. The reigning poverty and backwardness of Assam has always been analysed in the context of abnormal growth of population due to continuous influx of migrants that is suppose to be tremendously pressurising on land-man ratio with of course recognizing the competition for natural resources, economic opportunities and even cultural identity as the main reasons behind recurring economic, social and ethnic conflicts in the State.

Assam has had its share of failures and successes on economic front since independence. If one is to analyse the little success and big failures achieved on this front by the two alternate ruling parties, the national party – the Congress (I), and the regional party – the AGP in the State, it is the national party that seems to have had an upper hand in successes achieved in the economic front in the State, than the regional party, the AGP, which is burdened rather with more failures on economic front. *The question, therefore, remains open that have the failures in the economic front, really has affected election politics in the State?*

Economic considerations, more specifically, the political economy of the State has its own course of influences over the electoral politics in the State. The relative backwardness of the State, despite resource affluences, has led to the popular belief that the cause of this backwardness is rather exogenous. This belief, when politically interpreted, upheld the view that Assam's case is more of "relative deprivation" than that of "relative decelerations". This has created a visible cleavage separating regional sentiments from the national affiliations. During the course of six year long Assam movement, this sense of differences became even more pronounced leading to the emergence of the AGP as a strong regional party overthrowing the Congress from the seats of power. Notably, identifying the relative backwardness as a case of relative derivation and popularly believing the reasons responsible for this being exogenous continued even in the later phases as well with the notion of region narrowed down to the lines of ethnicity and community. This political economy of the State needs to be put in proper perspective when one tries to analyse the election politics in the State.

REFERENCES

Apter, David (1964). *Ideology and Discontent*. New York: Free Press.

Assam Development Report 2002. Planning Commission, Government of India.

Assam: The Pre- Poll Panorama (2001). A Freelance Peace. *Vedanti: Burning Assam*, Back Issues, http//www.vedanti.com.

Barpujari,Indrani (Forthcoming). "Illegal Migrants (Determination by Tribunals) Act and Assam–Promulgation and Repeal: A Contextual Analysis". New Delhi: Akansha.

Bhushan, Chandra (2004). *Terrorism and Separation in North-East India*. Delhi: Kalpaz.

Campbell, Angus *et.al* (1968). *Elections and the Political Order*. New York: John Wiley and Sons.

CMIE, Public Finance 2002.

Das, Samir K. (2004). *ULFA (United Liberation Front of Assam): A Political Analysis*. Delhi: Ajanta Publications.

Economic Survey, Assam 2001.

Economic Survey, Assam 2002-2003.

Election Commission of India. Various years, http://www.eci.gov.in

Guruswamy, Mohan (2005). *Left Behind: A Case Study of Assam*. Centre for Policy Alternatives (CPA), New Delhi.

Goswami, Sandhya (2004). "Mixed Verdict". *Economic and Political Weekly*. Vol XXXIX, No. 51. December 18-24.

Hussain, Wasbir (2001). "Elections under the Shadow of the Gun". *Economic and Political Weekly*. Vol XXXVI, No. 5 & 6. February 3-10.

McClosky, Herbert and Harold Dahlgren (1959). "Primary Group Influence on Party Loyalty". *American Political Science* Review: 53. pp. 757-76.

Mill, John Stuart (1962). *Considerations on Representative Government.* Chicago: Henry Regnery Company. p. 170.

Myron Weiner (1978). *India at the Polls: The Parliamentary Elections of 1977.* Washington: American Enterprise Institute.

Pakem, B. (1997). *Insurgency in Northeast India.* New Delhi: Omson Publication.

Palmer, Norman D. (1976). *Election and Political Development: The South Asian Experience.* New Delhi: Vikas. P.1.

Police Records, Government of Assam.

Rosenau, James N. (1973). *The Dramas of Politics.* Boston: Little, Brown. p. 171.

Sahni, Ajai (2002). "Survey of Conflicts & Resolution in India's Northeast". *Faultlines–Writings on conflict and resolution.* Volume 12, New Delhi: Bulwark Books. May.

Statistical Handbook of Assam, 1999, Government of Assam.

Vedanti - Burning Assam (Earlier Issues). Various Issues. http://www.vedanti.com.

CHAPTER 2

Nomination Process

Assam Politics: *A Review*

Historically, one of the strongest bastions of the Congress (I)[1] with a record uncontested primacy of the party winning almost all the seats to the Lok Sabha between 1946 and 1978, Assam for the first time came under a non-Congress (I) dispensation in March 1978. In the election to the State Assembly that followed the lifting of the national Emergency in 1977, a new party, the Janata Party headed by Golap Barbora[2] succeeded to wrest the seat of power in the State from the Congress (I), which ruled the State for five assembly terms consecutively since Independence. However, the infighting within the party led to its downfall from the helm of power in less than two years. The Barbora ministry failed to hold on to power. The party rather followed a carbon copy route of the developments at the Centre. It was a re-enactment of a political drama, which led to the toppling of the Moraji Desai government and installation of the ministry headed by Choudhury Charan Singh. Barbora's cabinet colleague, Jogen Hazarika, revolted and formed a new party called the Asom Janata Party and eventually formed the Government after toppling the ministry of Golap Barbora

[1] In Assam, the Congress party reigned supreme from the moment of the nation's Independence until 1978, one year following the lifting of the emergency and formation of the first non-Congress Government at the Centre.

[2] The Janata Party government could survive only for a brief period from 3rd March 1978 to September 1979.

on September 4, 1979. Hereafter, Assam experienced the installation of three successive short-lived ministries headed by (i) Jogen Hazarika, from September 9 to December 12, 1979, (ii) Syeda Anowara Taimur, a Congress (I) leader who had only 11 party followers in 1978 but could manage to secure the majority support and survived for seven months from December 6, 1980 to June 30, 1981, and (iii) Keshab Gogoi, from January 13, 1982 to March 19, 1982. This was a period of grim political uncertainty which witnessed the onset of the Assam movement and also the birth of an insurgent group called the United Liberation Front, Asom (ULFA).

This was followed by a difficult chapter in Assam's history when factional politics and defection led to a constitutional breakdown of the machinery of the Government leading to the imposition of President's Rule in the State keeping the Assembly under animated suspension, coupled with the beginning of the six year Assam movement and outbreak of insurgency related and communal violence. And, finally on the ground of 'constitutional compulsions'[3], inspite of popular opposition on the part the Assamese[4], the Union Government went ahead with the bloodstained election of February 1983 amidst the Assam agitation in its full swing. Finally, the Central government under Rajiv Gandhi signed the Assam Accord on August 15, 1985 with the leaders of the Assam agitation.

The conclusion of the Accord marked the end of Assam movement against the foreign nationals. The State saw the first explicit regional party, the Asom Gana Parishad[5], come

---

[3] An expression used by the Election Commission then.

[4] The Assam agitation was in full swing at the time of holding the 1983 Assembly election. The election was rejected by the people of Assam on demand of the expulsion of Bangladeshi nationals illegally staying in Assam and the removal of their names from the electoral rolls.

[5] The Asom Gana Parishad (AGP) was born in October 1985, two months after the signing of the Assam Accord on August 15, 1985. The signing of the Accord brought to an end the six-year-long Assam agitation led by the All Assam Students' Union (AASU) and other non-political platforms under the name of All Assam Gana Sangram Parishad (AAGSP).

to power after a decisive victory in December 1985. This was supposed to be a path-breaking development when a group of young and inexperienced leaders of a regional party took the rein of power, an achievement considered to be unparallel in the history of student movement in the country and elsewhere. But from the very beginning of its innings, the AGP leadership, instead of taking credible steps to redeem the promises made during the electioneering remained euphoric about its poll performance and was least concerned about the issues of governance. All this led to the party's failure at the seat of power. The AGP failed to mobilise a wider support base in the State. Tracing the history of the party to the Assam agitation, it is only natural that with the support base it mobilised during the Assam agitation, it could gather a rather narrower social base in its fold to the exclusion of those in the margin but a vast majority to reckon with. However, the contours of regional politics did change in the two decades since the signing of the Assam Accord with the AGP succeeding in making inroads into the marginal and marginalised social base of the State. This has been proved well by the party's wins in the Assembly election 1996[6]. This win is a matter of history now. The failure to live up to the promises made led the party, quite expectedly, not only to draw a blank in the 1999 Lok Sabha election but also to lose the political office in the State in the Assembly election of May 2001, winning only 20 seats in the 126 member Assembly. More suicidal than these losses for the party are the internal fallouts within the party today, with clearly defined factions, who are set on a battle to the finish.

---

[6] Three well researched articles provide some detailed understanding of the 1996 election in Assam which threw the Congress out of the State power and reduced its strength in the Lok Sabha as shown in Table 2.2, see Samir Kumar Das, "An Interpretation of the Assam Elections of 1996", Apurba Kumar Baruah, "Assam Elections 1996: The Congress Debacle" and Sandhya Goswami, "Assam Lok Sabha Election, 1996: An Analysis" in Girin Phukon and Adil-ul-Yasin (eds), *Working of Parliamentary Democracy and Electoral Politics in North East India* (New Delhi: South Asian Publishers, 1998).

The vertical split of the party in November 2005 when former Chief Minister Prafulla Kumar Mahanta floated a new party called the AGP (Progressive) after he was expelled from the party which he presided over since its inception till 2001, proves where regionalism exists in the State politics of Assam.

Table 2.1
Seats won by AGP, BJP and Congress (I) and Other Parties (1991 to 1999 Lok Sabha elections)

Party	Seats won (1991)	Seats won (1996)	Seats won (1998)	Seats won (1999)
Indian National Congress (INC)	8	5	10	10
Bharatiya Janata Party (BJP)	2	1	1	2
Asom Gana Parishad (AGP)	1	5	0	0
ADC/ASDC	1	1	1	0
CPM	1	1	0	0
CPI (ML) (L)				1
UMFA	0	0	1	0
Ind	1	1	1	1

Source: www.electionnext.com

Regionalism, as an ideology no more remains the AGP's exclusive domain today. Unlike the AGP, the Congress (I), with its electoral needs, however, has succeeded in enlarging the party's social base over the years by building alliances vertically as well as horizontally not only with the religious and linguistic minorities but also with the other marginalised groups like the tea garden labourers and the adivasis. The Congress was back with a bang in the 1991 Lok Sabha election, winning majority of the seats in the heartland of the Assamese dominated constituencies which had returned the AGP candidates to the Assembly in 1996. Since then the Congress (I) has been making heavy inroads into its support base. The coming back of the Congress (I) in 1991 Assembly election, after brief interlude, and again in 2001, and its performance in the 13th and 14th Lok Sabha polls of 1999 and 2004, especially the later victories, testify to the fact. Once more a reinvigorated Congress seemed to be back to its bastion for a considerable period of time, at least till the next election.

Amidst the regional force and the national power there seems to be an emerging alternative power in the State - yet another national power but with a regional touch. The Bharatiya Janata Party (BJP), an up coming national party with a low profile was making inroads slowly but surely. The win of Bijoya Chakraborty in the 13th Lok Sabha poll from the Gauhati Parliamentary constituency testifies to the fact that the party which was supposed to have its base in the Barak valley was making inroads into the Brahmaputra valley as well. The popular sentiments in the State dilly dallying for long between the regional force, the AGP, and the national power, the Congress (I), seemed to be fixing its mind in taking BJP's *Hindutva* ideology into its fold and giving a rare chance to the party to prove its worth in the coming years.

The Left parties made a significant impact in the State in the 1978 Assembly election winning 24 seats, the CPI (M) alone bagged 11. It is argued that the left performance shocked the chauvinist elements which took up the foreign national issue to spearhead attack on the left parties.[7]

Elections: *Post 1998*

In the 13th Lok Sabha poll 1999, the Indian National Congress (INC) won 10 out of the 14 seats. The seats, which the party won were Silchar (Santosh Mohan Dev), Barpeta (A F Golam Osmani), Dibrugarh (Paban Singh Ghatowar), Dhubri (Abdul Hamid), Lakhimpur (Ranee Narah), Mangaldoi (Madhab Rajbangshi), Kaliabar (Tarun Gogoi), Karimganj (Nepal Chandra Das), Jorhat (Bijoy Krishna Handique), and Tezpur (Moni Kumar Subba). The remaining four seats went to the BJP (Bijoya Chakraborty in Gauhati and Rajen Gohain in Nowgong), the ASDC (Dr. Jayanta Rongpi in Diphu) and an Independent (Kokrajhar). The INC had an impressive performance with 38.42 per cent votes in its favour. While the AGP with a blank was relegated to the background, the BJP had reasons to feel encouraged at its performance succeeding to secure two seats and occupying the second position in terms of voters' choice.

The trend continued with the Congress domination in the 2001 Assembly election in which it regained the seat of power at Dispur virtually routing the ruling AGP. The party was on the winning spree as it swept the Panchayat elections of 2001-02. In the 11th Assembly election in the State, the Congress defeated the four-party alliance led by the Asom Gana Parishad (AGP)[8], winning 71 of the 125 seats. The defeat for the AGP and BJP alliance was more than obvious with AGP abandoning its former allies of the 1996 Assembly election and lending the hand of support to the BJP at the last hour, which was unacceptable to certain BJP leaders

---

[7] Hiren Gohain, "Cudgel of Chauvinism", *Economic and Political Weekly*, February 23, 1980, pp.418-20. Also see Abu Nasar Saied Ahmed (ed), *National Question in Assam: The EPW 1980-81 Debate* (New Delhi: Akansha, 2006), Introduction.

[8] The new alliance included the AGP, the BJP, the All Bodo Students' Union (ABSU) and the Autonomous State Demand Committee (United).

like Hiranya Bhattacharya[9]. There were oppositions in the AGP camp as well, with some of the dissidents of the party joining the camp of the Congress.

With the new alliance in the background and the failure on the part of the ruling AGP to deliver to the satisfaction of the masses, the 11th Assembly poll in 2001 was not an uncertain game. The bad governance of the AGP during its tenure was more than enough for its disastrous performance in the 11th Assembly elections. The AGP could win only twenty seats, while the BJP, the ABSU and the ASDC (U) won eight, nine, and two respectively. The most shocking result was Prafulla Mahanta's own defeat in the Dispur constituency[10]. He finished third from Dispur, behind Congress (I)'s Robin Bordoloi, the winner, and Atul Bora, party Convenor of the Trinamool Gana Parishad and Mahanta's one-time trusted lieutenant. The results came as a shock to several Ministers and senior AGP leaders. The losers included the AGP stalwarts like Chandra Mohan Patowary, Kamala Kalita, Moidul Islam Bora, Nurul Hussain, Pradip Hazarika, Ramendra Narayan Kalita, Rekharani Das Boro and Thaneswar Boro.

The BJP's position was no better. The alliance with the AGP could not improve BJP's position. Though the BJP could double its strength in the Assembly by winning eight of the 44 seats it contested but this was too small an achievement to call for celebrations. The party had performed creditably in the 1999 Lok Sabha elections by winning about 29.84 per cent of the votes and its popularity had been soaring since

---

[9] A new party, the Asom Bharatiya Janata Party (ABJP) was formed under the presidentship of Hiranya Bhattacharya, one of the founder members of the BJP in the State and former Inspector General of Police, in 2001. The Asom Bharatiya Janata Party (ABJP) is a breakaway group of the Bharatiya Janata Party in Assam. Bhattacharya had objected to the decision of the BJP to align with the Asom Gana Parishad. However, the Asom BJP contested the 2001 State Assembly poll unsuccessfully.

[10] Mahanta could also win the Barhampur seat only by a margin of about 5,000 votes.

then. Hence, it was quite natural that the mood of the party was upbeat when the 11th Assembly election was announced. The party planned to put up candidates in over 80 constituencies. Problems began, however, the day the party decided to ally itself with the AGP. Though the State leadership opposed the move, the Central leaders forced it into the alliance with the hope to resist the Congress coming to power in the State. Unfortunately, this alliance proved to be a disaster for the party, yet again.

One of the facts that stood out was that for the first time in the State's history, the Assembly had no members from the Left parties[11]. The relentless attack on the Left parties during the period of the Assam movement led to the erosion of their support base to a great extent. It was compounded by the fact that the Left parties lived in a divided house, and therefore, performed miserably at the time of all the elections.

Table 2.2
Results of the 11th Assembly Election in Assam (2001)

Party	Contested Seats	Seats Won	Total Votes Received	Percentage of Total Votes Polled	Percentage of Votes in Contested Seats
1	2	3	4	5	6
Indian National Congress	126	71	4230676	39.75	39.75
Asom Gana Parishad	77	20	2130118	20.02	32.35
Independents	393	19	2076642	19.51	21.04
Bharatiya Janata Party	46	8	995004	9.35	26.31

(Contd...)

[11] In the 1996 Assembly House, The CPI and the CPI (M) had at least three and two seats respectively.

1	2	3	4	5	6
Nationalist Congress Party	62	3	267173	2.51	5.2
Autonomous State Demand Committee (United)	5	2	118610	1.11	29.45
Samata Party	19	1	83815	0.79	5.45
Samajwadi Party	23	1	109822	1.03	5.83
All India Trinamool Congress	23	1	58361	0.55	2.96
Autonomous State Demand Committee (Progressive)	5	0	98032	0.92	24.34
Amra Bangalee	1	0	422	0	0.63
Lok Jan Shakti Party	11	0	9051	0.09	0.9
Lok Shakti	3	0	1764	0.02	0.78
People's Democratic Front	7	0	35147	0.33	5.31
Revolutionary Communist Party Of India (Rasik Bhatt)	2	0	576	0.01	0.33
Samajwadi Janata Party (Rashtriya)	8	0	2345	0.02	0.32

(Contd...)

1	2	3	4	5	6
United Bodo Nationalist Liberation Front	13	0	16687	0.16	1.4
United Minorities Front, Assam	9	0	43712	0.41	5.54
United Reservation Movement Council of Assam	7	0	16901	0.16	2.5
United Tribal Nationalists Liberation Front	1	0	4185	0.04	5.32
Communist Party Of India (Marxist-Lennist) (Liberation)	9	0	20847	0.2	3.22
Janata Dal (Secular)	5	0	1690	0.02	0.39
Janata Dal (United)	6	0	7645	0.07	1.49
Muslim League	5	0	1230	0.01	0.3
Rashtriya Janata Dal	6	0	2378	0.02	0.47
Revolutionary Socialist Party	3	0	2905	0.03	0.84
Communist Party of India	19	0	116889	1.1	7.68
Communist Party of India	22	0	189349	1.78	10.65

Source: www.electionnext.com

Immediately after the swearing–in ceremony, the Chief Minister Tarun Gogoi had declared that his government would evolve a comprehensive plan to solve many of the pending works in the State, and one would be the holding of the long-awaited Panchayat elections in the State by the end of the year. Abiding by the promise, the much awaited Panchayat polls were on brisk preparations in the State in the second half the year 2001. Despite the previous AGP Government announcing the Panchayat elections in Assam every now and then, it had been four years since they were last held[12]. The Panchayat elections in the State were held towards the end of December 2001. The elections were to be held in 24,890 Gaon Panchayats[13], 203 Anchalik Panchayats[14] and for 470 Zila Parishad[15] constituencies in the 21 plain districts of the State in which 1.20 crore voters were expected to exercise their franchise.

The verdict of the general masses was in favour of the Congress. The Congress came out victorious in 243 Zila Parishads, 951 Anchalik Parishads and 983 Gaon Panchayats[16].

---

[12] The Panchayat elections were due in 1997 but the AGP Government deferred them indefinitely presumably because of the fear of being routed. In the absence of the Panchayat polls, development works were adversely affected at the grass-roots level. Eventually, the Congress conducted the elections in December 2001 redeeming its election promise.

[13] In case of the Gaon Panchayat constituencies, 1,990 seats were reserved for SC and 2,760 for ST candidates. Out of the 1,990 SC seats and 2,760 ST seats, 670 and 910 seats respectively were reserved for women.

[14] In case of the Anchalik Panchayat, 199 and 276 seats were reserved for the SC and for ST respectively. Out of these, the women were to get a share of 91 seats from those reserved for the ST and 67 seats from those reserved for the SC.

[15] Reservation of seats for SC/ST and women candidates was made as per the Assam Panchayat Act, 1994. Accordingly 36 out of 470 ZPCs were reserved for SC and 54 for ST candidates, and 10 SC seats were reserved for women.

[16] Results of Panchayat lections, Assam, (2001-02), *Assam Tribune*, 5th January, 2002. The Panchayat elections were not held on party line but candidates secured party support for which it was easy to identify the party affiliations of most of the candidates.

Table 2.3
No. of Constituencies, Panchayat Polls, Assam (2001-02)

Constituency	Numbers
Total Constituencies: Zila Parishad	
Zila Parishad Constituencies	470
Vacant	1
Deferred	79
Uncontested Constituencies	1
Total Constituencies where elections were held	389
Constituency: Anchalik Parishad	
Total Anchalik Panchayat Constituencies	2,489
Vacant	6
Deferred	335
Uncontested Constituencies	29
Total Constituencies where elections were held	2,119
Constituency: Gaon Panchayat	
Total Constituencies	24,890
Vacant	219
Deferred	3,350
Uncontested Constituencies	1,672
Total Constituencies where elections were held	19,649

Source: State Election Commission, Assam

Nominations: *The Act of Balancing Power*

Looking back, while the Congress nominated all the seating MPs and the former MPs, in the 13th Lok Sabha election, the BJP tried with new faces like Bijoya Chakraborty (Gauhati), Parimal Sukla Baidya (Karimganj), Ramani Kanta Deka (Barpeta) and Ram Prasad Sharma (Tezpur). The ASDC as always had its electoral understanding with left parties, more particularly, the CPI (ML) as Dr. Jayanta Rangpi had a long association with it.

Taking the 13th and the 14th Lok Sabha polls of the State in the background, a few case studies pertaining to the prestigious Lok Sabha constituencies in the State have been taken up to attempt an understanding of the politics of nomination of candidates of the important regional and national parties for the 14th Lok Sabha election.

A FEW CASE STUDIES

(A) Dhubri Lok Sabha Constituency

The Background

Dhubri happens to be a Lok Sabha constituency in which the majority of the voters mostly belong to the minority Muslim community. It includes ten Assembly constituencies in which the Muslim electorate constitutes 50 to 90 per cent of the populace. With this demographic character, Dhubri has always given a result in the Lok Sabha polls, which is a forgone conclusion. Out of the seven Lok Sabha polls since 1977 (Table 2.4 [A&B]), it was only in the 1984 Lok Sabha poll that the Congress failed in retaining the seat. Abdul Hamid[17], an independent candidate from the district won the 1984 poll defeating his nearest rival Nurul Islam from the Congress by winning a vote percentage of 25.91. Barring this election, the Congress has been winning the seat since 1977 with more or less a stable vote percentage ranging between 35 to 50 per cent with only a low of 26.53 per cent during the Lok Sabha poll of 1991, when Nurul Islam succeeded in defeating his arch rival Dinesh Chandra Sarkar from the BJP. The 13th Lok Sabha poll of 1999 was a contest between Abdul Hamid from the Congress and Dr. Pannalal Oswal from the BJP. Abdul Hamid won the poll with a margin of 34.58 per cent votes.

---

[17] Abdul Hamid later on joined the Congress and won the Lok Sabha seat in 1998 from this constituency.

13th Lok Sabha Poll Result
Winner: *Abdul Hamid(INC)*
Votes Secured: *2,79,812*
Runner-up: *Dr. Pannalal Oswal (BJP)*
Votes Secured: *2,58,472*
Abdul Hamid wins by 21,340 votes

Table 2.4 [A]
Dhubri Lok Sabha Constituency (Percentage of valid votes cast in favour of contesting parties)

Party Abbreviation	Current Party Status	2004	1999	1998	1996	1991	1984	1977
1	2	3	4	5	6	7	8	9
AGP	S	30.1	NC	NC	23.24	7.39	NC	NC
AIIC (T)		NE	NC	NC	5.47	NC	NC	NC
BJP	N	10.45	31.95	24.18	21.79	19.62	NC	NC
BLD		NE	NC	NC	NC	NC	NC	45.5
CPI	N	NE	7.14	10.59	NC	8.22	NC	NC
ICS		NE	NC	NC	NC	NC	16.06	NC
ICS (SCS)		NE	NC	NC	NC	8.75	NC	NC
INC	N	43.61	34.58	50.04	40.1	26.53	23.99	45.68
JD		NE	NC	NC	NC	11.67	NC	NC
JNP		NE	NC	NC	NC	NC	2.13	NC
JP		NE	NC	NC	NC	0.85	NC	NC
MUL	S	0.41	NC	NC	NC	NC	NC	NC
NAGP			NC	NC	NC	2.39	NC	NC
NCP	N	NC	2.05	NC	NC	NC	NC	NC
SP	S	NC	NC	8.66	2.28	NC	NC	NC
UMF		NE	NC	NC	NC	4.64	NC	NC

Source: www.eci.gov.in
**Although the Congress has been the winner since 1977, a vote swing did take place in favour of the BJP in 1996 and 1999.*

Nomination: The Process and the Grounds of Selection of Candidates

Just before the 2004 Lok Sabha Poll, the BJP was in the midst of chaos due to internal conflict. Dhubri district

Committee President of BJP, Sushil Das, and former MLA Dhruba Kumar Sen were in favour of Jayashree Goswami Mahanta, wife of Prafulla Kumar Mahanta, former Chief Minister of Assam. She sought the ticket from BJP for this constituency. Both Mr. Das and Mr. Sen were involved in secret plans to put up Mrs. Mahanta's nomination from BJP in the constituency[18]. Though Jayashree Goswami Mahanta was expected to be a preferred candidate in the Hindu belt, however, she being a member of AGP, and wife of the then AGP President and former Chief Minister of Assam, her inclination to join the BJP generated a lot of suspicion and controversy. Since the BJP was divided on the issue, it became obvious that Jayashree Goswami Mahanta would contest the election as an independent candidate from the district.

The BJP party workers of the minority cell protested the nomination of yet another woman candidate, Jabeen Borbhuyan[19] from the district. Some of them even put the BJP district office on fire and some took 'Amaran Annasan' (fast unto death) to protest her nomination. But even in the teeth of strong opposition, the BJP decided to field Jabeen Borbhuyan on the ground that she being a resident of Dhubri and belonging to the immigrant Muslim community carried the prospect of wooing her community which constituted the majority of the population in the district.

The district Congress Committee of Dhubri, on the other hand, was divided into two groups – Abdul Hamid's group and Anowar Hussain's group. There was sharp rivalry between the two groups. Both Hamid and Hussain fought for individual nominations from the party. There had been allegations of corruption against Abdul Hamid on grounds

---

[18] The two leaders even supposedly had threatened the newspapers not to report about their preference for Mrs. Mahanta as the BJP candidate from the district. As appeared in vernacular dailies.

[19] Jabeen Borbhuyan had the rare distinction of being BJP's sole woman Muslim candidate in the country.

Table 2.4 [B]

Dhubri Lok Sabha Constituency (List of winning candidates)

Year	Voters in *000	Voter Turnout (Percentage)	Winner			Runner-up		
			Candidate Name	Percentage	Party	Candidate Name	Percentage	Party
2004	863.59	75.1	Anowar Hussain	43.61	INC	Afzalur Rahman	30.1	AGP
1999	825.53	78.58	Abdul Hamid	34.58	INC	Dr. Prannalal Oswal	31.95	BJP
1998	773.08	73.65	Abdul Hamid	50.04	INC	Dr. Prannalal Oswal	24.18	BJP
1996	810.65	87.08	Nurul Islam	40.1	INC	Onkarmal Agarwal	23.24	AGP
1991	749.08	84.79	Nurul Islam	26.53	INC	Dinesh Chandra Sarkar	19.62	BJP
1984	642.85	86.77	Abdul Hamid	25.91	IND	Nurul Islam	23.99	INC
1977	340.93	67.71	Ahmad Hussein	45.68	INC	Nurul Islam	45.5	BLD

Source: www.eci.gov.in

of misuse of the MP funds. The local print media not only flashed his failure as an MP but also highlighted the erosion of his support base. The district Congress Committee opposed Hamid's[20] candidature and sent letters to Digvijay Singh expressing its strong opposition to his nomination. Close on the heels of the developments, ten MLAs and ministers from the Congress strongly opposing Hamid's candidature argued that there was no chance of him being elected in the forthcoming election. A campaign waged by the MLA, Wazed Ali Choudhury, in New Delhi, and joined by five other MLAs against Hamid's nomination was too strong to be ignored. The group went a step further and requested Digvijay Singh not to give Hamid the party ticket to contest the election from the district. Meanwhile, some other Congress workers were also campaigning for another aspirant, Matiur Rahman Mandal. Amidst the chaos, the Congress High Command ultimately decided to put up Anowar Hussain who projected to be more popular[21].

The AGP put up Afzalur Rahman, a former Congress minister who resigned from the party and joined the AGP in 1996 as the party candidate from the Dhubri constituency. The decision dismissed speculations floated by the media that Jayashree Goswami Mahanta would be given the party nomination. It was Afzalur Rahman, seemingly a single choice for the AGP, who claimed that AGP always stood with the general people[22]. The AGP leadership too was in favour of Afzalur Rahman in this constituency who seemed to be the strongest candidate from the constituency. Rahman

---

[20] Though the nomination was not clear as yet, Hamid had already started campaigning and demanded that he would surely get the ticket as he had the support from all sections of the society in the constituency.

[21] Being dissatisfied, Hamid ordered his loyals to campaign for the AGP. But he did not receive the expected support from his followers. As appeared in vernacular dailies.

[22] He gave the statement in an election meeting held on 10th March 2004 where above twenty thousand people were present. *Asomiya Pratidin,* 11th March, 2004.

belonging to the immigrant Muslim community had considerable support from a substantial section of his community. Considering his popularity, he was also offered the ticket from the BJP and the JD (U). However, he decided to go with the AGP's offer as he was in the party since 1996, and, therefore, filed his nomination from the AGP.

14th Lok Sabha Poll Result
Winner: *Anowar Hussain (INC)*
Votes Secured: *3,76,588*
Runner-up: *Afzalur Rahman (AGP)*
Votes Secured: *2,59,966*
Anowar Hussain wins by 1,16,62 votes

It is interesting to note that all the parties, knowing fully well that in a Muslim dominated constituency only a Muslim could win, nominated Muslim candidates only. It proves in unmistakable terms that primordial affiliations do play a role in the nomination process.

Table 2.5
Contestants in Dhubri Lok Sabha Constituency (1999 and 2004)

Dhubri					
1999			2004		
Candidate	*Party*	*Votes*	*Candidate*	*Party*	*Votes*
Abdul Hamid	**Indian National Congress**	279812	Anowar Hussain	**Indian National Congress**	376588
Dr. Pannalal Osawal	**Bharatiya Janata Party**	258472	Afzalur Rahman	**Asom Gana Parishad**	259966
Afzalur Rahman	**Independent**	174879	Jabeen Borbhuyan	**Bharatiya Janata Party**	90215

(Contd...)

Candidate	*Party*	*Votes*	*Candidate*	*Party*	*Votes*
Alauddin Sarkar	**Communist Party of India**	57735	Dr. Motiur Rahman Mondal	**Independents**	47230
Ahmed Hussain	**Nationalist Congress Party**	16611	Listi Rabha	**Independents**	23835
Minhar Ali Mandal	**Independents**	11892	Jayashree Goswami Mahanta	**Independents**	22311
Prabir Kumar Rabha	**Independents**	5785	Shajahan Sheikh	**Independents**	15094
Safior Rahman Talukdar	**Ajeya Bharat Party**	3883	Radha Ballav Adhikary	**Independents**	12572
			Minhar Ali Mandal	**Independents**	7562
			Gandhi Nath	**Independents**	4686
			Mohor Uddin Mondal	**Muslim League**	3533

Source: www.electionnext.com

(B) Dibrugarh Lok Sabha Constituency

The Background

The Dibrugarh Parliamentary constituency has traditionally been a Congress stronghold. Congress candidates have been winning this seat since the first Lok Sabha poll since independence. Even in 1977 election when there was a Janata wave, the Congress candidate Haren Bhumij turned out victorious (Table 2.6 [A&B]), securing at least 50 per cent of the votes. The constituency has about 9.78 lakh voters, out of which the tea garden labourers comprise 2.5 lakh, Bengali Hindus about 1.2 lakh and Hindi speaking people about 1 lakh. The Congress candidate Pawan Singh Ghatowar has been winning the Dibrugarh seat since 1991. Ghatowar, who is the President of the Assam Pradesh Congress Committee (APCC), belongs to the tea tribe community, which makes up for about 50 per cent of the votes in the Dibrugarh district. In 1998, Ghatowar won the seat securing as high as 64.4 per cent of the votes. Though Ghatowar retained the seat in 1999 also, the Congress vote share declined to 48.57 percent. In 2004, Ghatowar lost the seat to the AGP candidate Sarbananda Sanowal.

13th Lok Sabha Poll Result
Winner: ***Paban Singh (INC)***
Votes Secured: ***2,70,863***
Runner-up: ***Ajit Chaliha (BJB)***
Votes Secured : ***2,03,747***
****Paban Singh Ghatowar wins by 67,116 votes***

Table 2.6 [A]

Dibrugarh Lok Sabha Constituency (Percentage of valid votes cast in favour of contesting parties)

Party Abbreviation	Current Party Status	2004	1999	1998	1996	1991	1984	1977
1	2	3	4	5	6	7	8	9
AGP	S	35	13.62	8.25	31.34	21.96	NC	NC
AIIC (T)		NE	NC	NC	3.33	NC	NC	NC
BJP	N	32.06	36.54	25.59	9.05	5.74	NC	NC
BLD		NE	NC	NC	NC	NC	NC	44.31
CPI (ML) (L)	S	1.56	NC	NC	NC	NC	NC	NC
ICS (SCS)		NE	NC	NC	NC	2.13	NC	NC
INC	N	27.02	48.57	64.4	50.68	50.68	50.53	50.27
JNP		NE	NC	NC	NC	NC	1.87	NC
NAGP		NE	NC	NC	NC	7.25	NC	NC
SHS	S	NC	0.23	0.23	NC	NC	NC	NC

Source: www.eci.gov.in

**All along a Congress constituency, the party faced the worst defeat in 2004. The vote swing which started in 1999 in favour of BJP, ultimately went in favour of AGP, the party which finally captured the seat in 2004.*

Table 2.6 [B]

Dibrugarh Lok Sabha Constituency (List of winning candidates)

Year	Voters in *000	Voter Turnout (Percentage)	Winner			Runner-up		
			Candidate Name	Percentage	Party	Candidate Name	Percentage	Party
2004	631.24	65.08	Sarbananda Sonowal	35	AGP	Kamakhya Tasa	32.06	BJP
1999	578.81	61.2	Paban Singh Ghatowar	48.57	INC	Ajit Chaliha	36.54	BJP
1998	381.06	40.31	Paban Singh Ghatowar	64.4	INC	Ajit Chaliha	25.59	BJP
1996	591.3	70.32	Paban Singh Ghatowar	50.68	INC	Israil Nanda	31.34	AGP
1991	518.52	64.71	Paban Singh Ghatowar	50.53	INC	Dipen Tanti	21.96	AGP
1984	480.5	52.27	Haren Bhumji	50.68	INC	Nagen Saikia	41.38	IND
1977	248.9	49.5	Haren Bhumji	50.27	INC	Golap Borbora	44.31	BLD

Source: www.eci.gov.in

Nomination: The Process and the Grounds of Selection of Candidates

The support of the tea tribe community has been playing a decisive role in the elections in the constituency. The tea tribe has traditionally backed the Congress but they seemed to have become disenchanted with the Congress lately. Several leaders of the Assam Tea Tribes Students' Association (ATTSA) joined the BJP, chief amongst them being Kamakhya Prasad Tasa, General Secretary and former President of the Association. The major grievances of the tea tribes were the failure of the Congress to revive the Assam Tea Corporation Ltd (ATCL) gardens which had been bankrupt for several years causing great hardship for the tea labourers and the failure of the Congress to book the culprits in the Khobang tea estate firing incident in the Tinsukia district during the Durga Puja Bonus impasse, the year before the 2004 Lok Sabha poll. The stalling of the development works for the tea community under the Congress government was also raised by the tea tribe leaders like Kamakhya Prasad Tasa who was known to enjoy a great deal of popularity among the youths of the tea tribes. It appeared that they were not so disillusioned with the party as such, but they had grievances against Ghatowar, who hardly cared to take up the problems of the constituency for possible solutions, despite being in power for eight long years.

The tea tribe student leader, Kamakhya Prasad Tasa, joined the Bharatiya Janata Party (BJP) on February 22, 2004 just on the eve of the election. He resigned from the post of the General Secretary of the Assam Tea Tribes Students' Association (ATTSA) on January 24, 2004. Though the BJP did not clarify as to why it welcomed a person who till a couple of weeks ago was in the Congress, it was certain that Tasa would get the nomination from the BJP in the Dibrugarh Lok Sabha constituency. The BJP earlier tried with Ajit Chaliha, local caste Hindu tea planter more than once to challenge the Congress bastion but failed miserably. It held that since the tea tribe had a strong hold in the constituency, Tasa might be a challenge to the State Congress President, Pawan Singh Ghatowar, the sitting MP from the constituency. Internal conflict had sharpened in the district BJP. Zila Yuva Mancha of the BJP in the district and some party leaders accused BJP district President, Nakul Baruah, who himself was an aspirant for the party nomination, for his dictatorial role in sending the names for the Lok Sabha seat of Dibrugarh. They also sent a letter to the High Command about these issues. Finally, the BJP decided to field Tassa in this tea tribe dominated constituency. The nomination of Tasa, a young leader from the tea community created an extreme situation for Ghatowar.

It was supposed that the division of the tea tribe vote was largely the advantage for the AGP candidate. The AGP General Secretary, Hitendra Nath Goswami, announced the name of Sarbananda Sonowal as the candidate from AGP in Dibrugarh Lok Sabha constituency as he had the possibilities of being elected from the constituency. Sarbananda Sonowal, a young leader of the party, who played a major role in the All Assam Students' Union (AASU) during his days as a student leader, was elected to the Assam Assembly in 2001 from the Moran Assembly constituency, which is a part of Dibrugarh Lok Sabha constituency, defeating, Jibantara Ghatowar, wife of Paban Singh Ghatowar, by amassing a vote percentage of 42.64 per cent. His election to the Assembly defeating a candidate belonging to the tea tribe clearly indicated that there had been erosion in the Congress support base among the tea tribe labourers in favour of the AGP. This was the major consideration for AGP to nominate Sonowal from the prestigious Dibrugarh parliamentary constituency. Further, it was argued that Sonowal had been working with the people of Moran constituency, and in a way he had been expanding his support base. To Sonowal's good fortune, the All Assam Tai Ahom Students' Union (AATASU), which had a base among the predominant Ahom community in the constituency, announced that it would support Sonowal. The AATASU organized mass campaigns for him in the remote villages of the district. Having had a good impression as a student leader in rural areas, his strong stand on Illegal Migrants (Determination by Tribunals) (Act) [IM(DT) Act] clearly worked in his favour. AATASU criticising the former MPs from the constituency even distributed some letters in support of Sarbananda Sonowal.

Meanwhile, the CPI (ML) announced Subhash Sen, AICCTU State Secretary, as the candidate from Dibrugarh, knowing fully well that its candidate in case of defeat would forfeit the security deposit. It took the election as a vehicle to make its presence felt in Upper Assam. Yet another reason for nominating Sen was that he could penetrate deep into the rural areas which would help the party to create a support base in the constituency. It appeared that a few individuals, including a Professor at Dibrugarh University, took interest in the process of nominating Sen as the party candidate.

14th Lok Sabha Poll Result
Winner: *Sarbananda Sonowal (AGP)*
Votes Secured: ***2,20,944***
Runner-up: Kamakhya Tasa ***(BJP)***
Votes Secured: ***2,02,390***
****Sarbananda Sonowal wins by 18,554 votes***

Table 2.7
Contestants in Dibrugarh Lok Sabha Constituency (1999 and 2004)

Dibrugarh					
1999			2004		
Candidate	***Party***	***Votes***	***Candidate***	***Party***	***Votes***
Paban Singh Ghatowar	Indian National Congress	270863	Sarbananda Sonowal	Asom Gana Parishad	220944
Ajit Chaliha	Bharatiya Janata Party	203747	Kamakhya Prasad Tasa	Bharatiya Janata Party	202390
Biju Phukan	Asom Gana Parishad	75932	Paban Singh Ghatowar	Indian National Congress	
Brij Pradhan	Communist Party Of India (Marxist-Lennist) (Liberation)	5019	Badhram Rajgarh	Independents	15894
Ramnarayan Singh	Shiva Sena	1276	Subhas Sen	Communist Party Of India (Marxist-Lennist) (Liberation)	9843
Mansharam Patowari	Independents	837	Amrit Borgohain	Independents	6251
Paban Singh Ghatowar	Indian National Congress	270863	Titus Bhengra	Samata Party	5329
Ajit Chaliha	Bharatiya Janata Party	203747			
Biju Phukan	Asom Gana Parishad	75932			
Brij Pradhan	Communist Party Of India (Marxist-Lennist) (Liberation)	5019			
Ramnarayan Singh	Shiva Sena	1276			

Source: www.electionnext.com

(C) Gauhati Lok Sabha Constituency

The Background

The Gauhati Lok Sabha constituency happens to be the most prestigious constituency in the State. Being the gateway to India's Northeast, it has a special status. Its importance as the capital of the premier State also needs to be underscored. A witness to the ups and downs and electoral victories of different parties since independence (Table 2.8 [A&B]), the Constituency has been the focal point of all political activities. In the recent times, the Congress has captured this parliamentary seat thrice, in 1991, 1998 and 2004, followed by the Asom Gana Parishad who won twice in 1985 and 1996, and the sole victory that BJP registered was in 1999. Despite its victories, the Congress support base has declined in terms of percentage of votes polled from 49.57 per cent in 1998 to 40.06 percent in 2004.

In the 1984 Lok Sabha election, the AGP won 60.9 per cent of the votes, compared to the Congress' 17.7 per cent. In the next election held in the State, in 1991, the Congress not only improved its position by capturing 23.8 per cent of the votes, but also could recapture the seat. The seat went to Kirip Chaliha from the Congress, who won by 44,805 votes over his nearest rival, Asraf Ali of Natun Asom Gana Parishad. Although, the Congress could further improve its tally to 30.71 per cent in 1996, AGP's Prabin Chandra Sharma wrested back the seat from Congress' Bhubaneswar Kalita with a vote margin of 11,4,397 or 44.30 per cent.

The Gauhati Parliamentary constituency was the jewel in BJP's crown in the 1999 poll. It was one of the two seats with which the saffron party had opened its account in the Brahmaputra Valley for the first time. The constituency, traditionally a Congress bastion, was thus wrested by the BJP when Bijoya Chakrabarty drubbing the high-profile Bhubaneshwar Kalita of the Congress went to win it. Bijoya Chakrabarty's victory margin was impressive with 75,238 votes or a vote percentage of 45.95 per cent in an 11-cornered contest.

But the repeat of the previous feat by the then Union Minister for Water Resources, Bijoya Chakrabarty, seemed extremely difficult during the 14th Lok Sabha poll in the State, since the Congress Chief Minister Tarun Gogoi was all out to win the seat for his party. The Union Minister was also facing flak from her own party men as a section of the BJP leaders held her responsible for the party's debacle in the Guwahati Municipal Corporation's (GMC) elections, for she was the overall in-charge of that GMC elections. BJP could manage to win only 13 seats in the GMC elections.

13th Lok Sabha Poll Result
Winner: *Bijoya Chakrabarty (BJP)*
Votes Secured: *3,84,771*
Runner-up: *Bhubaneswar Kalita (INC)*
Votes Secured: *3,09,533*
Bijoya Chakrabarty wins by 75,238 votes

Table 2.8 [A]

Gauhati Lok Sabha Constituency (Percentage of valid votes cast in favour of contesting parties)

Party Abbreviation	Current Party Status	2004	1999	1998	1996	1991	1984	1977
1	2	3	4	5	6	7	8	9
AGP	S	20.51	14.21	21.44	44.3	16.57	60.9	NC
AII (T)		NE	NC	NC	0.67	NC	NC	NC
BJP	N	33.13	45.95	27.31	19.42	7.55	NC	NC
BLD		NE	NC	NC	NC	NC	NC	52.52
CPI	N	NC	NC	NC	NC	4.21	3.06	7.79
ICS		NE	NC	NC	NC	NC	0.93	NC
INC	N	40.06	36.96	49.57	30.71	23.84	17.72	39.69
JP		NC	NC	NC	NC	1.15	NC	NC
NAGP		NE	NC	NC	NC	17.54	NC	NC
NGP	N	NC	1.58	NC	NC	NC	NC	NC
SHS	S	NC	NC	NC	0.11	NC	NC	NC
SP	S	0.28	0.23	0.77	0.52	NC	NC	NC

Source: www.eci.gov.in

****The support swing in the Gauhati Parliamentary constituency rather shows a pendulum type phenomenon. Way back in 1991, it was the INC who won the seat with a vote percentage of 23.84, thereafter in 1996, the vote swing was in favour of the AGP (44.3 per cent) again to come back to the Congress in 1998 (49.57). In 1999, the votes favoured the BJP (45.95 per cent) again to fall on the Congress' lap in 2004 (40.06).***

Table 2.8 [B]
Gauhati Lok Sabha Constituency (List of winning candidates)

Year	Voters in *000	Voter Turnout (Percentage)	Winner			Runner-up		
			Candidate Name	Percentage	Party	Candidate Name	Percentage	Party
2004	881.78	61.18	Kirip Chaliha	40.06	INC	Bhupen Hazarika	33.13	BJP
1999	858.03	63.33	Bijoya Chakrabarty	45.95	BJP	Bhubaneswar Kalita	36.96	INC
1998	592.54	43.81	Bhubaneswar Kalita	49.57	INC	Manoranjan Goswami	27.31	BJP
1996	872.51	74.57	Prabin Chandra Sarmah	44.3	AGP	Bhubaneswar Kalita	30.71	INC
1991	746.04	69.89	Kirip Chaliha	23.84	INC	Asaf Ali	17.54	NAGP
1984	720.67	82.36	Dinesh Goswami	60.93	IND	Bhagaban Lahkar	17.72	INC
1977	291.6	52.7	Renuka Devi Barkataky	52.52	BLD	Dinesh Chandra Goswami	39.69	INC

Source: www.eci.gov.in

Nomination: The Process and the Grounds of Selection of Candidates

The prestigious Gauhati constituency with eleven candidates on the fray was the highpoint of Assam's 14th Lok Sabha poll[23].

On the eve of the ensuing 14th Lok Sabha poll, Bijoya Chakrabarty blaming the State government for not initiating the development projects sponsored by her MP fund, declared on her own that she would be the candidate from the BJP contesting the forthcoming Lok Sabha poll from the Gauhati Lok Sabha constituency. The self-proclamation failed to impress the local media as it started highlighting the discordant voice of her party colleagues including the top State leaders like Indramoni Bora and Rajen Gohain. The infighting within the party indicated that the BJP was not going to retain the seat, should Chakrabarty be given the party nomination. To utter surprise of everyone, the BJP found Dr. Bhupen Hazarika[24], a new member of the party, a potential threat to the other candidates from the constituency. It was held that a cultural icon of international repute, Dr. Hazarika, commanded tremendous respect from all sections of the society and the State that took pride in him.

Though a new entrant in BJP, Dr. Hazarika was not an unknown figure to politics. He left behind his past political career to dedicate himself to music and writings, perhaps his first love. Dr. Hazarika was elected to the Assam

---

[23] 14, 39,904 voters were to decide the fate of the candidates from this prestigious constituency.

[24] Dr. Hazarika, in his early years, was associated with the Indian People's Theatre Association (IPTA), which was known for its left leanings. He had never been a member of any Communist party though. But it was with the left parties' support that he, as an independent candidate, contested and won the Assembly poll from Naoboicha in 1967. He was an MLA till 1972. He later distanced himself not only from the IPTA, but also from the leftist ideologues and cultural activists. However, his decision to join a political party at the age of 78 did shock many of his old pals, cultural luminaries and intelligentsia. His decision invoked sharp and harsh criticism as the common masses did not want him to be under the banner of any political party.

Legislative Assembly in 1967 from Naoboicha constituency, but was defeated in 1972 when he contested from the Mangaldoi parliamentary constituency. Perhaps the people of the State did not like to see him as a political figure belonging to any party. Hence, the general masses were taken aback when Dr. Hazarika announced that he found the BJP, a party with a humanist approach, and immediately after joining the party, expressed his desire to contest the election from Gauhati. It was obvious that to be on the safe side, the BJP decided to give the nomination in favour of Dr. Hazarika. The BJP closing all discussions and controversies regarding the party's nomination of candidate finally declared Dr. Hazarika as the party candidate from the Gauhati constituency. The declaration came from the party's All India General Secretary, Pramod Mahajan. The BJP high command, therefore, deprived the former BJP MP, Bijoya Chakrabarty[25].

For the 14th Lok Sabha poll, twenty-three Congress leaders had sought nominations from the Congress in this constituency. The BJP's nomination of candidate for this constituency was supposed to influence the nomination process of the Congress candidates. Though Tarun Gogoi asserted that Dr. Bhupen Hazarika was not a factor for the Congress but he and his party did try their best to find out a worthy and heavyweight who had all possibilities to defeat Dr. Hazarika. Bhubaneswar Kalita, Pankaj Bora, Kirip Chaliha, Dr. Haren Das, Akan Bora were among those who had sought tickets from the Congress. Meanwhile, Dr. Bhumidhar Barman, Minister of Health and Family Welfare, Assam, proposed the name of Renuka Devi Barkataki, who happened to be a trade union leader. It was but natural that the whole process led to a sharp controversy.

---

[25] Immediately after the nomination of Hazarika, the supporters of Bijoya Chakrabarty organised protest rallies and meetings against Dr. Hazarika's nomination and deprivation of Bijoya. Ten men and women shaved their hairs in support of that. These protests were organised in the Judges Field, Guwahati. Bijoya's supporters also created chaos in a training camp of the BJP and demanded reassessment of the candidates list. They also shouted slogans like 'Bhupen hatao, BJP bachao'.

Within the Congress, there was an Upper Assam vs. Lower Assam controversy as well. A few ministers and MLAs from the Congress demanded that party workers from lower Assam only should be given tickets in the Gauhati Lok Sabha constituency[26]. The proposal offered by an MLA from Gauhati was supported by a Cabinet and a State Minister. The Congress General Secretary Akan Bora, and Kirip Chaliha condemned the proposal as undemocratic and unconstitutional. In the midst of these controversies, the media floated a rumour that the Congress was considering Dr. Mamoni Raisom Goswami, an eminent literary figure and winner of Jyanpith award, as its candidate for the Gauhati seat. Dr. Goswami, however, lost no time in issuing a statement dismissing the rumour.

Ultimately, resting all speculations and controversies and sidestepping even Kirip Chaliha and Haren Das, Tarun Gogoi declared that Bhubaneswar Kalita, would be the candidate from the Congress from the prestigious Gauhati Lok Sabha constituency. Bhubaneswar Kalita, unwilling to contest the election from this constituency, however, refused the offer. On Kalita's refusal, the name of Kirip Chaliha was forwarded. Sidelining the other eight MLAs' offer to fight from the Gauhati constituency, Gogoi offered the ticket ultimately to Kirip Chaliha, the former MP from the State who represented the constituency from 1991 to 1996.

The AGP was supposed to offer the ticket to Bhrigu Kumar Phukan[27] and Samujjal Bhattacharyya to contest from Gauhati. But Samujjal Bhattacharyya went on to clarify that he had no intentions of joining active politics. On this, it was announced by the party that Bhrigu Kumar Phukan was to be given another chance to return to the AGP, or he might as well be extended with outside support from the party's side. It is noteworthy that Phukan was one of the key figures who staged a vertical split in the AGP in 1990 to

[26] The controversy arose among the leaders of the party after a meeting that was held at Bhumidhar Barman's government residence concerning the issue of tickets.

[27] Bhrigu Kumar Phukan, one of the top leaders of the historic anti-foreigner agitation, which had swept the State between 1979 and 1985, was contemplating returning back to the AGP after finding that there was no significant place for him in the NCP.

form a new party called Natun-Asom Gana Parishad. He rejoined the party in 1996 with a hope that he would be fully rehabilitated. To his utter dismay, he found only lukewarm response from the AGP after the party marched back to capture power at Dispur in 1996. Thereafter, he preferred maintaining discreet silence till he joined the NCP. His home coming was rewarded and the party decided to put up Bhrigu Kumar Phukan[28]. His return to the party after a long hiatus generated enthusiasm among the workers in his Assembly constituency of Jalukbari.

The Trinamool Gana Parishad's (TGP)[29] party Secretary, Atul Bora, meanwhile announced that it would come into ally with any poll party which was ready to leave the Gauhati constituency for the TGP. The image of Deben Dutta, the leader of the Consumer Protection Movement in the State, being very bright among the voters of Guwahati city, was thought of as somebody who could attract the voters in his favour. A well-known educationist and a public face, Dutta[30] got the nomination from the TGP.

14th Lok Sabha Poll Result
Winner: *Kirip Chaliha (INC)*
Votes Secured: *3,53,250*
Runner-up: *Bhupen Hazarika (BJP)*
Votes Secured: *2,92,099*
Kirip Chaliha wins by 61,151 votes

[28] Eight local committees of Jalukbari AGP protested against Bhrigu Phukan's home coming, as they believed that because of the division in NCP and his existenceless, Phukan had come back to AGP. He harboured no good wishes for AGP. Bhrigu Phukan founded the the Asom Jatiya Sanmilan (AJS), a new political party after leaving the Asom Gana Parishad in 1998. In March 2001 the AJS General Secretary, Hemanta Barman, and many other members joined the Indian National Congress. Thereafter Bhrigu Phukan left the party and rejoined AGP to contest the 11th Legislative Assembly election from the AGP. On the other hand, the AJS contested as a part of the Rashtriya Democratic Alliance, on a Nationalist Congress Party symbol.

[29] Trinamool Gana Parishad (TGP), was founded as a splinter-group of Asom Gana Parishad in 2000. The party led by Atul Bora allied with the BJP in the State Assembly election, 2001.

[30] Moreover, the highly educated people were in favour of Deben Dutta in Guwahati. This was revealed by a survey carried out in Dimoria and Guwahati city by the Newspaper group *Asomiya Pratidin*.

Table 2.9
Contestants in Gauhati Lok Sabha Constituency (1999 and 2004)

Gauhati					
1999			2004		
Candidate	*Party*	*Votes*	*Candidate*	*Party*	*Votes*
Bijoya Chakrabarty	Bharatiya Janata Party	384771	Kirip Chaliha	Indian National Congress	353250
Bhubaneshwar Kalita	Indian National Congress	309533	Bhupen Hazarika	Bharatiya Janata Party	292099
Durga Das Boro	Asom Gana Parishad	119034	Bhrigu Kumar Phukan	Asom Gana Parishad	180856
Suniti Sonowal	National Congress Party	13241	Deven Dutta	Trinamool Gana Parishad	14933
Biren Rabha	Independents	4293	Rajat Chandra Rabha	Independents	14489
Dr. Phukan Chandra Boro	Independents	1987	Sumitra Das	Independents	11240
Nawaziz Ara Begum	Samajwadi Party	1933	Kazi Nekib Ahmed	Independents	3089
Mrinal Kanti Chowdhury	Ajeya Bharat Party	481	Dhwajen Brahma	Independents	2586
Bhumidhar Pathak	Independents	333	Bhabani Boro	Independents	2554
			Bhubaneswar Barman	Samajwadi Party	2466
			Nipon Dhoula	Social Action Party	2299
			Umesh Chandra Das	Independents	1914

Source: www.electionnext.com

(D) Jorhat Lok Sabha Constituency

The Background

The Congress has been bestowed with the power to win almost every Lok Sabha poll from this constituency since 1977 except the 1984 poll (Table 2.10 [A&B]) when Parag Chaliha, an AGP candidate defeated Bijoy Krishna Handique from the Congress by winning a vote percentage of 57.12. In rest of the elections, since the first Lok Sabha poll held in 1952, the Jorhat Lok Sabha constituency has been the den of the Congress all the way. Two interesting facts deserve attention. First, it was the present Chief Minister of Assam, Tarun Gogoi, who gave a boosting win to the Congress from the constituency in 1977 achieving a vote percentage of 49.44. Second, five consecutive wins for the Congress from the constituency since 1991 have been brought by a single personality, Bijoy Krishna Handique. This young tea planter from Jorhat, after losing the first election battle in 1984 to Parag Chaliha has never looked back. Though the vote percentage for the Congress had come down to 33.54 in the 14th Lok Sabha poll, Handique could collect as high a vote percentage of 48.31 and 65.13 in the 1999 and 1998 Lok Sabha polls respectively for the Congress. This he could achieve because of the tea garden vote bank, which was in his favour. It is noteworthy that Handique is a leading tea planter and owns a number of tea gardens located in Jorhat District.

However, of late, the Congress seems to be losing the traditional vote bank of the tea garden labourers. Formerly 2 lakh voters from 115 tea gardens within the constituency that covers both Jorhat and Sibsagar districts determined the fate of the candidates. But because of the division in the vote banks, the Congress had to face a strong opposition from Drupad Borgohain, a Rajya Sabha member belonging to the CPI.

Although the AGP has remained the runner up most of the time, the vote percentage of the party has been abysmally low in the district. In the 13th Lok Sabha poll, however, it was Janaki Nath Handique from the BJP who captured the second position. The Congress gradually was losing the traditional vote bank of the tea garden labourers. But BJP was slowly but surely building its base in some areas of the district.

13th Lok Sabha Poll Result
Winner: *Bijoy Krishna Handique (INC)*
Votes Secured: *3,04,690*
Runner-up: *Janaki Nath Handique (BJP)*
Votes Secured: *2,05,330*
Bijoy Krishna Handique wins by 99,360 votes

Table 2.10 [A]
Jorhat Lok Sabha Constituency (Percentage of valid votes cast in favour of contesting parties)

Party Abbreviation	Current Party Status	2004	1999	1998	1996	1991	1984	1977
1	2	3	4	5	6	7	8	9
AGP	S	14	18.74	16.37	40.71	24.14	57.12	NC
AIIC (T)		NE	NC	NC	4.32	NC	NC	NC
BJP	N	22.47	32.55	14.34	5.64	NC	NC	NC
BLD		NE	NC	NC	NC	NC	NC	39.91
CPI	N	25.84	NC	NC	NC	NC	11.4	10.65
INC	N	33.54	48.31	65.13	47.99	44.9	37.57	49.44
JD		NE	NC	NC	NC	NC	NC	NC
JD (S)	S	NC	NC	NC	NC	0.4	NC	NC
JNP		NE	NC	NC	NC	NC	2.45	NC
NAGP		NE	NC	NC	NC	6.95	NC	NC
NCP	N	0.4	NC	NC	NC	NC	NC	NC

Source: www.eci.gov.in

***A swing is noticed which had taken place against the Congress in 1999 and 2004 elections against the Congress in this constituency. But that did not adversely affect the election fortune of the sitting MP, Bijoy Krishna Handique. The swing went in favour of the BJP in 1999 and CPI in 2004.**

Table 2.10 [B]
Jorhat Lok Sabha Constituency (List of winning candidates)

Year	Voters in *000	Voter Turnout (Percentage)	Winner			Runner-up		
			Candidate Name	Percentage	Party	Candidate Name	Percentage	Party
2004	666.84	61.85	Bijoy Krishna Handique	33.54	INC	Dhrupad Borgohain	25.84	CPI
1999	649.49	64.72	Bijoy Krishna Handique	48.31	INC	Janaki Nath Handique	32.55	BJP
1998	346.46	34.54	Bijoy Krishna Handique	65.13	INC	Deba Kumar Bora	16.37	AGP
1996	677.37	72.35	Bijoy Krishna Handique	47.99	INC	Bhadreswar Buragohain	40.71	AGP
1991	563.63	66.01	Bijoy Krishna Handique	44.9	INC	Paragehar Chaliha	24.14	AGP
1984	525.44	72.3	Parag Chaliha	57.12	IND	Bijoy Krishna Handique	37.57	INC
1977	311.01	53.1	Tarun Gogoi	49.44	INC	Dulal Chandra Barua	39.91	BLD

Source: www.eci.gov.in

Nomination: The Process and the Grounds of Selection of Candidates

Bijoy Krishna Handique from the Congress could win the previous four Lok Sabha elections because of the tea garden labour vote banks, especially in the Sibsagar district, which were ever supportive. As allegations flashed in the print media that Handique did not channelise the MP funds in the desired manner, besides Jorhat, his popularity seemed to wane in the Sibsagar district as well. For once, people from Geleki were so unhappy with Handique and Hemoprava Saikia, a Minister in the Tarun Gogoi Cabinet hailing from Nazira within the Jorhat Lok Sabha constituency, for their failure to fulfill the promises that they even threatened to boycott the election. Despite these allegations, it was Handique who was nominated from the Congress to fight the 14th Lok Sabha poll (Table 2.11). The reasons seemed obvious. He was the sitting MP representing the constituency since 1991. Further, as a tea planter he had a strong financial background and was capable of bearing the election expenses without depending on the party pool.

Handique's main opponent, Dhrupad Borgohain, was on the other hand gaining popularity, as he in his six-year term, as a member of Rajya Sabha, served the people of the constituency to their satisfaction. Besides, there was an impression that Borgohain's public relations had been far better than Handique's and he had also consolidated his influence among the tea garden voters in the Sibsagar district. As the CPI felt that the election wind was in favour of Dhrupad Borgohain, he was given the party ticket to contest the election. Asom Jatiyatabadi Yuva Chatra Parishad (AJYCP) President, Hamidur Rahman, also urged the people to vote for Borgohain not on the basis of the party he represented, but as an individual figure who always worked for the people.

The AGP offered the ticket to Dulal Baruah. Mr. Baruah

had been shifting his party affiliation quite frequently since 1983 when he left the Janata Party. After some bewildering political positions during the Assam movement, he joined the AGP and then the BJP, and again returned to the AGP a few months before the 2004 Lok Sabha election. It was a foregone conclusion that Dulal Baruah would lose the election but at the same time he would take away a slice of the support base of Dhrupad Borgohain.

14th Lok Sabha Poll Result
Winner: *Bijoy Krishna Handique (INC)*
Votes Secured: *2,23,624*
Runner-up: *Drupad Borgohain (CPI)*
Votes Secured: *1,72,332*
Bijoy Krishna Handique wins by 51,292 votes

Table 2.11
Contestants in Jorhat Lok Sabha Constituency (1999 and 2004)

Dirugarh					
1999			2004		
Candidate	*Party*	*Votes*	*Candidate*	*Party*	*Votes*
Bijoy Krishna Handique	**Indian National Congress**	304690	Bijoy Krishna Handique	**Indian National Congress**	223624
Janaki Nath Handique	**Bharatiya Janata Party**	205330	Dhrupad Borgohain	**Communist Party of India**	172332
Deba Kumar Bora	**Asom Gana Parishad**	118194	Devananda Borgohain	**Bharatiya Janata Party**	149820
Pradip Kumar Gogoi	**Nationalist Congress Party**	2530	Dulal Chandra Baruah	**Asom Gana Parishad**	93353
			Raj Kumar Dowerah	**Revolutionary Communist Party of India (Rasik Bhatt) (R)**	16691
			Joyram Mout	**Samata Party**	11015

Source: www.electionnext.com

(E) Lakhimpur Lok Sabha Constituency

The Background

The Lakhimpur constituency, with a majority of the plain tribe, the Misings dominating it, has been a constituency in which the Congress has won the Lok Sabha polls four times since 1977. Starting the winning row in 1977 (Table 2.12 [A&B]) with Lalit Kumar Doley winning the seat for the Congress, it has seen victories in the constituency in the Lok Sabha polls of 1991, 1998 and 1999. Twice, that is in 1998 and 1999, Ranee Narah, a woman candidate from the Congress has won the seat for the party. In the 13th Lok Sabha poll of 1999, Ranee Narah won the seat with a margin of 34.41 percentage of votes. An important fact to be noted here is that it was Sarbananda Sonowal, the current MP from Dibrugarh Parliamentary constituency who lost to Ranee Narah in 1999. The lone time when the AGP succeeded in winning from this constituency is in 1996, when Dr. Arun Kumar Sarma won the seat for the AGP.

13th Lok Sabha Poll Result
Winner: *Ranee Narah (INC)*
Votes Secured: ***2,55,925***
Runner-up: *Sarbananda Sonowal (AGP)*
Votes Secured: ***2,01,402***
****Ranee Narah wins by***
54,523 votes

Table 2.12 [A]
Lakhimpur Lok Sabha Constituency (Percentage of valid votes cast in favour of contesting parties)

Party Abbreviation	Current Party Status	2004	1999	1998	1996	1991	1984	1977
1	2	3	4	5	6	7	8	9
AGP	S	37.61	27.08	22.05	33.06	21.1	NC	NC
AIIC (T)		NE	NC	NC	3.77	NC	NC	NC
BJP	N	21.14	24.81	19.41	8.5	NC	NC	NC
BLD		NE	NC	NC	NC	NC	NC	35.39
CPI	N	NC	NC	NC	NC	5.4	16.32	NC
INC	N	34.09	34.41	40.05	32.54	31.36	NC	59.06
JD		NE	NC	NC	1.95	NC	NC	NC
JD (S)	S	NC	0.17	NC	NC	NC	NC	NC
JNP		NE	NC	NC	NC	NC	4.09	NC
JP		NC	NC	NC	NC	1.04	NC	NC
LKD		NE	NC	NC	NC	NC	3.46	NC
NAGP		NE	NC	NC	NC	1.88	NC	NC
NCP	N	NC	0.74	NC	NC	NC	NC	NC
PTCA		NC	NC	NC	NC	2.73	NC	NC
RSP	S	1.47	NC	NC	NC	NC	NC	NC
SP	S	NC	0.17	NC	NC	NC	NC	NC

Source: www.eci.gov.in

****Basically, Lakhimpur has been a Congress constituency like Jorhat and Dibrugarh. But the erosion in support base of the Congress is quite visible in this constituency. The benefit of this swing has gone to the AGP. It is the AGP which captured the seat in 1996 and 2004.***

Table 2.12 [B]
Lakhimpur Lok Sabha Constituency (List of winning candidates)

Year	Voters in *000	Voter Turnout (Percentage)	Winner			Runner-up		
			Candidate Name	Percentage	Party	Candidate Name	Percentage	Party
2004	800.02	71.01	Dr. Arun Kumar Sarmah	37.61	AGP	Ranee Narah	34.09	INC
1999	767	72.31	Ranee Narah	34.41	INC	Sarbananda Sonowal	27.08	AGP
1998	705.16	66.66	Ranee Narah	40.05	INC	Dr. Arun Kumar Sarmah	22.05	AGP
1996	707.59	76.79	Dr. Arun Kumar Sarmah	33.06	AGP	Bolin Kuli	32.54	INC
1991	642.54	72.41	Bolin Kuli	31.36	INC	Iswar Prasanna Hazarika	21.1	AGP
1984	531.88	73.14	Gakul Saikia	50.22	IND	Nameswar Pegu	16.32	CPI
1977	287.88	51.79	Lalit Kumar Doley	59.06	INC	Mohananda Bora	35.39	BLD

Source: www.eci.gov.in

Nomination: The Process and the Grounds of Selection of Candidates

The Congress thought of nominating Ranee Narah from Lakhimpur for the ensuing 14th Lok Sabha poll. However, the anti Ranee Narah MLAs in the Congress declared that they were not ready to take the responsibility of the result, she being nominated. There had been allegations doing rounds that she failed as a committed MP in the constituency during the period 1998 to 2004. The print media too was vocal in creating a negative image of Mrs. Narah. The grassroots workers of the party too revolted against her and declared openly their unwillingness to work for her. Nevertheless, despite the mounting pressure on the Congress High Command against Narah's nomination[31], she did succeed in securing the nomination for three reasons - (i) she was the lone woman candidate the party could identify who had the prospects of winning the election, (ii) she had been the sitting MP from the constituency since 1998, and (iii) she was the wife of Bharat Narah, who was a Minister in the Tarun Gogoi Ministry. Again, the fact that Ranee Narah was a Muslim by birth and went on to marry Bharat Narah, a person belonging to the Mising community, infact had added an advantage to her candidature. It was, therefore, obvious that Ranee Narah got the nomination from the party[32] (Table 2.13). It was assumed that the two organisations, Takam Mising Porin Kebang (TMPK) and Mising Mimag Kebang (MMK)[33] would support the Congress in spite of the sharp rivalry between Bharat Narah and Ranee Narah, and between the two organisations TMPK and

---

[31]It is interesting to note here that while Ranee Narah was given the party nomination, Abdul Hamid was denied the same from Dhubri on the ground that his public image was alarmingly negative.

[32] Dileswar Tanti was offered the Ministership to seek cooperation for Ranee Narah in the election.

[33] Both the Mising political organisations TMPK and MMK are fighting for the Sixth Schedule status of the Misings under the Constitution of India.

MMK. Bharat Narah, after a secret meeting with Ranoj Pegu[34] (Advisor, TMPK and MMK), declared that the two organizations would only play an impartial role in the forthcoming election. However, the Lakhimpur district Unnayan Sangram Parishad questioned the Congress about voting a person to power, who was not only an anti Mising but corrupt as well. This perhaps indicated that Ranee Narah was destined to lose the election.

The AGP, on the other hand, made a well-calculated move and offered the party ticket to Dr. Arun Sarma, who was known to be more popular than Ranee Narah in the constituency. Dr. Sarma was elected from the constituency in 1996 and during his brief tenure till 1998 Sarma could cultivate public relations in a formidable manner. The AGP learnt a lesson in 1999 by denying Dr. Sarma a ticket when it went on to offer the same to Sarbananda Sonowal who lost to Ranee Narah. The party this time shifted Sarbananda Sonowal to Dibrugarh, his home constituency, freeing roads to nominate Dr. Sarma, a candidate capable of snatching the constituency from the unpopular Ranee Narah.

Uday Shankar Hazarika, who got the nomination from BJP, was also expected to capture some votes because of the BJP's induced popularity image in the country.

14th Lok Sabha Poll Result
Winner: *Arun Kumar Sarma (AGP)*
Votes Secured: *3,00,865*
Runner-up: *Ranee Narah (INC)*
Votes Secured: *2,72,717*
Arun Kumar Sarma wins by 28,148 votes

[34] Though it was alleged that Ranoj Pegu had come to a secret understanding with the Congress and that the TMPK and MMK favoured the Congress, he denied that. But the Mising voters expressed their serious reaction against the so-called betrayal of Ranoj Pegu. Behind the understanding with Ranee, it was assumed that it was the ambition of Pegu to become an MLA or MP in the coming days which made him to go into a secret understanding with the Congress. His movement demanding the Sixth Schedule was just a political issue. Inspite of these allegations, Pegu reiterated his anti Ranee stand.

Table 2.13
Contestants in Lakhimpur Lok Sabha Constituency (1999 and 2004)

Lakhimpur					
1999			2004		
Candidate	***Party***	***Votes***	***Candidate***	***Party***	***Votes***
Ranee Narah	**Indian National Congress**	255925	Arun Kumar Sarma	**Asom Gana Parishad**	300865
Sarbananda Sonowal	**Asom Gana Parishad**	201402	Ranee Narah	**Indian National Congress**	272717
Udai Shankar Hazarika	**Bharatiya Janata Party**	184533	Uday Shankar Hazarika	**Bharatiya Janata Party**	169123
Ranoj Pegu	**Independents**	89963	Hekjal Wood	**Independents**	19710
Balin Kuli	**Nationalist Congress Party**	5527	Puspa Gogoi	**Revolutionary Socialist Party**	11757
Isak Karkoria	**Independents**	2030	Padmeswar Phukan	**Samata Party**	7888
Rafiqul Latif Baruah	**Janata Dal (Secular)**	1287	Rabin Deka	**Independents**	4905
Minu Buragohain	**Samajwadi Party**	1233	Biju Narah	**Independents**	4456
Chinu Saikia	**Ajeya Bharat Party**	1222	Sunmoni Das	**Lok Jan Shakti Party**	2948
Sidananda Kaman	**Independents**	701	Ghanashyam Bhattarai	**Independents**	2886
			Isak Korkoria	**Independents**	2765

Source: www.electionnext.com

(F) Mangaldoi Lok Sabha Constituency

The Background

Since 1977, the Mangaldoi parliamentary constituency has been won thrice by the Congress, once each by the AGP and the BJP (Table 2.14 [A&B]). The Congress registered wins in 1991, 1998 and 1999, while the AGP in 1996 and the BJP, a new entrant, won the seat in the 14th Lok Sabha poll of 2004. It is Madhab Rajbangshi who has won the seat twice for the Congress. In 1991, the winning candidate from the Congress party was Prabin Deka. In the 13th Lok Sabha poll of 1999, Madhab Rajbangshi once again won the seat for the Congress defeating his nearest rival Munindra Singha Lahkar of the BJP by a vote percentage of 34.09. Another interesting aspect to note in the district is the strong hold of BJP here, which was only gaining strength with each passing day.

13th Lok Sabha Poll Result

Winner: *Madhab Rajbangshi (INC)*

Votes Secured: *2,83,749*

Runner-up: *Munindra Singha Lahkar (BJP)*

Votes Secured: *2,67,315*

Madhab Rajbangshi wins by 16,434 votes

Table 2.14 [A]
Mangaldoi Lok Sabha Constituency (Percentage of valid votes cast in favour of contesting parties)

Party Abbreviation	Current Party Status	2004	1999	1998	1996	1991	1984	1977
1	2	3	4	5	6	7	8	9
AGP	S	17.71	18.59	18.32	33.25	21.39	NC	NC
AIIC (T)		NE	NC	NC	NC	NC	NC	NC
BJP	N	40.74	32.11	22.2	15.59	NC	2.07	NC
BLD		NE	NC	NC	NC	NC	NC	56.05
ICS		NE	NC	NC	NC	NC	NC	NC
ICS (SCS)		NE	NC	NC	NC	12.76	NC	NC
INC	N	37.22	34.09	41.78	20.66	24.02	11.17	38.81
JD		NE	NC	NC	1.1	NC	NC	NC
JNP		NE	NC	NC	NC	NC	2.31	NC
JP		NE	NC	NC	NC	1.44	NC	NC
NAGP		NE	NC	NC	NC	12.34	NC	NC
PTC		NE	NC	NC	NC	NC	9.88	NC

Source: www.eci.gov.in

* *It has been a Congress constituency till 1999. Even then from 1998 onwards there has been a visible swing in favour of the BJP which ultimately captured power in the constituency in 2004. It may be noted that though the Congress improved its performance in 2004, it had to concede defeat as BJP was successful in drawing AGP's votes to its fold.*

Table 2.14 [B]
Mangaldoi Lok SabhaConstituency (List of winning candidates)

Year	Voters in *000	Voter Turnout (Percentage)	Winner			Runner-up		
			Candidate Name	Percentage	Party	Candidate Name	Percentage	Party
2004	848.94	70.17	Narayan Chandra Borkataky	40.74	**BJP**	Madhab Rajbangshi	37.22	**INC**
1999	858.53	72.75	Madhab Rajbangshi	34.09	**INC**	Munindra Singha Lahkar	32.11	**BJP**
1998	705.75	59.91	Madhab Rajbangshi	41.78	**INC**	Munindra Singha Lahkar	22.2	**BJP**
1996	835.01	79.57	Birendra Prasad Baishya	33.25	**AGP**	Prabin Deka	20.66	**INC**
1991	724.3	75.75	Prabin Deka	24.02	**INC**	Birendra Prasad Baishya	21.39	**AGP**
1984	650.38	82.63	Saifuddin Ahmed	45.81	**IND**	Imran Shah	22.13	**IND**
1977	303.1	54.1	Hiralal Patowary	56.05	**BLD**	Dharanidhar Das	38.81	**INC**

Source: www.eci.gov.in

Nomination: The Process and the Grounds of Selection of Candidates

Though Madhab Rajbangshi won the seat for the Congress in 1998 and 1999, he was not the hot favourite among the Congress party workers for the 2004 Lok Sabha poll. It was declared that above 40,000 Congress workers would go on non-cooperation in the ensuing election if Rajbangshi was offered the ticket. The party workers of Nalbari district especially were so upset because of the alleged misdeeds of Rajbangshi that they even went on to the extent of demanding an alternative candidate from the constituency. Despite the demand, when Rajbangshi was given the party ticket, considering the fact that he had won the seat in last two elections, many Congress leaders refused to take an active part to campaign for Rajbangshi[35]. It was reported in a section of the press that Rajbangshi had the backing of Tarun Gogoi. There was no presentable candidate to challenge his candidature. It provided enough ground to him to get the nomination despite his negative image in the party and the looming threat of non-cooperation by the grassroots workers of the party.

The BJP decided to go with Narayan Borkataky, who happened to be the President of the State unit of the party with a reportedly clean image (Table 2.15). It appeared that the party sensed the profound organizational weaknesses of the Congress candidate and did not take much time to announce the candidature of Borkataky, though he did not have the experience of contesting any elections so far.

The AGP trying to strengthen its hold in the constituency,

---

[35] The Congress party workers were so much fed up with Rajbangshi that some of them even went ahead and campaigned for the AGP and some chose to remain completely silent when the party ticket was given to Rajbangshi. He also faced opposition from MLA, Uttara Kalita, and Madan Kalita. The clashes had emerged out of the conflict regarding the distribution of MP funds. Rajbangshi did not receive the support of Bhubaneswar Kalita, the Minister for Industries in the Tarun Gogoi Ministry and a powerful personality in the Assam Pradesh Congress Committee, for the same issue in the beginning.

tried to capitalize the weakness of the Congress candidate and inexperience of the BJP candidate to its advantage by nominating Apurba Bhattacharjee from the constituency, a less known figure in the party echelon.

> **14th Lok Sabha Poll Result**
> **Winner:** ***Narayan Chandra Borkataky (BJP)***
> **Votes Secured:** ***3,45,863***
> **Runner-up:** ***Madhab Rajbangshi (INC)***
> **Votes Secured:** ***3,15,997***
> ****Narayan Chandra Borkataky wins by 29,866 votes***

Table 2.15
Contestants in Mangaldoi Lok Sabha Constituency (1999 and 2004)

Mangaldoi					
1999			2004		
Candidate	***Party***	***Votes***	***Candidate***	***Party***	***Votes***
Madhab Rajbangshi	**Indian National Congress**	283749	Narayan Chandra Borkataky	**Bharatiya Janata Party**	345863
Munindra Singha Lahkar	**Bharatiya Janata Party**	267315	Madhab Rajbangshi	**Indian National Congress**	315997
Birendra Prasad Baishya	**Asom Gana Parishad**	154711	Apurba Bhattacharjee	**Asom Gana Parishad**	315997
Rabi Ram Brahma	**Independents**	110650	Bhupendra Nath Kakati	**Independents**	15046
Binai Khungur Basumatary	**United Tribal Nationalists Liberation Front**	8429	Shaheda Begum	**Samata Party**	10863
Quazi Syed Kutubuddin	**Ajeya Bharat Party**	3657	Aroon Baruah	**Independents**	8209
Chathu Ram Das	**Independents**	2819	Tridip Pati Singha	**Independents**	6862
Bhupendra Nath Kakati	**Independents**	1068			

Source: www.electionnext.com

(G) Silchar Lok Sabha Constituency

The Background

Excepting the 1977 Lok Sabha poll (Table 2.16 [A&B]), when Rashida Haque Choudhury from the Congress won the seat, ever since the Silchar parliamentary constituency has been a battlefield between Santosh Mohan Dev from the Congress and Kabindra Purkayastha from the BJP. Santosh Mohan Dev had won the seat in 1980, 1984, 1996 and 1999, while Kabindra Purkayastha had won it in 1991 and 1998 and had been the runner up in 1996 and 1999. Of course, the vote share of the Congress has been more than that of the BJP. The CPM too once has had a hold in the constituency which can be gathered from the fact that its party candidate Noorul Huda had been the runner up in the elections of 1980 and 1984. In the 13th Lok Sabha poll of 1999, which was won by the Congress in the constituency, the winner, Santosh Mohan Dev from the party could amass a vote percentage of 55.54.

13th Lok Sabha Poll Result
Winner: *Santosh Mohan Dev (INC)*
Votes Secured: *3,29,256*
Runner-up: *Kabindra Purkayastha (BJP)*
Votes Secured: *2,21,504*
Santosh Mohan Dev wins by 1,07,752 votes

Table 2.16 [A]

Silchar Lok Sabha Constituency (Percentage of valid votes cast in favour of contesting parties)

Party Abbreviation	Current Party Status	2004	1999	1998	1996	1991	1984	1980	1977
1	2	3	4	5	6	7	8	9	10
AGP	S	NC	NC	NC	NC	2.61	NC	NC	NC
AIIC (T)		NE	NC	NC	0.64	NC	NC	NC	NC
BJP	N	36.98	37.36	**37.05**	30.45	**38.87**	NC	NC	NC
CPM	N	3.29	NC	27.78	21.67	36.81	39.08	NC	44.26
INC	N	**40.48**	**55.54**	33.85	**42.69**	16.73	**48.88**	NC	**55.74**
INC (I)		NE	NC	NC	NC	NC	NC	**52.01**	NC
INC (U)		NE	NC	NC	NC	NC	NC	46.98	NC
JNP		NE	NC	NC	NC	NC	NC	NC	NC
NAGP		NE	NC	NC	NC	1.7	NC	NC	NC
NCP	N	NC	0.97	NC	NC	NC	NC	NC	NC
SP	S	16.41	NC	NC	NC	NC	NC	NC	NC

Source: www.eci.gov.in

**The Congress experienced a swing against the party in 1996 and 2004. The swing went in favour of the BJP in 1998. Even then the Congress was successful in capturing back the seat again in 1999.*

Table 2.16 [B]
Silchar Lok Sabha Constituency (List of winning candidates)

Year	Voters in *000	Voter Turnout (Percentage)	Winner			Runner-up		
			Candidate Name	Percentage	Party	Candidate Name	Percentage	Party
2004	608.23	69.18	Santosh Mohan Dev	40.48	INC	Kabindra Purkayastha	36.98	BJP
1999	608.53	73.52	Santosh Mohan Dev	55.54	INC	Kabindra Purkayastha	37.36	BJP
1998	650.38	78.68	Kabindra Purkayastha	37.05	BJP	Santosh Mohan Dev	33.85	INC
1996	592.25	78.62	Santosh Mohan Dev	42.69	INC	Kabindra Purkayastha	30.45	BJP
1991	555.11	75.73	Kabindra Purkayastha	38.87	BJP	Noorul Huda	36.81	CPM
1984	473.2	75.69	Santosh Mohan Dev	48.88	INC	Noorul Huda	39.08	CPM
1980	376.01	66.54	Santosh Mohan Dev	52.01	INC (I)	Rashida Haque Choudhury	46.98	INC (U)
1977	255.92	54.31	Rashida Haque Choudhury	55.74	INC	Noorul Huda	44.26	CPM

Source: www.eci.gov.in

Nomination: The Process and the Grounds of Selection of Candidates

For the 14th Lok Sabha poll, it was feared that the election process in Silchar might become a false and fatal one because the administration (both the police and civil officers) was in favour of the Congress who could go to any extent for a Congress win in the district. Amidst these allegations, Santosh Mohan Dev was nominated by the Congress as the party candidate for the ensuing parliamentary election (Table 2.17). Dev, a former Union Minister, has been the winner in the last two elections. The choice was obvious. So is the case with the BJP candidate Kabindra Purkayastha, who has won the election in 1996 and became the Minister in the BJP led Government. Although he was defeated in 1998 and 1999 elections by his arch rival Santosh Mohan Dev, he was undoubtedly the best bet that the party could offer.

14th Lok Sabha Poll Result

Winner: *Santosh Mohan Dev (INC)*

Votes Secured: *2,46,215*

Runner-up: *Kabindra Purkayastha (BJP)*

Votes Secured : *2,24,895*

Santosh Mohan Dev wins by 21,320 votes

Table 2.17
Contestants in Silchar Lok Sabha Constituency (1999 and 2004)

Silchar					
1999			2004		
Candidate	***Party***	***Votes***	***Candidate***	***Party***	***Votes***
Santosh Mohan Dev	**Indian National Congress**	**329256**	Santosh Mohan Dev	**Indian National Congress**	**246215**
Kabindra Purkayastha	**Bharatiya Janata Party**	**221504**	Kabindra Purkayastha	**Bharatiya Janata Party**	**224895**
Abdul Muhib Mazumder	**Independents**	**29060**	Anowar Hussain Laskar	**Samajwadi Party**	**99820**
Subhash Mohan Deb	**Nationalist Congress Party**	**5737**	Noorul Huda	**Communist Party Of India (Marxist)**	**20020**
Chittaranjan Sukhlabaidya	**Independents**	**1338**	Samarendra Ghosh	**Independents**	**4990**
Saumitra Nath	**Independents**	**1235**	Alok Sen	**Samata Party**	**4517**
Rajendra Kumar Sinha	**Independents**	**1181**	Benu Bhushan Nath	**Independents**	**1720**
Amiya Kanti Das	**Independents**	**1000**	Ashutosh Das	**Independents**	**1673**
Kantimoy Deb	**Independents**	**683**	Kantimoy Deb	**Independents**	**1530**
Jowahar Lal Goala	**Independents**	**581**	Kshitindra Sarkar	**Independents**	**1434**
Narayan Choudhury	**Independents**	**573**	Manoranjan Das	**Independents**	**1419**
Nazmul Haque Laskar	**Independents**	**546**			
Gopal Chakraborty	**Independents**	**173**			

Source: www.electionnext.com

(H) Tezpur Lok Sabha Constituency

The Background

The Tezpur parliamentary constituency has always been a hub for the Congress. The Congress has succeeded in retaining the seat six times continuously since 1984 (Table 2.18 [A&B]). To start with, it is Bipin Pal Das who won the seat for the Congress in 1984, Swarup Upadhayaya in 1991 and Iswar Prasanna Hazarika in 1996. Thereafter, Moni Kumar Subba has won the seat for the Congress for three consecutive polls. In the 13th Lok Sabha poll, Subba won the seat with a vote percentage of 34.09 defeating Ram Prasad Sharma of the BJP.

13th Lok Sabha Poll Result
Winner: *Moni Kumar Subba (INC)*
Votes Secured: *2,30,884*
Runner-up: *Ram Prasad Sarmah (BJP)*
Votes Secured: *2,05,178*
Moni Kumar Subba wins by 25,706 votes

Table 2.18 [A]

Tezpur Lok Sabha Constituency (Percentage of valid votes cast in favour of contesting parties)

Party Abbreviation	Current Party Status	2004	1999	1998	1996	1991	1984	1977
1	2	3	4	5	6	7	8	9
AGP	S	30.48	30	21.65	31.41	23.18	NC	NC
AIIC (T)		NE	NC	NC	6.19	NC	NC	NC
BJP	N	22.88	30.3	24.6	12.99	5.98	NC	NC
BLD		NE	NC	NC	NC	NC	NC	51.22
CPI (ML) (L)	S	3.42	NC	NC	NC	NC	NC	NC
ICS		NE	NC	NC	NC	NC	3.16	NC
INC	N	40.27	34.09	45.16	32.46	41.89	31.62	48.78
JD		NE	NC	NC	2.34	NC	NC	NC
JNP		NE	NC	NC	NC	NC	28.69	NC
LKD		NE	NC	NC	NC	NC	5.81	NC
NAGP		NE	NC	NC	NC	10.9	NC	NC
NCP	N	NC	0.39	NC	NC	NC	NC	NC
PTC		NE	NC	NC	NC	NC	12.86	NC
RJD	S	NC	0.13	NC	NC	NC	NC	NC
SP	S	NC	NC	NC	0.74	NC	NC	NC

Source: www.eci.gov.in

****It has been a Congress bastion since 1984 despite certain swings against it in 1996 and 1999.***

Table 2.18 [B]
Tezpur Lok Sabha Constituency (List of winning candidates)

Year	Voters in *000	Voter Turnout (Percentage)	Winner			Runner-up		
			Candidate Name	Percentage	Party	Candidate Name	Percentage	Party
2004	719.77	71.52	Moni Kumar Subba	40.27	INC	Padma Hazarika	30.48	AGP
1999	705.45	72.62	Moni Kumar Subba	34.09	INC	Ram Prasad Sarmah	30.3	BJP
1998	674.29	69.45	Moni Kumar Subba	45.16	INC	Iswar Prasanna Hazarika	24.6	BJP
1996	677.45	79.35	Iswar Prasanna Hazarika	32.46	INC	Harsha Bahadur Biswakarma	31.41	AGP
1991	608.32	75.49	Swarup Upadhayaya	41.89	INC	Purna Narayan Sinha	23.18	AGP
1984	538.33	80.07	Bipin Pal Das	31.62	INC	Purna Narayan Sinha	28.69	JNP
1977	267.33	58.43	Purna Narayan Sinha	51.22	BLD	Bijoy Chandra Bhagabati	48.78	INC

Source: www.eci.gov.in

Nomination: The Process and the Grounds of Selection of Candidates

For the 14th Lok Sabha poll in Tezpur, *son of the soil* factor surfaced as the main ground for nomination of candidates from various parties. Moreover, the people of Tezpur wanted to see one of its local candidates being elected. Hence, Moni Kumar Subba from the Congress and G.L. Agarwal from the BJP seemed outsiders to them.

For the Congress, the lottery baron, Moni Kumar Subba, was not the instant choice either as the party candidate from the Tezpur Parliamentary constituency despite his two wins in 1998 and 1999 from the constituency. Subba's victory margin in 1999 too was considerably less than in the previous years. Moreover, party men in the Congress camp at Tezpur were rather dissatisfied with the unclean image of Subba. Despite Subba belonging to the Nepali community, even the All Assam Nepali Students' Union (AANSU) declaring him as the enemy of the whole nation, urged the people to wipe out Moni Kumar Subba forever from Tezpur. However, money power[36] could override this lapse on the part of Subba's character, and though his behaviour did create dissatisfaction among his own party men and his own community, he made his escape good and yet again was nominated as a Congress candidate to fight the 14th Lok Sabha poll.

On the other hand, the efforts of the third major contestant, BJP's G.L. Agarwal, were undermined by

[36] Moni Kumar Subba happened to be the richest politician of Assam during the 14th Lok Sabha poll with assets worth Rs.19 crore according to his affidavit submitted along with his nomination papers. According to Subba's affidavit, his total asset was Rs.19 crore and his personal jewellery was worth Rs.74 lakh. His first wife had jewellery worth Rs.38 lakh and his second wife had Rs.14 lakh. Money power and corruption have been dominating the Indian elections scene for a considerable period of time. At the time of each election the issue of corruption is prominently focused to be forgotten soon after the poll. For some analyses on the issue see Philip Oldenburg, "Corruption as an issue" in Subrata K. Mitra and James Chiriyandath, *Electoral Politics in India: A Changing Landscape* (New Delhi: Segment Books, 1992).

murmurs of discontentment among the BJP cadres in Tezpur[37]. Locked in a battle of wits, the Tezpur Rashtriya Sevak Sangh (RSS) backed from supporting G.L. Agarwal as the organisation was in support of the candidature of Ram Prasad Sharma[38] who was the runner-up in the 1999 Lok Sabha poll from the district. The RSS did not withdraw their decision even after being requested by Arun Sathe, G. L. Agarwal and MLA Ranjit Dutta. Like Subba, even Agarwal had to face other allegations as well[39]. Nevertheless, it was G. L. Agarwal, who got the nomination from the BJP in Tezpur.

The AGP workers of Tezpur became enthusiastic when Padma Hazarika, the son of the soil was offered the ticket. Padma Hazarika filed his nomination showing the strength of 20 thousand supporters (Table 2.19). To the common electorate, it was a tussle between Subba and Agarwal though the latter's unfamiliar face was a disadvantage, despite the fact that he was the proprietor of two daily newspapers and financially a well off person.

14th Lok Sabha Poll Result
Winner: *Moni Kumar Subba (INC)*
Votes Secured: *2,89,847*
Runner-up: *Padma Hazarika (AGP)*
Votes Secured: *2,19,402*
Moni Kumar Subba wins by 70,445 votes

---

[37] According to the BJP party cadres, Padma Hazarika had a "son of the soil" image there, whereas G.L. Agarwal was perceived as a candidate from outside. It was, therefore, natural for the BJP cadres to express fear at the nomination of G.L. Agarwal from the party to fight the Tezpur parliamentary seat.

[38] Despite his loss to Moni Kumar Subba in 1999, R.P. Sharma was seen as a grassroots level worker, who worked for the people in the district. An unconfirmed but highly reliable source narrated a story that Moni Kumar Subba directly helped Agarwal to get the BJP ticket in order to ward off a potentially strong contender R. P. Sharma.

[39] G.L. Agarwal had to pay a debt of 92 crore to the ASCARD Bank. The workers association expressed dissatisfaction about it and held Agarwal responsible for the death of the bank.

Table 2.19
Contestants in Tezpur Lok Sabha Constituency (1999 and 2004)

Tezpur					
1999			2004		
Candidate	***Party***	***Votes***	***Candidate***	***Party***	***Votes***
Moni Kumar Subba	**Indian National Congress**	230884	Moni Kumar Subba	**Indian National Congress**	289847
Ram Prasad Sarmah	**Bharatiya Janata Party**	205178	Padma Hazarika	**Asom Gana Parishad**	219402
Dr. Kosheswar Bora	**Asom Gana Parishad**	203141	Ghisa Lal Agarwal	**Bharatiya Janata Party**	164662
Joseph Kandulna	**Independents**	17626	Rubul Sarma	**Communist Party Of India (Marxist-Lennist) (Liberation)**	24595
Bibek Das	**Communist Party of India (Marxist-Lennist) (Liberation)**	8855	Dipen Tanti	**Independents**	21262
Kul Bahadur Chetry	**Nationalist Congress Party**	2657			
Syed Hussain Ali Shah	**Independents**	1893			
Noor Jaman Ahmed	**Independents**	1234			
Ilman Tanti	**Independents**	1232			
Helena Murmur	**Independents**	1197			
Kanak Khaund	**Independents**	891			
Mohibullah	**Rashtriya Janata Dal**	882			
Purnanarayan Sinha	**Independents**	838			
Abul Khayer	**Independents**	694			

Source: www.electionnext.com

REFERENCES

Ahmed, Abu Nasar Saied (2006) (eds.), *Nationality Question in Assam: The EPW 1980-81 Debate*. New Delhi: Akansha. Introduction.

Amar Asom (2004), January 19.

Amar Asom (2004), January 24.

Amar Asom (2004), February 1.

Amar Asom (2004), February 9.

Amar Asom (2004), February 11.

Amar Asom (2004), February 14.

Amar Asom (2004), February 15.

Amar Asom (2004), February 17.

Amar Asom (2004), February 18.

Amar Asom (2004), February 19.

Amar Asom (2004), February 23.

Amar Asom (2004), February 24.

Amar Asom (2004), March 1.

Amar Asom (2004), March 8.

Amar Asom (2004), March 12.

Amar Asom (2004), March 13.

Amar Asom (2004), March 15.

Amar Asom (2004), March 16.

Amar Asom (2004), March 20.

Amar Asom (2004), March 22.

Amar Asom (2004), March 24.

Amar Asom (2004), March 25.

Amar Asom (2004), March 26.

Amar Asom (2004), March 27.

Amar Asom (2004), March 29.

Amar Asom (2004), March 31.

Amar Asom (2004), April 1.

Amar Asom (2004), April 4.

Amar Asom (2004), April 5.

Amar Asom (2004), April 9.

Amar Asom (2004), April 19.

Amar Asom (2004), April 23.

Amar Asom (2004), April 26.

Baruah, Apurba Kumar (1998). "Assam Elections 1996: The Congress Debacle" in Girin Phukon and Adil-ul-Yasin (eds), *Working of Parliamentary Democracy and Electoral Politics in North East India.* New Delhi: South Asian Publishers.

Das, Samir Kumar (1998). "An Interpretation of the Assam Elections of 1996" in Girin Phukon and Adil-ul-Yasin (eds), *Working of Parliamentary Democracy and Electoral Politics in North East India.* New Delhi: South Asian Publishers.

ElectionNext, www.electionnext.com, 2004.

Gohain, Hiren (1980). "Cudgel of Chauvinism", *Economic and Political Weekly*, February 23, pp.418-20.

Goswami, Sandhya (1998). "Assam Lok Sabha Election, 1996: An Analysis" in Girin Phukon and Adil-ul-Yasin (eds), *Working of Parliamentary Democracy and Electoral Politics in North East India.* New Delhi: South Asian Publishers.

Indian Express, www.indianexpress.com, 2001.

Prabhakar, M.S. (2004), "From Agitation to Governance", www.flonnet.com, Vol 21, Issue 08.

__________. (2004), "Northeastern Challenges", www.flonnet.com, Vol 21, Issue 08.

Pratidin (2004), February 25.

Pratidin (2004), February 29.

Pratidin (2004), March 2.

Pratidin (2004), March 3.

Pratidin (2004), March 5.

Pratidin (2004), March 6.

Pratidin (2004), March 8.

Pratidin (2004), March 11.
Pratidin (2004), March 14.
Pratidin (2004), March 20.
Pratidin (2004), March 24.
Pratidin (2004), March 26.
Pratidin (2004), March 28.
Pratidin (2004), March 29.
Pratidin (2004), March 30.
Pratidin (2004), March 31.
Pratidin (2004), April 1.
Pratidin (2004), April 3.
Pratidin (2004), April 4.
Pratidin (2004), April 5.
Pratidin (2004), April 6.
Pratidin (2004), April 17.
Pratidin (2004), April 19.
Pratidin (2004), April 20.
Pratidin (2004), April 21.
Pratidin (2004), April 22.
Pratidin (2004), April 23.
Pratidin (2004), April 27.
Pratidin (2004), April 30.
Pratidin (2004), May 11.
Pratidin (2004), May 15.
Pratidin (2004), May 17.
Pratidin (2004), May 18.
Pratidin (2004), May 21.
Pratidin (2004), May 22.

CHAPTER 3

Ethnicity and Vote Bank Politics

No interpretation of election trends and results can be complete without an indepth analysis of the participation and behaviour of the ethnic composition in a multicultural country like India. One hardly needs to underscore the role of ethnicity in Indian politics as it has been institutionalized in social infrastructure of the country[1]. Ethnicity mobilizes support base for political action. Its manifestation as a social class[2] is evident in various social and political processes. Election is one such political process in which ethnicity based mobilization is visible prominently. That is why communities vote *en mass* and *en-bloc* in support of primordial interests. Assam too is not an exception. Since post 1972 reorganization of the State, which created the two separate States of Meghalaya and Mizoram, two religious communities remain significant in Assam: Hindus and Muslims; two languages dominate the two valleys of the Brahmaputra and the Barak:

[1] Rajni Kothari, *Politics in India* (Boston: Little, Brown and Co., 1970), "Social Infrastructure" Chapter VI, and Kothri's "Introduction: Caste in Indian Politics" an early version of which appeared as an introduction to his earlier edited work entitled, *Caste in Indian Politics* (New Delhi: Orient and Longman, 1970). Also see Paul R. Brass, *Ethnicity and Nationalism: Theory and Comparison*, (New Delhi: Sage Publications, 1991), Chapter 1.

[2]One of the finest expressions and analysis on social class is found in Andre′ Bete′ille, *Social Class*, (Guwahati: Foundation Day Lecture of OKDISCD, 2005).

Assamese and Bengali[3]. In addition to them, the tea tribe community being conscious of their demographic composition spread all over the State also constitutes an important component having significant voice in the game of power sharing. Table 3.1 provides a clue to the understanding of these primordial communities and their share of votes in the last State Assembly election, 2001. The tribal resurgence post-1972 is a recent phenomenon in the State, so is their high voting turnout[4]. This is despite the fact that the dominant tribal segment in Assam was reduced to 12.5 per cent of the total population in the State after reorganization of the State in 1972.

A significant feature of elections in Assam has been the Congress centric phenomenon since 1952. India has been governed under the 'Congress System' for much of its post-colonial period. Consequently, the Congress Party was able to maintain its control of the State government for so long despite its failure to sufficiently serve the Assamese middle class interests. The uncontested primacy of Congress is demonstrated by its ability to win nearly all seats to the Lok Sabha between 1952 and 1977 (Table 3.1). It also reveals that the other political entities have failed to muster enough support base to challenge the Congress.

The Assam agitation saw the birth of the first regional party, the Asom Gana Parishad, which went on to win the 1985 election later that year. The AGP, however, was not destined to last long in power. Despite the initial soft electoral competition on the part of Congress, the AGP was unable to maintain its position as the representative party for a

---

[3] S. K Chaubey, *Electoral Politics in North East India* (Madras: Universities Press, 1985). Chapter II, p.63.

[4] The voting turnout of the tribal population in Assam has been always less than 50 per cent till 1972 when it jumped to 57 per cent due mainly to the growth of tribal consciousness. For some details see Myron Weiner and John Osgood Field, "How Tribal Constituencies Vote" in their edited book *Studies in Electoral Politics in Indian States*, Vol. II (New Delhi: Manohar, 1975). Chapter II.

Table 3.1
Congress' Performance in Assam in Lok Sabha Elections (1952-1996)

Year	Total Seats	Seats won	Percentage of seats won
1952	12	11	92
1957	12	12	100
1962	12	12	100
1967	14	14	100
1971	14	13	93
1977	14	10	72
1980	14	2	14
1991	14	8	57
1996	14	5	36

Source: www.electionnext.com

Table 3.2

Category-wise analysis of the performance of political parties in the State Assembly Poll, 2001

Category	Seats	Turn-out	INC		AGP+		RDA		Left		Others		Independent	
			Category-wise analysis											
			Seats Won	Vote Share	Seats Won	Vote Share	Seats Won	Vote Share	Seats Won	Vote Share	Seats Won	Vote Share	Seats Won	Vote Share
High Muslim Population	36	76.8	79	32.6	10	30.8	2	3.5	1	5.2	2	5.6	2	17.3
Tea Garden Areas	28	72	19	41.1	8	35.8	0	1.8	0	3.0	0	1.7	1	8.6
High S.T. Population	19	76.9	8	30.3	11	44.7	0	0.7	0	1.4	0	9.8	0	13.1

Source: "On Predictable Line", *Frontline*, Vol.18, Issue 11, May 26-June 8, 2001

majority of the region's inhabitants. It, therefore, could not engage itself in the political bargaining, which was the need of the hour amidst the newly rising identity crisis among the ethnic groups in the State.

On a close analysis, a few failures on the part of the AGP become distinct. First, the demographics of Assam were not as favorable to the dominant ethnic group (Table 3.3).

Table 3.3
Population by Language (1991) and Religion in Assam (2001)

Language	Percentage	Religion	Percentage
Assamese	58	Hindus	64.89
Bengali	22	Muslims	30.92
Bodo	5	Christians	3.70
Hindi	5	Sikhs, Buddhists and Jains	0.36
		Others	0.09
Others	10	Religion not stated	0.04

Source: Statistical Hand Book, Assam, 2000 and 2004

Note: Figures of *language wise distribution of population* indicate discrepancies, as they do not add up to 100.

Perhaps as a result of this, the nature of Assamese sub-nationalism was itself different than in other states, taking on both an exclusionary discourse and an emphasis on 'higher order concerns' found in the 'cultural realm.'[5] The second

[5] Benjamin O. Rogus, "Ethnic Parties and Centre-State Relations: The Case of Assam in Northeast India", San Francisco State University, 2001. http://www.bss.sfsu.edu.

factor, the ultimate failure of the Assam Movement to transform itself into a territorially pan-Assam movement, hindered the AGP's electoral efforts as the ethnic groups like the Bodos[6], Karbis, and Misings as well, came to reject AGP's conception of Assamese nationalism. Mere emphasis on social mobilization at the expense of political mobilization in the State only sounded at once the death nail for the AGP in State politics. This act of emphasis on social mobilization on the part of the AGP also led to a simultaneous inspiring of a counter-mobilization and grouping by an important segment of the Bengali Muslim population in the State. The consolidation of the Bengali Muslim vote behind the Congress helped facilitate the party's return in 1991, while a tribal insurgency for an independent Bodoland further relegated the AGP's chances of occupying power in the State.

In the 1991 Lok Sabha election, the AGP was able to garner only one seat and despite a brief respite in 1996, the AGP fared even worse in subsequent elections (Refer to Table 2.1 in Chapter 2). The AGP was apparently been sandwiched between the primary vote getters, the BJP and a reinvigorated Congress Party.

The Muslims: *A Decisive Electorate*

The Muslim population in Assam constituting more than 30 per cent of the total population of the State (Census, 2001) is a major part of the socio-cultural and economic mosaic of the State[7]. Since 1911, there has been a steady rise in the population in Assam and along with it, the Muslim component has also seen a rising trend (Table 3.4).

---

[6] The Bodos, in fact, launched their own separatist insurgency adding additional troubles to the beleaguered AGP government.

[7] For some understanding see M. Kar, *Muslims in Assam Politics* (New Delhi: Omson, 1990) and Bimal J. Dev and Dilip K. Lahiri, *Assam Muslims: Politics and Cohesion* (New Delhi: Mittal, 1985).

Table 3.4
Proportion of Muslim Population within Decadal Population Variation in Assam

Year	Decadal Population Variation		Year	Proportion of Muslim Population	
	Assam	India		Assam	India
1901-11	16.99	5.75	1911	16.23	22.39
1911-21	20.48	-0.31	1921	-	-
1921-31	19.91	11.00	1931	22.78	23.49
1931-41	20.41	14.22	1941	-	-
1941-51	19.93	13.31	1951	24.68	9.91
1951-61	34.98	21.51	1961	25.30	10.71
1961-71	34.95	24.80	1971	24.56	11.21
1971-81	23.36	24.69	1981	-	-
1981-91	24.24	23.82	1991	28.43	12.12
1991-01	18.85	21.34	2001	30.91	13.42

Source: Various *Census Reports.*

Table 3.5

Voting pattern in Muslim – dominated Assembly segments, Lok Sabha Election, 2004 (Assam) (in *Per cent*)

Assembly Constituency	Turnout	INC	BJP	AGP	UMFA	CPI/CPI (M)		Others/ Ind
1	2	3	4	5	6	7	8	9
(i) Barpeta								
Abhayapuri North	78.45	35.61	10.50	35.92	8.80	6.37		2.80
Baghbor	76.33	45.52	1.87	11.78	12.58	5.03	23.22	
Barpeta	76.26	36.31	13.27	23.00	7.17	3.11	17.14	
Chenga	74.17	45.78	10.26	26.11	1.22	5.76	10.87	
Jania	73.74	45.47	3.20	6.97	21.09	11.33	11.97	
Sarbhog	67.02	19.49					80.51	
Sarukhetri	71.08	27.50	13.66	9.85	3.18	12.91	32.90	
(ii) Dhubri								
Bilasipara East	76.29	47.90	7.45	38.38				6.27
Bilasipara West	71.10	52.45	3.19	22.90			21.46	
Dhubri	74.23	51.20	13.70	21.82			13.28	

(Contd...)

1	2	3	4	5	6	7	8	9
Goalpara East	69.91	45.10	20.20	20.06			14.64	
Goalpara West	74.47	24.36	10.43	43.33			21.88	
Gauripur	77.97	43.00	6.17	42.16				8.67
Jaleswar	75.40	33.52	4.93	54.34				7.21
Mankachar	79.12	38.42	4.18	22.60			34.80	
South Salmara	76.39	52.62	0.75	31.70			14.93	
(iii) Kaliabor								
Dhing	74.46	45.15		12.25			42.50	
Rupahihat	76.00	34.78		14.34			50.88	
Samaguri	77.67	47.47		29.38			23.15	
(iv) Mangaldoi								
Dalgaon	78.20	63.75	24.78	7.02				4.45
Mangaldoi	72.31	44.50	27.73	22.69				5.08
(v) Nowgong								
Hojai	67.42	36.10	51.62	7.96	2.75			1.57
Jamunamukh	65.40	49.32	17.56	29.46	1.66			2.01
Laharighat	73.08	55.65	35.19	5.90	1.22			2.04
Nowgong	62.87	37.01	44.27	15.61	1.24			1.85

Source: Mixed Verdict, Sandhya Goswami, *Economic and Political Weekly*, Vol XXXIX No. 51, December 18-24, 2004

Note: The table has been modified to bring the Assembly constituencies under their respective Parliamentary constituencies

The election scenario in the State, mostly after the surfacing of regionalism in Assam politics with the emergence of the regional party like the Asom Gana Parishad (AGP) rather reflects the increasing pressure of the centrifugal forces distinct in the narrow local interests of the multiple linguistic and ethnic communities. The State's ethnic demography always impinging on state politics has been to a great extent the decisive factor for the winning note of many a candidate in the elections to both the State Assemblies as well as to the Lok Sabha constituencies. It has been found that to win in a constituency, the support base of the dominant groups is a must.

There are twenty-three Assembly constituencies in the State in which the Muslims constitute 50 to 90 per cent of the total population. In seven other Assembly constituencies, they are a numerical strength of 40 to 49 per cent. In other words, the Muslims constitute the decisive factor in 30 out of 126 Assembly constituencies[8]. Table 3.6 read together with Table 3.7, presents a clear picture of the dominant Muslim factor in Assam's electoral politics.

Table 3.6

Muslim dominated Assembly constituencies in Assam (2001 Assembly election)

No. and name of the constituency		Total votes	Muslim votes	% of Muslim votes
4	Karimganj South	1,26,049	79,953	63.43
5	Badarpur	1,06,071	59,142	55.43
6	Hailakandi	1,06,687	53,333	49.99
8	Algapur	1,08,208	55,846	51.61

(Contd...)

[8] Abu Nasar Saied Ahmed, "Participation of Muslims in Governance: A Case of the Muslims of Assam" in K.N. Jahangir and M.A. Jawaid (eds) *Minorities in India in the New Millennium* (New Delhi: Manas, forthcoming).

No. and name of the constituency	Total votes	Muslim votes	% of Muslim votes
10 Sonai	1,17,276	66,789	56.95
21 Mankachar	1,11,823	99,187	88.70
22 South Salmara	93,218	91,540	98.20
23 Dhubri	1,06,597	69,746	65.43
24 Gauripur	1,13,836	59,013	51.84
26 Bilasipara East	92,555	68,583	74.10
34 Abhayapuri North	91,246	46,864	51.36
38 Goalpara West	94,271	52,207	55.38
39 Jaleswar	84,038	69,019	82.13
43 Barpeta	1,17,712	58,538	49.73
44 Jania	1,04,455	95,921	91.83
45 Baghbor	80,734	77,157	95.57
46 Sarukhetri	1,17,797	65,401	55.52
47 Chenga	79,382	60,156	75.78
67 Dalgaon	1,23,222	90,543	73.48
81 Laharighat	1,05,016	59,670	56.82
83 Dhing	1,20,080	1,08,096	90.02
85 Rupahihat	1,10,036	88,744	80.65
90 Jamunamukh	1,10,957	92,960	83.78

Source: An Educational Study on Voting Behaviour of Electorate and Development works done in Constituencies of Assam (Guwahati; National Education Foundation, 2001)

Despite the dominance of the Muslim electorate in 23 Assembly constituencies and their substantial presence in seven more constituencies, they do not always return representatives from their own community as evident from Table 3.6. But the influence of the Muslims in these 30 constituencies is felt intensely at the time of elections.

Table 3.7
Number of Muslim MLAs in Assam since 1947

Year	Tota Sales	No. of Muslim MLAs	No. of Muslim contestants	% of Muslim electorate
1947	71	16 (22.53%)	NA	NA
1952	105	15 (14.28%)	61	22.06
1957	108	15 (13.88%)	36	22.06
1962	108	18 (16.66%)	62	23.3
1967	112	19 (19.96%)	72	23.3
1972	126	21 (16.66%)	78	24.56
1978	126	29 (23.01%)	166	24.56
1983	126	32 (25.39%)	130	24.56
1985	126	25 (19.84%)	225	24.56
1991	126	24 (19.04%)	328	25.6
1996	126	19 (15.07%)	351	25.6
2001	126	24(19.04%)	394	NA

Source: Assam Assembly Secretariat, Dispur, M. Kar, *Muslims in Assam Politics*, p. 161

It may be noted that since a Lok Sabha constituency covers a larger geographical area embracing several Assembly segments, the Muslim factor though is decisive only in three out of 14 Lok Sabha constituencies – Barpeta, Dhubri and Cachar, in some other constituencies such as Gauhati, Mangaldoi, Nowgong and Lakhimpur, it still plays a crucial factor. Therefore, no political party, including the BJP, could afford to dismiss the Muslim vote bank factor.

For the Muslims of Assam, issues like uniform civil code and demolition of Babri Mosque have never been election issues not to speak of the role as deciding factors in elections. But a highly political and sensitive issue like the IMDT has always played a balancing factor in all the elections in the State. The poll plank of the Congress in the State has always been the IMDT Act. By opposing a repeal of the IMDT Act, and assuring 'permanent land pattas' to these minorities - the Muslims residing in dominant pockets in the State as well as in the *char* (river island) areas, the party has successfully endeared itself to these people and has, therefore, been successful in capturing the minority dominant pockets in almost all elections in the State. Not only has the Congress support base in these dominant minority assemblies remained intact, the voting turnout in these pockets has been significantly high. In five Parliamentary constituencies of Barpeta, Dhubri, Kaliabor, Mangaldoi, and Nowgong, the majority of the voters in the Assembly segments of Abhayapuri North, Baghbor, Sarbhog, Jania, Barpeta, Chenga and Sarukhetri in Barpeta Parliamentary constituency, Bilasipara East, Bilasipara West, Dhubri, South Salmara, Goalpara East, Goalpara West, Mankachar, Jaleswar, Gauripur in Dhubri Parliamentary constituency, Dhing, Rupahihat and Samaguri in Kaliabor parliamentary constituency, Dalgaon and Mangaldoi in Mangaldoi Parliamentary constituency, and Hojai, Jamunamukh, Laharighat and Nowgong in Nowgong Parliamentary constituency are Muslims (Table 3.5). It has been found that out of ten Assembly segments in Dhubri, nine are Muslim dominated, while in the Barpeta Parliamentary constituency, the Muslims are a majority in seven out of ten Assembly segments. While in the Nowgong Parliamentary constituency, four out of nine Assembly segments are minority dominated. Moreover, their growing number, constitute a majority in the constituencies like Dhubri with 71 per cent, Barpeta with 56 per cent, Hailakandi with 55 per cent and Goalpara with 50 per cent[9]. A State in which religious diversity has been providing ample scope for polarization on religious lines, the voting behaviour of the Muslim population is certainly decisive. This Muslim populace, the ever-supporting Congress community failed

[9] As per the 1991 Census, the Muslim community constitutes a majority in Assam in the districts where the immigrants dominate.

the Congress only twice – in 1985 and 1996 since independence, when a split in the Muslim vote became inevitable due to the emergence of regional parties in the political scenario of the State. The voting pattern in Muslim dominated Assembly segments in Assam though indicate an 'always for the Congress' trend, there are certain hiccups. Analysis of the 2001 State Assembly election in the Muslim dominated constituencies can clearly bring out their contemporary voting behaviour. To cite here, in the 36 constituencies with a concentration of Muslim population 40 per cent and above in the State, the Congress (I) won 19 seats in 2001 Assembly poll, which is a loss of six seats when compared with the number of Assembly segments in which it had a lead in the Lok Sabha election of 1999. The Congress (I), therefore, got an overwhelming 57 per cent of the vote among Muslims, but one should recall that the AGP-BJP counter-mobilization also did not work in ten constituencies. In Nowgong, though being a Muslim dominated constituency (Table 3.8 [A]&[B]), the AGP candidate Girindra Kumar Barua won the seat with a vote percentage of 43.38 while Nripen Goswami from the Indian National Congress could secure a vote percentage of 33.40 only. In the Assembly constituency of Hojai (Table 3.9 [A]&[B]), where Ardhendu Dey of Congress (I) has been the winner of the Assembly elections in 1991, 1996 and 2001, it has been found that the Muslim electorate in the constituency has given 47.54 per cent of their votes to the Congress in the last Assembly election of 2001. While these two constituencies in Nowgong clearly show a tilt towards the BJP, the same trend seems to be catching Gauripur under Dhubri parliamentary constituency as well. Goalpara West and Jaleswar in Dhubri Lok Sabha constituency are also exceptions. The Muslim population in these two Assembly constituencies has heavily favoured the AGP.

But, a look at the Lok Sabha polls gives the picture of the minorities backing the Congress as usual. In the Muslim majority constituencies of Barpeta, Dhubri and Karimganj, it is Congress again which succeeded in winning from these three constituencies (Table 3.10, 3.11 and 3.12 and also refer Table 2.4 (B) in Chapter 2) in the 2004 Lok Sabha poll. An interesting trend noted in these constituencies is that the BJP since the 1998 Lok Sabha poll has well made a base in these Muslim majority constituencies. The runner up in these constituencies has been a BJP candidate, whether it is Parimal Suklabaidya in the Karimganj constituency or Dr. Pannalal Oswal from the Dhubri constituency. It indicates that the BJP has made an inroad in the Muslim dominated areas. To keep the trend on, as stated in Chapter 2, the BJP even had put up a Muslim woman candidate in the Dhubri Lok Sabha constituency in the Lok Sabha poll of 2004.

Autonomous District Council: *A Review*

Karbi-Anglong, along with the neighbouring North Cachar Hills District, has been enjoying autonomy under the provisions of the Sixth Schedule of the Constitution of India, an arrangement that considerably precedes the creation of the State of Meghalaya. It was the division of the composite State of Assam that led to the drawing of new administrative boundaries in 1970. The North Cachar Hills sub-division of the United Mikir and Cachar Hills District was upgraded to a district in 1970. The Mikir Hills District section was renamed as Karbi Anglong in 1976. Both the districts thus went on to have Autonomous Councils. However, it was the emergence of new social forces during the 80s that accentuated discontent over the state of affairs yet again, and, led to the movement for an autonomous State within Assam which later culminated into a Memorandum of Understanding (MoU) between the Autonomous State Demand Committee (ASDC), Karbi Anglong, and the Government of Assam in the presence of the Union Minister of Home Affairs[10].

[10] Consequent upon the understanding, the State government transferred another 14 departments (making a total of 30) including, Panchayat and Rural Development including DRDA, handloom and textiles, sports and youth welfare, town and country planning, transport, excise and finance (including sales tax, excise and professional tax) to the ADCs.

Table 3.8 (A)

Result of Nowgong Assembly constituency
Percentage of Valid Votes Caste in Favour of Contesting Parties

Party Abbreviation	Current Party Status	2001	1996	1991	1985	1983	1978
AGP	S	43.48	63.15	43.39	-	-	-
AICC (T)	NE	-	1.81	-	-	-	-
AITC	S	0.73	-		-		
BJP	N	-	4.9	-	-	-	-
CPI	N	-	-	-	0.69	-	13.02
CPM	N	-	-	-	1.68	5.44	15.44
INC	N	33.4	28.87	47.28	33.2	94.56	34.24
INC (I)	NE	-	-	-	-	-	2.89
JD	NE	-	-	0.77	-	-	-
JNP	NE	-	-	-	-	-	-
LKD	NE	-	-	-	0.3	-	33.35
NAGP	NE	-	-	3.94	-	-	-
SP	S	-	0.05	-	-	-	-
UMF	NE	-	-	1.25	-	-	-

Source: eci.gov.in

Table 3.8 (B)

List of Winning candidates: Nowgong Assembly constituency

Year	Voters in *000	Voter Turnout (Percentage)	Winner Candidate Name	Winner Percentage	Winner Party	Runner-up Candidate Name	Runner-up Percentage	Runner-up Party
2001	87.13	69.14	Girindra Kumar Barua	43.38	AGP	Nripen Goswami	33.40	INC
1996	86.21	77.30	Prafulla Kumar Mahanta	63.15	AGP	Mukut Sarma	28.87	INC
1991	71.61	74.28	Mukut Sarma	47.28	INC	Prafulla Kumar Mahanta	43.39	AGP
1985	68.59	79.38	Prafulla Kumar Mahanta	58.49	IND	Mukut Sarma	33.20	INC
1983	9.01	10.59	Mukut Sarma	94.56	INC	Bhupen Barbara	5.44	CPM
1978	41.20	64.03	Mukut Sarma	34.24	INC	Indreswar Goswami	33.35	JNP

Source: eci.gov.in

Table 3.9 (A)
Result of Hojai Assembly constituency
Percentage of Valid Votes Caste in Favour of Contesting Parties

Party Abbreviation	Current Party Status	2001	1996	1991	1985	1983	1978
AGP	S	-	34.85	11.21	-	-	-
AICC (T)	NE	-	0.25	-	-	-	-
BJP	N	41.8	22.49	22.64	4.92	-	-
CPI	N	-	-	-	-	15.43	23.49
CPM	N	-	-	-	12.99	-	12.31
ICS (SCS)	NE	-	-	0.46	-	-	-
INC	N	47.54	40.31	41.71	29.22	79.97	22.59
INC (I)	NE	-	-	-	-	-	5.06
JD	NE	-	-	1.23	-	-	-
JNP	NE	-	-	-	1.05	-	30.56
NAGP	NE	-	-	5.38	-	-	-
SP	S	4.55	-	-	-	-	-
UMF	NE	-	-	14.71	-	-	-

Source: eci.gov.in

Table 3.9 (B)

List of winning candidates: Hojai Assembly constituency

Year	Voters in *000	Voter Turnout (Percentage)	Winner			Runner-up		
			Candidate Name	Percentage	Party	Candidate Name	Percentage	Party
2001	108.85	72.54	Ardhendu Dey	47.54	INC	Rama Prasad Saha	41.80	BJP
1996	97.57	79.73	Ardhendu Kumar Dey	40.31	INC	Kamal Dutta	34.85	AGP
1991	84.34	77.17	Ardhendu Kumar Dey	41.71	INC	Sikha Sur Choudhury	22.64	BJP
1985	70.71	82.46	Santi Ranjan Das Gupta	37.81	IND	Sadhan Ranjan Sarkar	29.22	INC
1983	46.42	50.07	Sadhan Ranjan Sarkar	79.97	INC	Md. Aftaruddin Ahmad	15.43	CPI
1978	56.14	69.26	Santi Ranjan Das Gupta	30.56	JNP	Aftaruddin Ahmad	23.49	CPI

Source: eci.gov.in

Table 3.10
Dhubri Lok Sabha constituency (List of winning candidates)

Year	Voters in *000	Voter Turnout (Percentage)	Winner			Runner-up		
			Candidate Name	Percentage	Party	Candidate Name	Percentage	Party
2004	863.59	75.1	Anwar Hussain	43.61	INC	Afzalur Rahman	30.1	AGP
1999	825.53	78.58	Abdul Hamid	34.58	INC	Dr. Pannalal Oswal	31.95	BJP
1998	773.08	73.65	Abdul Hamid	50.04	INC	Dr. Pannalal Oswal	24.18	BJP
1996	810.65	87.08	Nurul Islam	40.1	INC	Onkarmal Agarwal	23.24	AGP
1991	749.08	84.79	Nurul Islam	26.53	INC	Dinesh Chandra Sarkar	19.62	BJP
1984	642.85	86.77	Abdul Hamid	25.91	IND	Nurul Islam	23.99	INC
1977	340.93	67.71	Ahmad Hossein	45.68	INC	Nurul Islam	45.5	BLD

Source: www.eci.gov.in

Table 3.11
Barpeta Lok Sabha constituency (List of winning candidates)

Year	Voters in *000	Voter Turnout (Percentage)	Winner			Runner-up		
			Candidate Name	Percentage	Party	Candidate Name	Percentage	Party
2004	762.68	70.9	A F Golam Osmani	35	INC	Kumar Deepak Das	26.07	AGP
1999	767.91	75.02	A F Golam Osmani	43.2	INC	Ramani Kanta Deka	31.35	BJP
1998	624.73	61.1	A F Golam Osmani	58.64	UMFA	Manjushree Pathak	21.85	BJP
1996	705.21	82.25	Uddhab Barman	36.75	CPM	Abdus Samad Ahmed	26.85	UMFA
1991	706.518	81.26	Uddhab Barman	30.44	CPM	Abdul Latif	22.62	INC
1984	651.16	89.04	Ataur Rahman	44 38	IND	Sirajul Hoque	35.54	IND
1977	355.26	63.57	Ismail Hossain Khan	56.96	INC	Biswa Goswami	43.04	BLD

Source: www.eci.gov.in

Table 3.12

Karimganj Lok Sabha constituency (List of winning candidates)

Year	Voters in *000	Voter Turnout (Percentage)	Winner			Runner-up		
			Candidate Name	Percentage	Party	Candidate Name	Percentage	Party
2004	671.49	68.58	Lalit Mohan Suklabaidya	47.81	INC	Parimal Suklabaidya	34.12	BJP
1999	695.54	73.75	Nepal Chandra Das	49.55	INC	Parimal Suklabaidya	43.33	BJP
1998	746.53	79.19	Nepal Chandra Das	39.7	INC	Swapan Kumar Das	38.26	BJP
1996	703.35	80.24	Dwaraka Nath Das	33.07	BJP	Sabita Das	28.24	INC
1991	619.17	77.24	Dwaraka Nath Das	39.2	BJP	Jatindra Chandra Das	30.79	JD
1984	513.27	75.76	Sudarsan Das	47.14	BJP	Nihar Ranjan Laskar	31.94	INC
1980	269.55	41.83	Nihar Ranjan Laskar	49.6	ICS	Kamdeb Das	22.03	CPM
1977	239.77	44.79	Nihar Ranjan Laskar	54.61	INC (I)	Lilamoy Das	41.63	BLD

Source: www.eci.gov.in

Karbi Anglong is a land where the Dimasas, Karbis, Khasis and Kukis besides the other minor tribes have lived in harmony for decades. For the past two decades this relationship of harmony has disappeared into oblivion and only ethnic conflicts reign supreme today[11]. The roots of these conflicts run deep. A plausible political context, however, seems to be the breakdown of the understanding that had existed between the Kuki National Army (KNA)[12] and the Autonomous State Demand Committee (ASDC), a district-level political party with indefinable links to one of the factions of the Communist Party of India (Marxist-Leninist). The ASDC was the ruling party in the District Council when the understanding was entered into.

The major political development in the last decade in this district is the split in the ASDC brought upon largely by ASDC leaders themselves, and the return of the Congress (I) to political office in these districts. Moulding further the complex situation is the recent emergence of the United People's Democratic Solidarity (UPDS) with its predictable agenda for a Karbi State purged of all non-Karbis. The split in the UPDS further and the emergence of a pro-talks faction, which signed a ceasefire agreement with the Central government in May 2002, compelled the anti-talk factions to assert themselves through violence. The Kukis, often reluctant to be driven by similar separatist urges in the district, are a natural target of the other militant outfits. The conflict has been more or less a continuation in the district but with different motivations.

---

[11] Recently, the district of Karbi Anglong witnessed a series of ruthless killings as a result of the armed clashes between the Dimasas and the Karbis. The trouble started on September 14, 2005 when three Dimasa auto rickshaw pullers were hacked to death allegedly by the Karbi militant outfit named UPDS which was retaliated by the Dimasas in the same manner of ruthlessness. Thereafter, several violent incidents took place which took the life of countless people.

[12] Kuki National Assembly (KNA) is the political organisation of the Kuki people in the district, with claims to a trans-regional ethnic and political identity.

The two autonomous districts namely, Karbi Anglong and North Cachar Hills constitute a single Parliamentary constituency and have five Assembly segments - Diphu, Bokajan, Howraghat, Haflong and Baithalangso. Therefore, the geographical area of the ADC is co-terminus with the Lok Sabha constituency covering both the districts. With a population size of 8,13,311 in the district of Karbi Anglong and 1,88,079 in the district of N.C. Hills, which make up around 3.76 per cent (2001 census) of the total population of the State, the Autonomous District constituencies has 58 per cent of the population as tribals, and of this, 76 per cent are Hindus. The ADCs mirror the multi ethnic and linguistic character of the State with tribes like Karbis, Kukis, Hmars, Dimasas, Nepalis, Kacharis and Tiwas, and the linguistic groups like Bengalis, Assamese, Biharis residing on the same land.

Going down electoral politics' history, as a tribal dominated constituency where the Karbis constitutes the largest ethic group (43 per cent) it used to elect invariably a Karbi representative only, as is evident from Table 3.13.

Table 3.13
Contestants in Autonomous District (Assam)

Candidate	Party	Votes
	1991	
Jayanta Rongpi	Autonomous State Demand Committee	139785
Biren Singh Engti	Indian National Congress	82004
Nigamananda Maithar	Asom Gana Parishad	44588
Brojen Langthasa	Independents	16061
Bapuram Singnar	Bharatiya Janata Party	14242

(Contd...)

Candidate	Party	Votes
	1996	
Jayanta Rongpi	**Autonomous State Demand Committee**	**180112**
Elwin Teron	**Indian National Congress**	**76982**
Gokul Ch. Hojai	**Independents**	**71998**
Gujar Teron	**Bharatiya Janata Party**	**10368**
James Hanse	**Independents**	**1760**
Kabon Timungpi	**Independents**	**687**
	1998	
Dr. Jayanta Rongpi	**Autonomous State Demand Committee**	**184241**
Biren Singh Engti	**Indian National Congress**	**79377**
Elwin Teron	**Independents**	**71095**
Pabitra Kr Kemprai	**Bharatiya Janata Party**	**46977**
Angelus Terang	**Independents**	**9636**
	1999	
Dr. Jayanta Rongpi	**Communist Party Of India (Marxist-Leninist) (Liberation)**	**208789**
Biren Singh Engti	**Indian National Congress**	**148914**
Elwin Teron	**Independents**	**27382**
Kabon Timungpi	**Independents**	**1751**
	2004	
Biren Singh Engti	**Indian National Congress**	**125937**
Elwin Teron	**Autonomous State Demand Committee**	**101808**
Dr. Jayanta Rongpi	**Communist Party Of India (Marxist-Leninist) (Liberation)**	**74399**
Ratan Teron	**Bharatiya Janata Party**	**57584**
Sanmoni Kemprai	**Independents**	**26713**
Chember G. Momin	**Independents**	**8003**
Sailendra Hasnu	**Asom Gana Parishad**	**3755**
Harsing Teron	**Samata Party**	**3178**

Source: www.electionnext.com

In this constituency of Assam, the CPI (ML) has been conducting a novel experiment of leading a nationality struggle. This is the only tribal region of Northeast where the secessionist militancy gave way to democratic movement for autonomy in the 1980s and the Autonomous State Demand Committee (ASDC) formed by CPI (ML) won the Karbi Anglong District Council election in 1988[13].

The present Central Committee member of CPI (ML), Jayanta Rongpi[14], won from this constituency in 1991 under the banner of Autonomous State Demand Committee (ASDC) (Table 3.13), polling 1,39,785 votes (47.13 per cent), defeating the sitting Congress MP, Biren Singh Engti by a margin of over 57,000 votes.

In 1996, he succeeded in retaining his seat improving the performance by getting 53 per cent votes. In 1998, he was again re-elected with a vote percentage of 47. And in 1999, Jayanta Rongpi contested the election under the CPI (ML) banner yet again and got the maximum votes so far, polling 2,08,789 votes (53.98 per cent). This victory earned a state recognized party status for CPI (ML).

Till the 13th Lok Sabha poll, the ASDC had its legislators from all the five Assembly segments of this parliamentary constituency. But the situation underwent drastic and complicated changes since then. The CPI (ML) and the ASDC suffered a vertical split in 2000 on allegations and counter allegations of corruption and misuse of its funds and most importantly, on the question of orientation of the autonomous state movement. The renegades in the name of ASDC (U)

---

[13] For details see Borsing Rongphar's *Karbi Anglongor Rajnaitik Itihas* (The Political History of Karbi Anglong), (Diphu: Fu Fu Publication, Karbi Anglong, 2005).

[14] The powerful movement for securing Autonomous State under Article 244 A of the Constitution in the hill districts of Karbi Anglong and North Cachar Hills earned this constituency the distinction of being the first to have sent a tribal MP of revolutionary left stream.

entered into alliance with the AGP and the BJP and compromised the struggle for an autonomous State[15].

In the Assembly election that took place in May 2001 (Table 3.14 to 3.18), the CPI (ML) candidates were defeated in all the five constituencies of the hill districts, the renegade ASDC (U) got two seats and the Congress won three. Later, the Congress captured power at both the District Councils of Karbi Anglong and North Cachar Hills.

However, in the 2004 Lok Sabha polls, the INC candidate Biren Singh Engti won with 31.38 per cent whereas the four-time winner, Jayanta Rongpi, could not even secure the runners up position. Elwin Teron (ASDC) emerged as the runner up with 25.36 per cent. Rongpi was relegated to the third position[16]. Despite, its decelerating performance in the elections, the CPI (ML) opposition stood firm on the path of struggle to achieve autonomous statehood.[17]

Thus it has been found that the decisive result in the elections in the Autonomous District Council is mainly the outcome of the inter-tribe politics, which has been gaining ground of late. Besides, the accusations and counter

---

[15] The ASDC (U) was also accused of hobnobbing with militant outfits like UPDS and even with Bodo Liberation Tigers (BLT).

[16] The Congress win was linked to the decline in the popularity of Dr. Jayanta Rongpi. There were various allegations of corruption against him.

[17] The CPI (ML) launched agitation following the Centre's decision to create three new states not giving due respect to the demand of the hill districts. The Party also opposed any attempt of encroaching upon the rights enjoyed by the Autonomous Council, and submitted a memorandum to the Centre opposing the Assam Government's conspiracy to dismember Karbi Anglong transferring part of it to Meghalaya. They also opposed the Clause 8 of Memorandum of Settlement with BLT to confer Hill Tribe ST (H) status to Bodos living in Karbi Anglong whereas the Congress and the ASDC led by Holiram Terong covertly agreed to support the Bodo demand. It was the outcome of the intrigue by Holiram led ASDC and Congress to woo Kuki Revolutionary Army (KRA) that killing of Karbis at the hand of KRA took place in December 2003. CPI (ML) exposed this treachery and demanded that KRA terrorists must be flushed out of Karbi Anglong and KRA be declared a banned outfit. The party also demanded that negotiations should be opened with anti-talk UPDS. In *Profiles of some Constituencies*, http://www.cpiml.org, 2004.

accusations against parties and political leaders[18], regional as well as national, has only added to the scenario of violence and confusion in the district. There has been also confusions and misunderstandings among the tribes already on war with each other over the question of nomination[19].

Jayanta Rongpi who could register wins in 1996, 1998, and 1999, lost the battle of wits in 2004 to Biren Singh Engti from the Congress. This was perhaps because of the split in the aim and conviction on the demand for autonomous statehood of the district. The ASDC, which split up into ASDC (U) and ASDC (P) not only ignited inter-ethnic clashes in the district but it also saw the end of peace prevalent in the district since 1980s. Certain facts and figures, therefore, stand out.

1. The Congress could win the seat after three consecutive defeats. This was a real achievement for the party in the hill district. But this win could not be crowned on Congress' head. This was perhaps a result of the splitting electorate consequent upon the split in the Holiram Terang led ASDC (ML) into ASDC (P) and ASDC (U).
2. The people, especially the Karbis, had woven a dream of an autonomous State under Article 244 A of the Indian Constitution, which inspired them to spearhead a massive movement under the leadership of Dr. Jayanta Rongpi. People expressing immense faith on him had elected him as their leader for three terms at a stretch.

---

[18]Prior to the 14th Lok Sabha poll, Biren Singh Engti accused Dr. Jayanta Rongpi as the culprit of ethnic conflict in Karbi Anglong. He told this after receiving green signal from the party High Command. He demanded that for the sake of electoral gain from the Kuki community, Rongpi had instigated the Karbi-Kuki conflict. *Amar Asom* 19th March 2004. There were also other accusations doing the rounds like the CPI (ML) all India General secretary accusing that only because of want of political gains the Congress and BJP were fully involved in the ethnic conflict in Karbi Anglong and North Cachar districts and flaring it up. *Amar Asom* 29th March 2004.

[19] Karbi-Dimasa clash emerged regarding BJP's candidate for Diphu LS constituency. Chanmoni Kamprai, former DHD leader and Ratan Terong, the President of Karbi Anglong district's BJP unit had given their candidature. Karbi Anglong unit and Uttar Cachar unit of the BJP on the other hand, had demanded their own candidate on ethnic lines.

But he seemed to belie the hopes and aspirations of the people when he could not convince a part of the ASDC on the question of autonomous statehood, which led to the ultimate split in the ASDC, Rongpi leading ASDC (P) and Holiram Terang leading the other faction ASDC (U). Hence his defeat was foreseen and a forgone conclusion.

3. The mistrust and hatred among the different tribes like the Karbis, Kukis, Hmars and Dimasas on many questions, especially on the question of total lack of minority group representation in the ADCs of the two districts, more particularly in Karbi Anglong, has created a violent situation of killings, arsons, and rampant fear in the district, which still continues. This too affected the election results of 2004 Lok Sabha poll.

Elections in Bodoland: *In the Shadow of the Bodo Movement*

The All Bodo Students' Union (ABSU) and the Bodo Peoples' Action Committee (BPAC) launched in March 1987 a movement for the creation of a separate State of Bodoland on the northern bank of the river Brahmaputra comprising 25, 878 sq.km area. The All Bodo Students' Union (ABSU) with its provocative slogan 'Divide Assam fifty-fifty' spearheaded the agitation for the creation of the Bodoland, in 1987. The total population within the proposed Bodoland was reckoned at 67,67,450 out of which, ST population was said to be 47, 41, 614 and the Bodo population 34,29,897 making the ST percentage as 70 and Bodo percentage as 51 based on voluntary census conducted by the ABSU-BPAC[20]. The Bodos suffered from a sense of relative deprivation and hence registered their grievances first in the form of a protest movement and eventually in the form of extreme militancy, with the end in view to have a separate Bodoland, a homeland

---

[20] Mentioned in *Three Member Experts Committee Report*, Vol. IV, 25th February 1991, Government of India, Ministry of Home Affairs. Although the latest census data is not available, the Bodo population in Kokrajhar District, which is said to have highest concentration of the Bodos, is estimated to be below 50%.

Table 3.14 (A)

Result of Halflong (ST) Assembly Constituency

		Percentage of Valid Votes Caste in Favour of Contesting Parties					
Party Abbreviation	Current Party Status	2001	1996	1991	1985	1983	1978
AIIC (T)	NE	-	6.34	-	-	-	-
ASDC	-	-	54.58	-	-	-	-
ASDC (P)	NE	29.29	-	-	-	-	-
ASDC (U)	NE	5.64	-	-	-	-	-
INC	N	45.44	33.3	61.73	61.24	41.97	31.09
JNP	NE	-	-	-	-	-	40.88
SAP	-	0.55	-	-	-	-	-

Source: www.eci.gov.in

Table 3.14 (B)
List of winning candidates: Halflong (ST) Assembly Constituency

Year	Voters in 1000	Voter Turnout (Percentage)	Winner			Runner-up		
			Candidate Name	Percentage	Party	Candidate Name	Percentage	Party
2001	75.65	71.41	Gobinda Ch. Langthasa	45.44	INC	Prakanta Warisa	29.29	ASDC (P)
1996	66.98	78.60	Samarjit Halflongbar	54.58	ASDC	Gobinda Ch. Langthasa	33.30	INC
1991	57.66	70.03	Gobinda Ch. Langthasa	61.73	INC	Jatan Kumar Thaosen	38.27	IND
1985	49.66	74.01	Gobinda Ch. Langthasa	61.24	INC	Ijiranbe	25.67	IND
1983	29.20	56.12	G.C. Langthasa	58.03	IND	Sonaram Thaosen	41.97	INC
1978	29.55	64.22	Sonaram Thaosen	40.88	JNP	S.C. Daolagupu	31.09	INC

Source: www.eci.gov.in

Table 3.15 (A)
Result of Diphu (ST) Assembly Constituency

Party Abbreviation	Current Party Status	Percentage of Valid Votes Caste in Favour of Parties					
		2001	1996	1991	1985	1983	1978
AGP	S	11.97	-	21.82	-	-	-
ASDC	-	-	41.8	-	-	-	-
ASDC (P)	NE	22.82	-	-	-	-	-
ASDC (U)	NE	26.03	-	-	-	-	-
BJP	N	1.81	4.32	2.6	-	-	-
INC	N	33.38	24.61	22.63	23.52	29.94	32.11
JD	NE	-	-	1.66	-	-	-
JNP	NE	-	-	-	6.68	-	57.69

Source: www.eci.gov.in

Table 3.15 (B)
List of winning candidates: Diphu (ST) Assembly Constituency

Year	Voters in 1000	Voter Turnout (Percentage)	Winner			Runner-up		
			Candidate Name	Percentage	Party	Candidate Name	Percentage	Party
2001	97.91	74.32	Bidyasing Engleng	33.38	INC	Babu Rongpi	26.03	IND
1996	80.11	80.11	Hemsing Tisso	41.80	ASDC	Lutsat Singson	29.05	INC
1991	70.05	70.05	Dipendra Rongpi	48.68	ADC	Kunjalal Hagjer	22.63	INC
1985	64.40	64.40	Sam Singh Hanse	26.46	IND	Bidyasing Engleng	23.52	INC
1983	51.75	51.75	Kaziasong	30.91	IND	Sertha Sing Terang	29.94	INC
1978	60.67	60.67	Gandhi Ram Timung	57.69	JNP	Sai Sai Terang	32.11	INC

Source: www.eci.gov.in

Table 3.16 (A)
Result of Baithlangso (ST) Assembly Constituency

		Percentage of Valid Votes Caste in Favour of Contesting Parties					
Party Abbreviation	**Current Party Status**	**2001**	**1996**	**1991**	**1985**	**1983**	**1978**
AGP	S	-	-	9.43	-	-	-
ASDC	-	-	55.56	-	-	-	-
ASDC (P)	NE	16.58	-	-	-	-	-
ASDC (U)	NE	40.77	-	-	-	-	-
BJP	N	-	4.37	-	-	-	-
INC	N	41.81	40.07	41.2	30.77	78.32	53.16
JNP	NE	-	-	-	-	-	46.84
RJD	S	0.84	-	-	-	-	-

Source: www.eci.gov.in

Table 3.16 (B)
List of winning candidates: Baithlangso (ST) Assembly Constituency

Year	Voters in 1000	Voter Turnout (Percentage)	Winner			Runner-up		
			Candidate Name	Percentage	Party	Candidate Name	Percentage	Party
2001	96.44	71.90	Rupon Singh Ronghang	41.81	INC	Holiram Terang	40.77	ASDC (U)
1996	89.90	75.04	Holiram Terang	55.56	ASDC	Khorsing Bey	40.07	INC
1991	75.19	68.30	Holiram Terang	49.37	ADC	Dhani Ram Rongpi	41.20	INC
1985	53.60	62.35	Holiram Terang	35.04	IND	Dhani Ram Rongpi	30.77	INC
1983	22.80	30.82	Dhani Ram Rongpi	78.32	INC	Rong Bong Kro	21.68	IND
1978	36.50	50.47	Dhani Ram Rongpi	53.16	INC	Roy Enghee	46.84	JNP

Source: www.eci.gov.in

Table 3.17 (A)
Result of Bokajan (ST) Assembly Constituency

		Percentage of Valid Votes Caste in Favour of Contesting Parties					
Party Abbreviation	**Current Party Status**	**2001**	**1996**	**1991**	**1985**	**1983**	**1978**
AGP	S	-	-	16.04	-	-	-
ASDC	-	-	57.94	-	-	-	-
ASDC (P)	NE	26.01	-	-	-	-	-
ASDC (U)	NE	34.82	-	-	-	-	-
BJP	N	-	-	1.8	-	-	-
INC	NE	-	-	-	-	7.44	-
JNP	N	30	15.85	24.26	30.48	58.32	33.52
RJD	NE	-	-	-	-	-	39.13

Source: www.eci.gov.in

Table 3.17 (B)
List of winning candidates: Bokajan (ST) Assembly Constituency

Year	Voters in 1000	Voter Turnout (Percentage)	Winner			Runner-up		
			Candidate Name	Percentage	Party	Candidate Name	Percentage	Party
2001	69.87	73.45	Jagat Sing Engti	34.82	ASDC (U)	Hidhinath Rongpi	30.00	INC
1996	61.47	82.55	Jagat Sing Engti	57.94	ASDC	Ashwen Jishing Rengma	23.08	IND
1991	54.96	72.91	Monsing Rongpi	54.91	ADC	Rajen Timung	24.26	INC
1985	35.90	62.97	Rajen Timung	30.48	INC	Dhani Ram Teron	29.30	IND
1983	18.82	39.34	Rajen Timung	58.32	INC	Rohini Kumar Dey	13.07	IND
1978	24.90	54.80	Bilton G. Momin	39.13	JNP	Chatra Sing Teron	33.52	INC

Source: www.eci.gov.in

Table 3.18 (A)
Result of Howraghat (ST) Assembly Constituency

Party Abbreviation	Current Party Status	2001	1996	1991	1985	1983	1978
		Percentage of Valid Votes Caste in Favour of Contesting Parties					
AGP	S	-	-	14.37	-	-	-
ASDC	-	-	54.16	-	-	-	-
ASDC (P)	NE	30.09	-	-	-	-	-
ASDC (U)	NE	39.1	-	-	-	-	-
BJP	N	-	1.14	-	-	-	-
ICS	NE	-	-	-	13.24	15.77	-
INC	N	29.34	18.66	7.95	25.58	48.25	37.62
JNP	NE	-	-	-	-	-	50.07

Source: www.eci.gov.in

Table 3.18 (B)

List of Winning Candidates: Howraghat (ST) Assembly Constituency

Year	Voters in 1000	Voter Turnout (Percentage)	Winner			Runner-up		
			Candidate Name	Percentage	Party	Candidate Name	Percentage	Party
2001	70.28	81.26	Dharamsing Teron	39.10	ASDC (U)	Rabi Kumar Phangcho	30.09	ASDC (P)
1996	61.03	86.35	Chandra Kanta Terang	54.16	ASDC	Brojen Langthasa	26.04	IND
1991	58.57	78.77	Babu Rongpi	57.02	ADC	Khorsing Engti	20.25	IND
1985	39.00	71.08	Khorsing Engti	36.92	IND	Dorsing Terong	25.58	INC
1983	23.80	45.46	Dorsing Terang	48.25	INC	Resulo Hemre Rengma	32.20	IND
1978	34.95	67.45	Barelong Terang	50.07	JNP	Dorsing Terang	37.62	INC

Source: www.eci.gov.in

for the Bodo community living in the lower part of Assam. As the Bodo movement for a separate homeland took an extreme form of violence resulting in indiscriminate killings, extortions, blowing up of bridges and railway lines and other infrastructure, the two militant factions the NDFB and the BLT continued with their violent activities till the negotiation for an agreement could be forged with the BLT in 2003. Eventually, the Bodoland Territorial Council (BTC) was formed and elections were held recently.

Leading the opposition on the concept of a separate Bodoland, on the other hand, was the Sanmilita Janagosthiya Sangram Samiti (SJSS)[21], an alliance of twenty-one non-Bodo organizations, which had for long opposed any concession to the Bodo nationalists. The SJSS derived its support from an important section of the Assamese people, the Koch Rajbangshi, who bear close ethnic links with the Bodos. Reservations and anxieties had also been expressed by organizations representing other non-Bodo populations living in the area — the Adivasis, the Nepalis and the tea garden labour communities. Another important segment of non-Bodo population in the envisaged Bodoland area, the Muslim peasantry of East Bengal ancestry, had also been at loggerheads with the Bodoland agitation, ending up more often than not as victims of violence.

The ABSU leaders, along with the leaders of the Bodo People's Action Committee (BPAC) signed the Bodoland Accord-I providing for the creation of a 'Bodoland Autonomous Council' (BAC) on February 20th 1993. However, the BAC did not work for various reasons, especially the limitations inherent in the Accord that gave birth to it. The

---

[21] The SJSS feared that curving out a separate territory for the Bodos will not only lead to the loss of the political identity of the non-Bodos but will also help the Bodos in driving out the non- Bodos, who have already been systematically attacking the non-Bodos to clear the proposed area for formation of the Bodoland.

rivalries between the Congress (I) and the Asom Gana Parishad (AGP) government, which was in office in Guwahati when the agitation began, too mired it[22].

The last settlement for the creation of the Bodoland Territorial Council (BTC), in which the National Democratic Alliance (NDA) government and Congress (I) governments in Delhi and Guwahati actively cooperated in the drafting of the Accord in 2002, saw apart from creating an autonomous self-governing body under the Sixth Schedule of the Constitution of India for the Bodos, address various socio-cultural, economic and educational concerns raised by the Bodos, the largest among the plains' tribes in the State.

Table 3.19
Contestants in Kokrajhar District (Assam)

Candidate	Party	Votes
	1991	
Satyendra Nath Brohmo Choudhury	**Independents**	426727
Louis Islary	**Indian National Congress**	163588
Birendra Chandra Boro	**Asom Gana Parishad**	140809
Samar Brahma Choudhury	**Plains Tribals Council Of Assam**	71027
	1996	
Louis Islary	**Independents**	185688

(Contd...)

[22] That hurriedly signed accord had faltered on various counts, the most important being the absence of a clear-cut geographical boundary for the BAC, which led ultimately to its denunciation by the Bodo groups who were initially party to the agreement. In fact, the conviction, continues to be widespread in Assam, and not merely among die-hard supporters of the AGP, that the Bodoland agitation was created, encouraged and even financed by the Congress (I) at that point of time, with a view to creating problems for the AGP government, the first seemingly coherent and viable regional political formation to challenge successfully the near-unbroken historic hegemony of the Congress (I) in Assam. *Promises and Problems*, M.S. Prabhakara.

Candidate	Party	Votes
Rabi Ram Brahma	**Independents**	**154134**
Pani Ram Rava	**Asom Gana Parishad**	**153540**
Lahendra Basumatary	**Indian National Congress**	**129037**
Charan Narzary	**Bharatiya Janata Party**	**122609**
Amrit Lal Basumatary	**Indian Congress (Socialist)**	**17160**
	1998	
Sansuma Khunggur Bwiswmuthiary	**Independents**	**192975**
Theodor Kisku Rapaz	**United Reservation Movement Council Of Assam**	**151543**
Binod Gayary	**Independents**	**140457**
Charan Narzary	**Bharatiya Janata Party**	**115875**
Premsing Brahma	**Indian National Congress**	**89470**
Louis Islary	**Asom Gana Parishad**	**47853**
Thaneswar Boro	**Plains Tribals Council Of Assam**	**12952**
Jamini Mohan Basumatary	**Independents**	**4041**
	1999	
Sansuma Khunggur Bwiswmuthiary	**Independents**	**334367**
Theodor Kisku Rapaz	**United Reservation Movement Council Of Assam**	**246942**
Gangadhar Ramchiary	**People's Democratic Front**	**172434**
Sri Premsing Brahma	**Indian National Congress**	**65234**
Anil Murmu	**Independents**	**63427**
Kanakeswar Narzary	**United Bodo Nationalist Liberation Front**	**7611**
	2004	
Sansuma Khunggur Bwiswmuthiary	**Independents**	**689620**
Sabda Ram Rabha	**Independents**	**205491**
Derhagra Mushahary	**Indian National Congress**	**61425**
Rajendra Mushahary	**Independents**	**10451**

Source: www.electionnext.com

Amidst violence in demand for a separate identity, Kokrajhar is perhaps the only Parliamentary constituency with ten Assembly segments in the State that has returned back independent candidates as winners since the 1991 Lok Sabha election. The population of the district stands at 905764, which is around 3.4 per cent of the total population of the State. Again, as mentioned earlier, the composition of the population in the district is multi-ethnic, with a large percentage of the non-Bodo population also residing in the district. The tribal population stands at around 41 per cent.

It is Satyendra Nath Brohmo Choudhury who was the winner in the 1991 poll. He won polling a total vote of 53 per cent. The Congress candidate Louis Islary was the runner up with 20 per cent of the votes. Louis Islary, though, was the winner in 1996 Lok Sabha poll, he won as an independent candidate. In the Lok Sabha polls of 1998, 1999 and 2004, held in the shadow of the Bodo Movement, the independent candidate Sansuma Khunggur Bwiswmuthiary[23], supported by the All Bodo Students' Union has been the winner. Moreover, in the 2004 poll, Bwiswmuthiary could amass a vote percentage of as high as 71 per cent. On the other hand, Sabda Rabha, the candidate supported by the non-Bodos like the Rajbangshis, Rabhas, minorities and Adivasis although could gather the second position, he could get a vote percentage of 21 only.

An interesting trend that has been noticed in the polls of 1998 and 1999 was that of Theodor Kisku Rapaz from the United Reservation Movement Council of Assam (URMCA) being the runner up in these two polls with a marginal difference in votes with the winner Sansuma Khunggur Bwiswmuthiary. On the other hand, the major political

---

[23] However, it was reported that rigging had been done by Sensuma's supporters in a massive way threatening the presiding and polling officers in a polling station at Kachugaon in Tamulpur legislative constituency. In Tamulpur his supporters captured some EVMs the day before the election. They were also accused of kidnapping some Adivasis. *Pratidin*, 21st April 2004.

parties like the Indian National Congress, the Asom Gana Parishad and even the BJP have failed to make inroads into the district till date.

In the 11th Assembly election of 2001 (Tables 3.20 to 3.29), except in the constituent assemblies of Gossaingaon, Barama and Bhabanipur, where the Congress could occupy the seats, the rest of the seven constituencies saw independent candidates come out as winners. In the three constituencies of Gossaingaon, Barama and Bhabanipur, it was AGP MLAs from whom the power was wrested by the Congress candidates in 2001. The Congress (I) made up for these losses in areas where the scheduled tribes constituted more than 25 per cent of the population. Although it did not get a major chunk of the scheduled tribe votes, it won three seats in non-Bodo areas, a big gain as compared to the Assembly elections of 1991 and 1996 when it won only one seat and none respectively.

The Tea Garden Belt of Upper Assam: *Class Politics*

As elsewhere in the country, the voting behaviour in the State is also smeared with *class politics*. The tea labourers' community in the State[24] comprising both workers and ex-workers, mostly belonging to the tribal groups, has a presence in the electoral politics of the State for many years. This community constituting around 52.27 lakhs or 21 per cent of the State's population, mostly concentrated in ten districts of the State, according to the 1991 Census is the deciding force for the outcome of many elections in 27 Assembly constituencies in the State[25]. The tea labour community,

[24] The tea community in the State is mostly concentrated in the tea belt area in the districts of Dibrugarh, Lakhimpur, Darrang and Sibsagar. As per the tea statistics of 2001, out of a total 40, 795 tea estates in Assam, 39, 922 are located in these four districts. Despite their numerical strength and long history in Assam stretching more than a century, they remain the 'outsiders' without the tribal status, as has been accorded to them in their place of origin, and are deprived of benefits availed by the other backward castes.

[25] This tea community is traditionally considered as a 'vote bank' for the Congress. This community has in fact played a decisive role in the victories of the Congress candidates of upper Assam. "Mixed Verdict", Sandhya Goswami, *Economic and Political Weekly*, vol. XXXIX no. 51, December 18-24, 2004.

Table 3.20 (A)

Result of Gossaingaon Assembly Constituency

Party Abbreviation	Current Party Status	Percentage of Valid Votes Caste in Favour of Parties					
		2001	1996	1991	1985	1983	1978
AGP	S	5.73	36.86	2.89	-	-	-
BJP	N	-	9.45	-	-	-	-
FBL	NE	-	-	-	-	-	5.64
ICS	NE	-	-	-	13.14	22.15	-
ICS (SCS)	NE	-	-	0.76	-	-	-
INC	N	54.92	27.04	24.98	39.52	41.72	35.18
INC (I)	NE	-	-	-	-	-	10.67
JNP	NE	-	-	-	-	-	22.64
PTC	NE	-	-	-	11.65	13.09	-
RSP	S	-	-	-	-	-	6.31

Source: www.eci.gov.in

Table 3.20 (B)
List of winning candidates: Gossaingaon Assembly Constituency

Year	Voters in 1000	Voter Turnout (Percentage)	Winner			Runner-up		
			Candidate Name	Percentage	Party	Candidate Name	Percentage	Party
2001	113.12	90.44	Mithias Tudu	54.92	INC	Dr. Bibhuti Bhusan Brahma	36.02	IND
1996	77.25	87.16	Rajendra Mushahary	36.86	AGP	Mithias Tudu	27.04	INC
1991	87.07	89.25	Tajendra Narzary	70.66	IND	Mithias Tudu	24.98	INC
1985	58.47	86.05	Mithias Tudu	39.52	INC	Helen Murmu	14.35	IND
1983	41.20	68.59	Mithias Tudu	41.72	INC	Samsul Haque	22.15	ICS
1978	43.60	74.83	Mithias Tudu	35.18	INC	Mathias Marandi	22.64	JNP

Source: www.eci.gov.in

Table 3.21 (A)

Result of Kokrajhar West (ST) Assembly Constituency

Party Abbreviation	Current Party Status	Percentage of Valid Votes Caste in Favour of Parties				
		2001	1996	1985	1983	1978
AGP	S	-	8.96	-	-	-
BJP	N	-	9.84	-	-	-
ICS	NE	-	1.37	31.08	11.15	-
INC	N	10.99	11.24	20.99	52.33	49.8
PTC	NE	-	-	16.68	18.61	40.16

Source: www.eci.gov.in

Table 3.21 (B)
List of winning candidates: Kokrajhar West (ST) Assembly Constituency

Year	Voters in 1000	Voter Turnout (Percentage)	Winner			Runner-up		
			Candidate Name	Percentage	Party	Candidate Name	Percentage	Party
2001	106.66	88.98	Hemendra Nath Brahma	71.51	IND	Lahendra Basumatary	11.96	IND
1996	85.51	87.23	Parameswar Brahma	27.56	IND	Jitendra Nath Roy	18.98	IND
1991	-	-	Amrit Lal Basumatary	UC	IND	-	-	-
1985	58.72	89.00	Ranendra Narayan Basumatary	31.08	ICS	Ranendra Narayan Basumatary	20.99	INC
1983	47.11	73.69	Ranendra Narayan Basumatary	52.33	INC	Thaneswar Narzary	18.61	PTC
1978	50.80	81.65	Ranendra Narayan Basumatary	49.80	INC	Thaneswar Narzary	40.16	PTC

Source: www.eci.gov.in

Table 3.22 (A)
Result of Kokrajhar East (ST) Assembly Constituency

Party Abbreviation	Current Party Status	Percentage of Valid Votes Caste in Favour of Parties					
		2001	1996	1991	1985	1983	1978
AGP	S	-	10.69	-	-	-	-
BJP	N	-	7.84	-	-	-	-
ICS	NE	-	-	-	15.3	8.73	-
INC	N	12.99	12.4	13.95	27.25	38.15	35.22
INC (I)	NE	-	-	-	-	-	3.87
PTC	NE	-	-	-	40.14	35.84	49.42
PTCA	-	-	-	6.81	-	-	-

Source: www.eci.gov.in

Table 3.22 (B)

List of winning candidates: Kokrajhar East (ST) Assembly Constituency

Year	Voters in 1000	Voter Turnout (Percentage)	Winner			Runner-up		
			Candidate Name	Percentage	Party	Candidate Name	Percentage	Party
2001	112.39	89.13	Pramila Rani Brahma	81.91	IND	Charan Narzary	12.99	INC
1996	88.23	83.13	Pramila Rani Brahma	45.09	IND	Chitta Ranjan Brahma	21.41	IND
1991	86.92	88.14	Pramila Rani Brahma	79.24	IND	Dhwajendra Brahma	13.95	INC
1985	64.38	87.46	Charan Narzary	40.14	PTC	Dambarudhar Brahma	27.25	INC
1983	42.15	67.44	Dambarudhar Brahma	38.15	INC	Samar Brahma Choudhury	35.84	PTC
1978	48.63	81.92	Samar Brahma Choudhury	49.42	PTC	Jagadish Chandra Brahma	35.22	INC

Source: www.eci.gov.in

Table 3.23 (A)
Result of Sidli (ST) Assembly Constituency

Party Abbreviation	Current Party Status	Percentage of Valid Votes Caste in Favour of Parties					
		2001	1996	1991	1985	1983	1978
AGP	S	-	-	7.7	-	-	-
BJP	N	-	9.59	-	-	-	-
CPM	N	-	-		-	14.17	-
ICS	NE	-	-	-	3.06	-	-
INC	N	7.92	14.01	13.07	31.06	41.27	42.68
INC (I)	NE	-	-	-	-	-	3.54
PTC	NE	-	-	-	47.51	14.74	51.06
PTCA	-	-	-	0.75	-	-	-

Source: www.eci.gov.in

Table 3.23 (B)

List of winning candidates: Sidli (ST) Assembly Constituency

Year	Voters in 1000	Voter Turnout (Percentage)	Winner			Runner-up		
			Candidate Name	Percentage	Party	Candidate Name	Percentage	Party
2001	116.81	83.38	Matindra Basumatary	72.61	IND	Andrias Hajoary	14.50	PDF
1996	94.48	79.82	Andrias Hajoary	32.60	IND	Chino Basumatary	28.70	IND
1991	102.45	87.17	Khiren Borgoyary	78.48	IND	Louis Islary	13.07	INC
1985	70.30	87.67	Janendra Basumatary	47.51	PTC	Luis Islary	31.06	INC
1983	48.32	62.68	Luis Islari	41.27	INC	Subhas Basumatary	27.74	IND
1978	58.11	80.85	Panchanan Brahma	51.06	PTC	Uttam Brahma	42.68	INC

Source: www.eci.gov.in

Table 3.24 (A)
Result of Bijni Assembly Constituency

Party Abbreviation	Current Party Status	Percentage of Valid Votes Caste in Favour of Parties				
		2001	1996	1991	1985	1978
AGP	S	-	25.96	6.45	-	-
AICC (T)	NE	-	0.49	-	-	-
BJP	N	-	9.47	-	-	-
CPM	N	14.83	-	15.64	25	-
ICS	NE	-	-	-	0.9	-
INC	N	24.44	15.83	21.33	8.91	24.23
INC (I)	NE	-	-	-	-	1.76
JNP	NE	-	-	-	-	23.12
NAGP	NE	-	-	3.38	-	-
NCP	N	0.25	-	-	-	-
PTC	NE	-	-	-	26.93	-
UMF	NE	-	-	0.22	-	-

Source: www.eci.gov.in

Table 3.24 (B)

List of winning candidates: Bijni Assembly Constituency

Year	Voters in 1000	Voter Turnout (Percentage)	Winner			Runner-up		
			Candidate Name	Percentage	Party	Candidate Name	Percentage	Party
2001	76.34	85.06	Romio Brahma	46.09	IND	Dhiresh Barman	24.44	INC
1996	72.29	84.68	Mohini Basumatary	40.60	IND	Ratneswar Ray	25.96	AGP
1991	70.54	87.18	Kamal Brahma	52.44	IND	Uday Chandra Das	21.33	INC
1985	54.28	87.18	Ganesh Bora	26.93	PTC	Parimal Chakraborty	25.00	CPM
1978	46.31	79.64	Padmalochan Boro	33.12	IND	Golak Chandra Patgiri	24.23	INC

Source: www.eci.gov.in

Table 3.25 (A)
Result of Sorbhog Assembly Constituency

Party Abbreviation	Current Party Status	Percentage of Valid Votes Caste in Favour of Parties					
		2001	1996	1991	1985	1983	1978
AGP	S	-	-	25.11	-	-	-
AIIC (T)	NE	-	6.31	-	-	-	-
AITC	S	0.84	-	-	-	-	-
BJP	N	28.7	10.36	-	-	-	-
CPM	N	25.65	43.67	33.13	39.33	36.74	59.77
INC	N	3.72	16.45	37.21	4.2	16.16	25.85
INC (I)	NE	-	-	-	-	-	1.11
JNP	NE	-	-	-	-	-	7.28
PTC	NE	-	-	-	-	11.79	-

Source: www.eci.gov.in

Table 3.25 (B)

List of winning candidates: Sorbhog Assembly Constituency

Year	Voters in 1000	Voter Turnout (Percentage)	Winner			Runner-up		
			Candidate Name	Percentage	Party	Candidate Name	Percentage	Party
2001	98.76	76.38	Samsul Haque	32.90	IND	Anilananda Pathak	28.70	BJP
1996	75.55	85.06		43.67	CPM		16.45	IND
1991	87.19	85.17	Samsul Haque	37.21	INC	Hemen Das	33.13	CPM
1985	70.21	87.08	Hemen Das	39.33	CPM	David Ledger	27.80	IND
1983	37.41	52.68	Hemen Das	36.74	CPM	Samsul Haque	32.24	IND
1978	51.48	73.90	Hemen Das	59.77	CPM	Pranita Talukdar	25.85	INC

Source: www.eci.gov.in

Table 3.26 (A)

Result of Bhabanipur Assembly Constituency

Party Abbreviation	Current Party Status	Percentage of Valid Votes Caste in Favour of Parties					
		2001	1996	1991	1985	1983	1978
AGP	S	15.86	37.46	21.99	-	-	-
AIIC (T)	NE	-	0.15	-	-	-	-
BJP	N	-	3.93	-	-	-	-
ICS	NE	-	0.84	-	0.32	-	-
ICS (SCS)	NE	-	-	20.8	-	-	-
INC	N	44.65	24.53	1.06	3.61	44.73	12.69
INC (I)	NE	-	-	-	-	-	8.3
JD	NE	-	-	5.08	-	-	-
JNP	NE	-	-	-	0.94	-	28.34
NAGP	NE	-	-	3.87	-	-	-
NCP	N	1.95	-	-	-	-	-
PTC	NE	-	-	-	16.15	26.52	-

Source: www.eci.gov.in

Table 3.26 (B)
List of winning candidates: Bhabanipur Assembly Constituency

Year	Voters in 1000	Voter Turnout (Percentage)	Winner			Runner-up		
			Candidate Name	Percentage	Party	Candidate Name	Percentage	Party
2001	76.63	81.44	Sarbananda Choudhury	44.65	INC	Milan Boro	37.34	IND
1996	65.37	83.90		37.46	AGP		24.65	IND
1991	68.29	82.47	Milan Boro	35.72	IND	Surendra Nath Medhi	21.99	AGP
1985	61.34	92.08	Surendra Nath Medhi	48.62	IND	Kanak Chandra Boro	22.78	IND
1983	17.22	28.42	Mir Abdul Halim	44.73	INC	Garga Narayan Narzary	26.52	PTC
1978	41.55	71.32	Tarini Charan Das	28.34	JNP	Purnanda Kherkatary	18.62	IND

Source: www.eci.gov.in

Table 3.27 (A)
Result of Tamulpur Assembly Constituency

		Percentage of Valid Votes Caste in Favour of Parties					
Party Abbreviation	**Current Party Status**	**2001**	**1996**	**1991**	**1985**	**1983**	**1978**
AGP	S	-	23.95	14.68	-	-	-
AIIC (T)	NE	-	9.86	-	-	-	-
BJP	N	-	4.64	-	-	-	-
CPI	N	-	-	-	2.14	11.53	-
INC	N	37.2	16.85	8.82	13.72	44.63	14.45
INC (I)	NE	-	-	-			1.93
JNP	NE	-	-	-	-	-	30.67
NAGP	NE	-	-	6.15	-	-	-
PTC	NE	-	-	-	20.16	25.9	-
PTCA	-	-	-	5.25	-	-	-

Source: www.eci.gov.in

Table 3.27 (B)
List of winning candidates: Tamulpur Assembly Constituency

Year	Voters in 1000	Voter Turnout (Percentage)	Winner			Runner-up		
			Candidate Name	Percentage	Party	Candidate Name	Percentage	Party
2001	108.41	82.09	Biswajit Daimary	53.21	IND	Padum Chauhan	37.20	INC
1996	89.50	79.99	Derhagra Mushahary	33.10	IND	Ramesh Mazumdar	23.95	AGP
1991	88.44	79.13	Derhagra Mushahary	24.25	IND	Ramesh Mazumdar	14.68	AGP
1985	70.27	82.92	Bhaben Narji	30.95	IND	Maneswar Boro	20.16	PTC
1983	30.67	50.17	Padam Bahadur Chouhan	44.63	INC	Abiram Boro	25.90	PTC
1978	44.23	73.53	Padam Bahadur Chouhan	30.67	JNP	Maneswar Boro	29.99	IND

Source: www.eci.gov.in

Table 3.28 (A)
Result of Barama Assembly Constituency

Party Abbreviation	Current Party Status	Percentage of Valid Votes Caste in Favour of Parties					
		2001	1996	1991	1985	1983	1978
AGP	S	-	23.95	14.68	-	-	-
AIIC (T)	NE	-	9.86	-	-	-	-
BJP	N	-	4.64	-	-	-	-
CPI	N	-	-	-	2.14	11.53	-
INC	N	37.2	16.85	8.82	13.72	44.63	14.45
INC (I)	NE	-	-	-			1.93
JNP	NE	-	-	-	-	-	30.67
NAGP	NE	-	-	6.15	-	-	-
PTC	NE	-	-	-	20.16	25.9	-
PTCA	-	-	-	5.25	-	-	-

Source: www.eci.gov.in

Table 3.28 (B)

List of winning candidates: Barama Assembly Constituency

Year	Voters in 1000	Voter Turnout (Percentage)	Winner			Runner-up		
			Candidate Name	Percentage	Party	Candidate Name	Percentage	Party
2001	89.67	77.46	Paniram Rabha	39.04	INC	Nageswar Choudhury	29.65	IND
1996	77.71	77.42	Rekha Rani Das Boro	39.41	AGP	Gangadhar Ramchiary	25.84	IND
1991	75.81	75.82	Pani Ram Rabha	30.04	NAGP	Rekha Rani Das Boro	26.85	AGP
1985	68.80	85.30	Rekha Rani Das Boro	54.54	IND	Alit Chandra Boro	32.04	PTC
1983	10.72	16.14	Alit Chandra Boro	86.26	PTC	Baikuntha Nath Das	13.74	INC
1978	38.47	65.58	Baikuntha Nath Das	36.25	INC	Alit Boro	34.63	PTC

Table 3.29 (A)
Result of Chapaguri (ST) Assembly Constituency

Party Abbreviation	Current Party Status	2001	1996	1991	1985	1983	1978
		Percentage of Valid Votes Caste in Favour of Parties					
AGP	S	-	36.82	32.69	-	-	-
AIIC (T)	NE	-	0.22	-	-	-	-
BJP	N	-	2.69	-	-	-	-
CPI (ML) (L)	S	1.77	-	-	-	-	-
ICS	NE	-	-	-	0.43	-	-
ICS (SCS)	NE	-	-	0.24	-	-	-
INC	N	7.95	8.06	4.48	7.62	18.2	11.09
INC (I)	NE	-	-	-	-	-	4.43
PTC	NE	-	-	-	37.71	-	32.87
PTCA	-	-	-	19.33	-	-	-

Source: www.eci.gov.in

Table 3.29 (B)

List of winning candidates: Chapaguri (ST) Assembly Constituency

Year	Voters in 1000	Voter Turnout (Percentage)	Winner			Runner-up		
			Candidate Name	Percentage	Party	Candidate Name	Percentage	Party
2001	92.92	83.88	Tijen Basumatary	70.30	IND	Suren Swargiary	8.02	IND
1996	82.55	80.96	Jagmohan Basmatary	40.16	IND	Suren Swargiary	36.82	AGP
1991	77.98	78.98	Suren Swargiary	32.69	AGP	Jog Mohan Barkachary	31.53	IND
1985	68.09	86.84	Suren Swargiary	47.83	IND	Chilarai Uzir	37.71	PTC
1983	6.56	10.33	Bimal Gayari	75.59	PTC	Ramdas Boro	18.20	INC
1978	41.43	71.33	Manik Chandra Das	33.42	IND	Khogendra Nath Boro	32.87	PTC

Source: www.eci.gov.in

constitutes the oldest amongst Assam's immigrant groups that was recruited by the British Tea Planters from present day Jharkhand, Andhra Pradesh, Bihar, Chhattisgarh, Orissa and Uttar Pradesh between 1861 and the early 20th century, to work as indentured labour in tea plantations in Assam, spread over the districts of western Assam, Morigaon, Nagaon, Sonitpur and Darrang in Middle Assam, Golaghat, Jorhat, Sibsagar, Dibrugarh and Tinsukia in eastern or upper Assam, North Cachar and Karbi Anglong districts in southern Assam and the Barak Valley. Belonging to the tribal groups such as Gonds, Kharias, Khonds, Kisang, Mundas, Nagesias, Oraons and Santhals, they settled down in Assam at the end of the contract period, some even left the tea plantations to settle in the surrounding agricultural lands before the expiry of the contract. The latter came to be known as the ex-Tea labour community that today lives in villages neighbouring the tea estates and provides casual labour to these estates depending on the seasonal demand.

The Indian National Trade Union Congress (INTUC), a labour organisation having allegiance to the Congress has made its presence felt through its affiliate, the *Assam Chah Mazdoor Sangha* among the tea garden workers in the State since 1947. However, the contemporary trends in electorate politics in the State show the declining influence of the Congress amidst the tea garden workers. The other parties like the Asom Gana Parishad (AGP) and the Bharatiya Janata Party (BJP) are spreading their influence among these workers as they have admitted their failure so far in realizing the impact of INTUC's reach and its ability to transform its influence among the tea garden workers to vote for the Congress. This perhaps will change the rules of the game, unbalancing the power equation of the Congress so far in these garden constituencies. From the INTUC's side, it seems that no attempts were made to address the socio-economic problems of the tea garden workers. The

Government too was often caught off side on coxing the management to take up right steps in providing relief to the tea garden workers. Most pathetic and grim conditions prevail among the tea garden workers in general and in Assam Tea Corporation (ATC)[26] gardens in particular, which are in the State sector.

There are many flaws in the Plantation Labour Act 1951, taking advantage of which, it is alleged, garden managements are exploiting the plantation workers and keeping them in a sub human condition. The garden managements are even violating the flawed Plantation Labour Act. There is also a failure on the part of the Assam Government in directing the tea estate managements to follow the law envisaged on wage policy, adopted in the second five-year plan in case of tea plantation workers. This has resulted in adoption of peculiar inconvenient policies by the management of the estates. Non-fulfillment of demands like the payment of full bonus and wages fixed by the State government thus has eroded the support base of the Congress among the tea garden workers. Most of the political parties in Assam have thus merely been using the issue of Adivasis and tea tribes as a 'political tool'.

The erosion in the vote bank of the Congress, therefore, has been caused by the alleged indifferent attitude of the party in ameliorating the ever-worsening conditions of plantation labourers in the State. With the rising educational level among the backward classes of the State (in spite of adverse educational environment) especially in the garden dominated areas, the younger generations of this helpless

[26] There are 14 gardens under the ATC. The Government in 2001 declared all the gardens sick and decided to sell all the gardens to a private company. Tea workers in Assam are paid much below the government stipulated minimum wage in violation of the Minimum Wages Act. Without their weekly wages the workers live in an artificially created famine-like situation. The workers of the ATC gardens are forced to fill their stomachs by taking wild vegetables obtained from nearby forests, and unknown roots of the jungle herbs due to which workers suffer from different stomach ailments and unknown diseases.

section of the populace of the State are gradually realising that they are being treated as a mere vote bank since independence by the Congress.

Meanwhile, CPI (ML)-led Asom Sangrami Chah Sramik Sangha (ASCSS) has been trying hard to emerge as an alternative organization of tea garden workers in Tinsukia, Dibrugarh, Sonitpur and Jorhat districts[27]. Though initially the ASCSS had no organization or even any contact with the Assam Tea Corporation (ATC) gardens, witnessing the growing unrest of the workers of the ATC gardens against the government's policy, the ASCSS planned to intervene in the situation to orient and guide the movement[28]. Out of the 14 gardens of the ATC, eight are in Jorhat and rest are in Nagaon, Golaghat and Sibsagar districts.

In March 2002, a memorandum was endorsed in a mass meeting of the members of the ATC gardens, ASCSS, AICCTU and CPI (ML) and was submitted to the government representative in the meeting itself.

The demands listed in the memorandum were:

1. All the pending wages and salaries of the ATC garden workers and employees should be released immediately.
2. Publish a white paper on ATC garden.
3. Restore the sanctity of law and apply the policy of uniform wages and bonus to every garden.
4. Implement election promises of the Congress and give Sunday wages to the workers, and
5. The Government must declare its position regarding the tea workers' demand during the next Assembly Session.

---

[27] It has been able to build the organization in more than 30 gardens.

[28] The ASCSS had organized a convention on the theme *Save the Workers of ATC Gardens* at Jorhat. A good section of second rung leaders and activists of the ACMS participated in the convention defying the obstruction of the State leaders. Representatives from all ATC gardens of Jorhat district were present. The convention resolved to organize the workers on a higher plane and a 'March' to the Assembly programme was organized on 6th April 2002 to pressurize the government to solve the workers' problems.

After submission of the memorandum, the leaders of the movement met and decided to formally resign from the ACMS[29] and work with the ASCSS. Secondly, they decided to organize workers in other ATC gardens, who had not yet been contacted. To facilitate that they decided to hold conventions in Nagaon and Golaghat. Thirdly, they decided to burn the effigy of Paban Singh Ghatowar in every garden to protest against his alleged apathy to his own people. Their programme was carried out as scheduled indicating the fact that the Congress was losing its ground slowly but steadily and a new struggling organization was gradually emerging. This lost battlefield for the Congress was evident in the election results too (Table 3.30 and also refer table 2.6 of Chapter 2). Paban Singh Ghatowar has been the winner from the constituency, who has been winning the Lok Sabha elections since 1991 with comfortable margins. He captured the seat in 1991 and 1996 by winning a vote percentage of 51 each. Then he went on to win the Lok Sabha election of 1998 as well, winning with a high vote percentage of 64. However, though he succeed winning in 1999 as well but his winning vote percentage came down to 49

Table 3.30

Contestants in Dibrugarh District (Assam)

Candidate	Party	Votes
	1991	
Paban Singh Ghatowar	**Indian National Congress**	243937
Dipen Tanti	**Asom Gana Parishad**	106017
Israil Nanda	**Natun Asom Gana Parishad**	35011
Kumud Bihari Das	**Bharatiya Janata Party**	27692

(Contd...)

[29] Pawan Singh Ghatowar is the President of ACMS.

Candidate	Party	Votes
Anil Barua	Indian Peoples Front	24966
Jogen Hazarika	Independents	14274
Phate Chandra Garodia	Indian Congress (Socialist - Sarat Chandra Sinha)	10265
Abraham Sanga	United Reservation Movement Council Assam	5945
Doli Das (W)	Independents	5058
Dharmananda Pandey	Independents	4968
Sitaram Bukardia	Independents	2584
Nurul Muda Ahmed	Independents	2005
	1996	
Paban Singh Ghatowar	Indian National Congress	281253
Israil Nanda	Asom Gana Parishad	173898
Harendra Narayan Dutta	Bharatiya Janata Party	50246
Mansharam Patowari	All India Indira Congress (Tiwari)	18463
Anil Kumar Barooah	Communist Party Of India (Marxist-Leninist) (Liberation)	11122
Dharmananda Pandey	Independents	6494
Ramnarayan Singh	Shiva Sena	3572
Padma Kumar Gohain	Independents	2874
Budhram Rajgarh	Independents	2425
Dipak Kumar Das	Independents	1936
Binod Agarwalla	Independents	1668
Phate Chand Garodia	Independents	1009

(Contd...)

Candidate	Party	Votes
	1998	
Paban Singh Ghatowar	Indian National Congress	234195
Ajit Chaliha	Bharatiya Janata Party	93073
Onkarmal Agarwal	Asom Gana Parishad	29985
Anil Kumar Barooah	Communist Party Of India (Marxist-Leninist) (Liberation)	3307
Israil Nanda	Independents	3095
	1999	
Paban Singh Ghatowar	Indian National Congress	270863
Ajit Chaliha	Bharatiya Janata Party	203747
Biju Phukan	Asom Gana Parishad	75932
Brij Pradhan	Communist Party Of India (Marxist-Leninist) (Liberation)	5019
Ramnarayan Singh	Shiva Sena	1276
Mansharam Patowari	Independents	837
	2004	
Sarbananda Sonowal	Asom Gana Parishad	220944
Kamakhya Tasa	Bharatiya Janata Party	202390
Paban Singh Ghatowar	Indian National Congress	170589
Badhram Rajgarh	Independents	15894
Subhas Sen	Communist Party Of India (Marxist-Leninist) (Liberation)	9843
Amrit Borgohain	Independents	6251
Titus Bhengra	Samata Party	5329

Source: www.electionnext.com

In the Assembly election of 2001, except the two constituencies of Moran and Duliajan, where the AGP candidate Sarbananda Sonowal and the BJP candidate Rameswar Teli won the elections respectively, in all other seven constituencies it was a Congress victory all the way. Until then the Congress had its grip among the tea garden workers. Hence it was able to repeat its history of wins in the constituencies of Dibrugarh, Lahowal, Tingkhong, Naharkatia, Tinsukia, Digboi and Margherita (Tables 3.31 to 3.39).

The lost battle for the Congress became even more evident with the defeat of Pawan Singh Ghatowar, the Congress kingpin and winner from the constituency for the last four consecutive Lok Sabha polls. Ghatowâr had to finally face defeat at the hands of Sarbananda Sonowal from the AGP who could amass a vote percentage of 35.

The scenario thus changed. It was only obvious that the Congress failed to retain its seat in the 2004 Lok Sabha poll from the Dibrugarh constituency, which went to Sarbananda Sanowal of AGP (Table 3.30). Paban Singh Ghatowar failed to retain the seat, which he had been winning since the 1991 Lok Sabha poll, and the Congress for the first time tasted defeat in this constituency in 52 years.

Hence it has been found that in the upper Assam belt, the dominant tea garden workers who normally voted for the Congress is now changing their stand. The field is open today in this constituency for the parties to safeguard the rights of the tea community and woo the voters away from an already wobbly Congress support base.

Table 3.31 (A)
Result of Moran Assembly Constituency

		Percentage of Valid Votes Caste in Favour of Contesting Parties					
Party Abbreviation	**Current Party Status**	**2001**	**1996**	**1991**	**1985**	**1983**	**1978**
AGP	S	42.64	45	17.91	-	-	-
AIIC (T)	NE	-	3.1	-	-	-	-
BJP	N	-	2.38	-	-	-	-
CPI	N	-	-	7.58	-	-	-
ICS	NE	-	-	-	0.3	1.18	-
INC	N	41.33	45.44	47.49	22.14	84.22	16.06
INC (I)	NE	-	-	-	-	-	29.35
JD	NE	-	1.05	1.98	-	-	-
JNP	NE	-	-	-	-	-	21.04
JP	-	-	-	0.87	-	-	-
LKD	NE	-	-	-	1.57	-	-
NAGP	NE	-	-	6.85	-	-	-
NCP	N	1.9	-	-	-	-	-

Source: www.eci.gov.in

Table 3.31 (B)
List of winning candidates: Moran Assembly Constituency

Year	Voters in 1000	Voter Turnout (Percentage)	Winner			Runner-up		
			Candidate Name	Percentage	Party	Candidate Name	Percentage	Party
2001	67.58	70.63	Sarbananda Sonowal	42.64	AGP	Jibontara Ghatowar	41.33	INC
1996	63.05	72.33	Joy Chandra Nagbanshi	45.44	INC	Kiran Kumar Gogoi	45.00	AGP
1991	53.42	66.04	Joy Chandra Nagbanshi	47.49	INC	Kiran Kumar Gogoi	17.91	AGP
1985	49.51	70.19	Kiron Kumar Gogoi	46.86	IND	Haren Gogoi	22.14	INC
1983	7.37	12.45	Joy Chandra Nagbanshi	84.22	INC	Banshi Barhai	9.00	IND
1978	38.30	63.22	Joy Chandra Nagbanshi	29.35	INC (I)	Dayananda Borgohain	21.04	JNP

Source: www.eci.gov.in

Table 3.32 (A)
Result of Dibrugarh Assembly Constituency

Party Abbreviation	Current Party Status	Percentage of Valid Votes Caste in Favour of Contesting Parties					
		2001	1996	1991	1985	1983	1978
AGP	S	-	29.89	23.42	-	-	-
AIIC (T)	NE	-	6.98-18.29	-	-	-	-
BJP	N	24.44	-	6.3	0.48	-	-
CPI (ML) (L)	S	1.64	-	-	-	-	-
ICS	NE	-	-	-	0.92	4.76	-
ICS (SCS)	NE	-	40.72	0.68	-	-	-
INC	N	67.57	-	42.38	44.87	91.96	26.48
INC (I)	NE	-	0.51	-	-	-	4.47
JD	NE	-	-	2.92	-	-	-
JNP	NE	-	-	-	0.69	-	57.84
JP	-	-	-	3.26	-	-	-
LKD	NE	-	-	-	0.41	-	-
NAGP	NE	-	-	9.3	-	-	-
NCP	N	2.63	-	-	-	-	-
RJD	S	0.43	-	-	-	-	-
SHS	S	-	0.93	-	-	-	-
SP	S	0.72	0.37	-	-	-	-

Source: www.eci.gov.in

Table 3.32 (B)

List of winning candidates: Dibrugarh Assembly Constituency

Year	Voters in 1000	Voter Turnout (Percentage)	Winner			Runner-up		
			Candidate Name	Percentage	Party	Candidate Name	Percentage	Party
2001	60.20	59.39	Dr. Kalyan Kumar Gogoi	67.57	INC	Ajit Chaliha	24.44	BJP
1996	58.17	66.20	Dr. Kalyan Kumar Gogoi	40.72	INC	Taranath Buragohain	29.89	AGP
1991	55.36	61.00	Keshab Gogoi	42.38	INC	Bhaskar Bora	23.42	AGP
1985	56.53	71.95	Keshab Gogoi	44.87	INC	Ananta Handique	37.32	IND
1983	5.61	8.71	Keshab Chandra Gogoi	91.96	INC	Ramesh Chandra Barooah	4.76	ICS
1978	39.06	65.62	Keshab Chandra Gogoi	57.84	JNP	Lakshi Prasad Dutta	26.48	INC

Source: www.eci.gov.in

Table 3.33 (A)

Result of Lahowal Assembly Constituency

		Percentage of Valid Votes Caste in Favour of Contesting Parties					
Party Abbreviation	**Current Party Status**	**2001**	**1996**	**1991**	**1985**	**1983**	**1978**
AGP	S	-	39.85	16.84	-	-	-
AIIC (T)	NE	-	5	-	-	-	-
BJP	N	23.15	1.76	1.27	-	-	-
CPI	N	6.55	-	6.44	3.78	11.89	11.56
ICS (SCS)	NE	-	-	0.43	-	-	-
INC	N	68.52	50.37	43.17	41.48	78.9	27.11
INC (I)	NE	-	-	-	-	-	6.94
JD	NE	-	1.33	2.92	-	-	-
JNP	NE	-	-	-	0.98	-	19.99
JP		-	-	3.26	-	-	-
NAGP	NE	-	-	9.3	-		-
NCP	N	1.09	-	-	-	-	-
SHS	S	-	0.75	-	-	-	-

Source: www.eci.gov.in

Table 3.33 (B)

List of winning candidates: Lahowal Assembly Constituency

Year	Voters in 1000	Voter Turnout (Percentage)	Winner			Runner-up		
			Candidate Name	Percentage	Party	Candidate Name	Percentage	Party
2001	63.56	64.95	Prithibi Majhi	68.52	INC	Rebati Phukan	23.15	BJP
1996	63.03	71.26	Prithibi Majhi	50.37	INC	Karuna Hazarika	39.85	AGP
1991	55.83	66.48	Haren Bhumij	43.17	INC	Karuna Hazarika	16.84	AGP
1985	48.01	67.68	Dipen Tanti	51.03	IND	Dipok Moormoo	41.48	INC
1983	11.25	19.14	Dipok Moormoo	78.90	INC	Sitaram Rajput	11.89	CPI
1978	35.44	59.30	Dipok Moormoo	27.11	INC	Nakul Patnaik	19.99	JNP

Source: www.eci.gov.in

Table 3.34 (A)

Result of Duliajan Assembly Constituency

		Percentage of Valid Votes Caste in Favour of Contesting Parties				
Party Abbreviation	**Current Party Status**	**2001**	**1996**	**1991**	**1985**	**1978**
AGP	S	-	-	26.31	-	-
AIIC (T)	NE	-	8.37	-	-	-
AITC	S	1.26	-	-	-	-
BJP	N	50.75	12.26	-	-	-
CPI	N	-	25.68	-	-	-
ICS	NE	-	-	-	0.76	-
INC	N	39.53	47.77	50.82	41.17	19.67
INC (I)	NE	-	-	-	-	14.59
JD	NE	-	-	1.53	-	-
JNP	NE	-	-	-	1.19	22.87
JP	-	-	-	1.23	-	-
NAGP	NE	-	-	12.63	-	-
SHS	S	-	0.57	-	-	-

Source: www.eci.gov.in

Table 3.34 (B)
List of winning candidates: Duliajan Assembly Constituency

Year	Voters in 1000	Voter Turnout (Percentage)	Winner			Runner-up		
			Candidate Name	Percentage	Party	Candidate Name	Percentage	Party
2001	70.78	63.10	Rameswar Teli	50.75	BJP	Amiya Gogoi	39.53	INC
1996	66.65	67.30	Amiya Gogoi	47.77	INC	Likheswar Gogoi	25.68	CPI
1991	60.12	65.79	Amiya Gogoi	50.82	INC	Diganta Saikia	26.31	AGP
1985	51.89	64.41	Amiya Gogoi	41.17	INC	Nakul Baruah	39.75	IND
1978	36.63	59.02	Jogen Hazarika	22.87	JNP	Indeswar Khound	19.67	INC

Source: www.eci.gov.in

Table 3.35 (A)
Result of Tingkhong Assembly Constituency

Party Abbreviation	Current Party Status	Percentage of Valid Votes Caste in Favour of Contesting Parties				
		2001	1996	1991	1985	1978
AGP	S	44.79	41.82	16.82	-	-
AIIC (T)	NE	-	1.06	-	-	-
BJP	N	-	1.44	-	-	-
CPI	N	-	-	-	-	10.95
CPM	N	2.6	-	-	-	-
ICS	NE	-	-	-	1.81	-
INC	N	45.37	44.86	47.35	34.4	21.88
INC (I)	NE	-	-	-	-	11.33
JD	NE	-	0.94	3.92	-	-
JNP	NE	-	-		1.05	31.64
LKD	NE	-	-		0.32	-
NAGP	NE	-	-	6.75	-	-
NCP	N	1.46	-	-	-	-
SP	S	1.26	0.43	-	-	-

Source: www.eci.gov.in

Table 3.35 (B)
List of winning candidates: Tingkhong Assembly Constituency

Year	Voters in 1000	Voter Turnout (Percentage)	Winner			Runner-up		
			Candidate Name	Percentage	Party	Candidate Name	Percentage	Party
2001	72.19	72.21	Etuwa Munda	45.37	INC	Anup Phukan	44.79	AGP
1996	68.09	74.90	Etuwa Munda	44.86	INC	Anup Phukan	41.82	AGP
1991	58.63	68.12	Prithibi Majhi	47.35	INC	Jogesh Bikash Chetia	16.82	AGP
1985	52.44	69.66	Atul Chandra Koch	44.99	IND	Paban Ghatuwar	34.40	INC
1978	43.01	65.23	Bhadreswar Gogoi	31.64	JNP	Bijoy Tanti	22.91	IND

Source: www.eci.gov.in

Table 3.36 (A)
Result of Naharkatia Assembly Constituency

Party Abbreviation	Current Party Status	Percentage of Valid Votes Caste in Favour of Contesting Parties				
		2001	1996	1991	1985	1978
AGP	S	19.63	-	24.01	-	-
AIIC (T)	NE	-	1.43	-	-	-
BJP	N	-	8.5	1.15	2.43	-
CPI	N	-	-	-	-	9.15
CPM (ML) (L)	S	1.11	-	-	-	-
CPM	N	9.59	35.29	29.12	18.51	26.84
INC	N	65.94	44.12	29.02	32.06	14.48
INC (I)	NE	-	-	-	-	14.09
JNP	NE	-	-	-	1.91	25.56
NAGP	NE	-	-	7.87	-	-

Source: www.eci.gov.in

Table 3.36 (B)

List of winning candidates: Naharkatia Assembly Constituency

Year	Voters in 1000	Voter Turnout (Percentage)	Winner			Runner-up		
			Candidate Name	Percentage	Party	Candidate Name	Percentage	Party
2001	66.83	68.18	Pranati Phukan	65.94	INC	Kusumbar Tairai Gogoi	19.63	AGP
1996	64.46	71.73	Pranati Phukan	44.12	INC	Sasha Kamal Handique	35.29	CPM
1991	61.67	69.04	Sasha Kamal Handique	29.12	CPM	Hari Phukan	29.02	INC
1985	57.69	75.75	Kusumbar Tairai Gogoi	42.80	IND	Khirud Saikia	32.06	INC
1978	39.91	67.69	Sasha Kamal Handique	26.84	CPM	Jonaram Neog	25.56	JNP

Source: www.eci.gov.in

Table 3.37 (A)
Result of Tinsukia Constituency

Party Abbreviation	Current Party Status	Percentage of Valid Votes Caste in Favour of Contesting Parties					
		2001	1996	1991	1985	1983	1978
AGP	S	-	21.75	20.05	-	-	-
AIIC (T)	NE	-	3.01	-	-	-	-
BJP	N	33.96	13.97	4.79	0.94	-	-
CPI	N	-	-	2.56	-	-	7.45
CPI (ML) (L)	S	2.71	-	-	-	-	-
CPM	N	-	-	-	17.19	30.53	-
ICS	NE	-	-	-	0.27	-	-
ICS (SCS)	NE	-	-	0.78	-	-	-
INC	N	51.49	55.22	58.08	42.83	63.17	13.71
INC (I)	NE	-	-	-	-	-	21.42
JD	NE	-	0.7	4.98	-	-	-
JNP	NE	-	-	-	1.38	-	50.1
JP	-	-	-	2.19	-	-	-
LKD	NE	-	-	-	0.37	-	-
NCP	N	0.9	-	-	-	-	-
SHS	S	-	0.26	-	-	-	-
SP	S	-	0.22	-	-	-	-

Source: www.eci.gov.in

Table 3.37 (B)
List of winning candidates: Tinsukia Constituency

Year	Voters in 1000	Voter Turnout (Percentage)	Winner			Runner-up		
			Candidate Name	Percentage	Party	Candidate Name	Percentage	Party
2001	71.20	61.17	Rajendra Prasad Singh	51.49	INC	Shio Shambhu Ojha	33.96	BJP
1996	69.70	69.93	Sudhangshu Coomer De Sirkar	55.22	INC	Hemanta Gohain	21.75	AGP
1991	60.54	61.92	Shio Sambhu Ojha	58.08	INC	Prokash Dutta	20.05	AGP
1985	53.14	69.37	Shio Sambhu Ojha	42.83	INC	Binod Goswami	26.14	IND
1983	17.07	24.80	Rajendra Nath Phukan	63.17	INC	Lallan Kr. Singh	30.53	CPM
1978	38.61	60.80	Golap Borborah	50.10	JNP	Rajendra Nath Phukan	21.42	INC (I)

Source: www.eci.gov.in

Table 3.38 (A)
Result of Digboi Constituency

Party Abbreviation	Current Party Status	2001	1996	1991	1985	1983	1978
		Percentage of Valid Votes Caste in Favour of Contesting Parties					
AGP	S	-	-	20.85	-	-	-
AIIC (T)	NE	-	2	-	-	-	-
BJP	N	30.2	11.26	5.59	3.07	-	-
CPI	N	2.64	13.15	-	-	-	-
CPI (ML) (L)	S	1.47	-	-	-	-	
CPM	N	-	-	-	-	20.87	-
ICS	NE	-	-	-	1.33	-	-
INC	N	60.22	61.98	63.75	58.54	72.23	10.58
INC (I)	NE	-	-	-	-	-	32.66
JD	NE	-	5.38	1.88	-	-	-
JD (U)	S	2.45	-	-	-	-	-
JNP	NE	-	-	-	0.8	-	32.45
JP	-	-	-	2.74	-	-	-
SAP	-	3.01	-	-	-	-	-
SHS	S	-	2.06	-	-	-	-

Source: www.eci.gov.in

Table 3.38 (B)
List of winning candidates: Digboi Constituency

Year	Voters in 1000	Voter Turnout (Percentage)	Winner			Runner-up		
			Candidate Name	Percentage	Party	Candidate Name	Percentage	Party
2001	60.89	63.48	Rameswar Dhanowar	60.22	INC	Bhaben Sharma	30.20	BJP
1996	59.70	69.96	Rameswar Dhanowar	61.98	INC	Munin Borah	13.15	CPI
1991	57.54	68.30	Rameswar Dhanowar	63.75	INC	Lila Bora	20.85	AGP
1985	51.12	72.43	Rameswar Dhanowar	58.54	INC	Dayanand Dowera	26.31	IND
1983	9.76	17.10	Rameswar Dhanowar	72.23	INC	Tupidhar Gogoi	20.87	CPM
1978	33.53	64.88	Rameswar Dhanowar	32.66	INC (I)	Niranjan Biswas	32.45	JNP

Source: www.eci.gov.in

Table 3.39 (A)
Result of Margherita Constituency

Percentage of Valid Votes Caste in Favour of Contesting Parties

Party Abbreviation	Current Party Status	2001	1996	1991	1985	1978
AGP	S	19.63	-	24.01	-	-
AGP	S	-	34.17	-		-
AITC	S	2.44	-	-	-	-
BJP	N	26.85	1.91	0.92	-	-
CPI	N	-	2.98	2.44	-	7.44
CPI (ML) (L)	S	1.68	-	-	7.2	-
ICS	NE	-	-	2.26	-	-
INC	N	**57.07**	**46.45**	**41.32**	-	14.18
INC (I)	NE	-	-	-	**66.66**	23.88
JD	NE	-	1.47	-	-	-
JD (U)	S	0.57	-		-	-
JNP	NE	-	-	1.47	-	**26.32**
JP	-	-	1.62	-	-	-
NAGP	NE	-	1.3	-	-	-
UMF	NE	-	0.42	-	-	-

Source: www.eci.gov.in

Table 3.39 (B)
List of winning candidates: Margherita Constituency

Year	Voters in 1000	Voter Turnout (Percentage)	Winner			Runner-up		
			Candidate Name	Percentage	Party	Candidate Name	Percentage	Party
2001	87.02	64.44	Pradyut Bordoloi	57.07	INC	Debojit Baruah	26.85	BJP
1991	66.01	68.38	Kul Bahadur Chetri	46.45	INC	Debojit Baruah	34.17	AGP
1985	60.41	69.59	Kul Bahadur Chetri	41.32	INC	Debojit Baruah	31.54	IND
1983	18.54	26.07	Kul Bahadur Chetri	66.66	INC	Bholanath Sur	14.57	IND
1978	40.23	63.81	Kul Bahadur Chetri	26.32	JNP	Liladhar Gogoi	23.88	INC (I)

Source: www.eci.gov.in

Elections in Tezpur: *Bargaining its Way to Wins*

Tezpur, under the Sonitpur district, which has a population size of 16,81,513, is a Parliamentary constituency that has nine Assembly segments. Sonitpur district which spreads over an area of 5324 sq. kms. on north bank of the Brahmaputra River is the second largest district of Assam after Karbi Anglong.

The people in the district are a non-homogeneous lot. They are a mosaic of ethnic groups. Majority of the people have Assamese language as their mother tongue though the others also use it, as a *lingua franca*. Other languages spoken are Bodo, Nepali, Bengali and Hindi.

The Nepali community, who constitute a big chunk of the population, is fairly dominant in the central and southern part of the district, especially in the Biswanath Chariali and Gohpur sub-divisions. The rough population pattern of the community shows that in Tezpur their number stands at 2.25 lakh[30], who have had a voice in the election battles in the constituency. Moreover, the returning MP from the constituency for the last three terms, Mani Kumar Subba, is a Nepali[31]. It is, therefore, necessary to focus on this community and study its role in election politics.

Mani Kumar Subba[32], probably the wealthiest MP from

[30] The Nepalis are spread across the State. They number 1.5 lakh in Dibrugarh, 1 lakh in Lakhimpur, 40,000 in Kaliabor and another 1 lakh in Guwahati. *The Sentinel*, April 7, 2004.

[31] But the Nepalis in the constituency do not have a consensus in voting Mani Kumar Subba to power for the simple fact that he is a Nepali. It has been found that the Chief Secretary of Gorkha Autonomous Council Demand Committee, Gillu Sharma, prior to the Lok Sabha poll, 2004 declared their support to the AGP candidates in the election as the party was more sympathetic towards the demands of the Nepali community living in Assam. The community is demanding special protected class with Constitutional safeguards.

[32] Mani Kumar Subba's original name is Mani Raj Limboo. Alleged to be a resident of Nepal, he was reportedly refused enrolment as an Indian voter in the 17 Central Pendam assembly segment in Sikkim in 1985. This followed a complaint lodged by Ashok Kumar Subba of the then Janata Party, who said he was a foreign national with a permanent address at Ekhabo Panchayat, Ward No 8, Taplezum District, Mechi Anchal, Nepal. Reports say he was born in village Sangsabu of Tamarkhola Ekhabu Gram Panchayat in Taplezum district and that in 1962 he came to Sikkim, then an independent country,

the Northeast[33], saw the rise to the politics' hot seat in Assam from the Tezpur constituency, supposedly with the aid of the money power which he amassed being the king of the

---

where he began his career as a cardamom plantation labourer. In 1965 he migrated to Tinsukia in Upper Assam, where he set up a gambling business. After some years, he went to Arunachal Pradesh and married a relative of the State's current chief minister, Gegong Apang. She is now said to be living in Harmotti, north Assam. This link brought him fortune and he became one of the biggest contractors in Arunachal Pradesh. In 1991, Assam Congress chief Hiteswar Saikia offered him a ticket to contest the election from the Naoboicha Assembly constituency. In December 1997, G K Pillai, Joint Secretary, Union home ministry, acting on a complaint from then Assam Chief Minister, Prafulla Kumar Mahanta, asked the Central Bureau of Investigation to inquire into allegations that Subba was a foreign national. On January 5, 1998, the CBI registered a preliminary case against him. There was also a case of defaulting in payments to the governments of Sikkim, Manipur and Nagaland while running lotteries on their behalf. But the biggest financial controversy that Subba is alleged to be involved in is the Nagaland State Lottery scam. His family owns MS Associates, a major player in the lottery business, which came under the scanner after the Comptroller and Auditor General detected a massive scam in the conduct of the Nagaland State Lottery in 1999. The CAG report dealt exclusively with the running of the Nagaland State Lottery, of which MS Associates had been appointed the 'State sole distributor' in 1994. In raids conducted at several places in Delhi, Kohima, Guwahati and Shillong, sack loads of documents were picked up. Finance ministry officials claimed some 'subsidiary' scams involving several politicians and industrialists were unearthed. Apparently, the State government earned only minuscule revenue from the lottery, which ran for four years and had a turnover of thousands of crores of rupees. While 91 per cent of the face value of tickets was to be paid as prize money, only 78 per cent was actually given away. The winners were thus cheated of Rs. 5,000 crore or Rs. 50 billion. 'In the absence of any evidence to the contrary, it can be assumed that this amount was not paid as prize money and was retained by the distributor,' the CAG report said. The audit began in 1997, a marathon exercise that scrutinised the running of the Nagaland State Lottery from 1993 through 1997. In these years, 83,254 lottery draws were conducted, of which the CAG examined 42,459. The CAG had calculated that of the Rs 38,297 crore (Rs 382.97 billion) worth of tickets printed, even a mere two per cent profit for the distributor, agents, and State government would work out to Rs 766 crore or Rs 7.6 billion. Even if the State government were to get half the profit, it should have been entitled to Rs 383 crore or Rs 3.83 billion. But it received only Rs 40.2 crore or Rs 400.2 million. Besides, the directorate made a practice of first depositing the receipts in a savings bank account for up to seven months before submitting them to the treasury. In *Rediff Special*, G. Vinayak, September 24, 2004.

[33] In his affidavit filed with the nomination papers for the 2004 general election, Mani Kumar Subba mentioned that he and his two wives were worth Rs 19.8 crore, i.e. Rs 190.8 million. For details refer to foot note 36, Chapter 2.

lottery business in the region. Since Subba became a member of the Assam Legislative Assembly in 1998, he has never looked back in politics. Immediately thereafter, Subba got the nomination to fight the 1998 Lok Sabha election from the constituency[34]. The Tezpur Lok Sabha seat since then has been the stronghold of Congress leader Mani Kumar Subba (Table 3.40).

Though time and again Subba has been alleged and branded as a corrupt politician, it was Sonia Gandhi, who after consulting legal experts including a former Chief Justice of India, overruled the objections and upheld the majority view of the Assam Pradesh Congress Committee while renominating him yet again in 1999[35]. To no surprise, subsiding all confusions, allegations and speculations, he won the election to the Lok Sabha once again in 1999. Subba engaged in a bitter contest with BJP's R. P. Sharma, defeated the latter in the last round by over 40,000 votes. He held on to his position in the 2004 Lok Sabha election as well. Subba retained the Tezpur seat, defeating Padma Hazarika of the AGP by nearly 70,000 votes, though there was a decline in the victory margin of the controversial Subba as compared to his last wins. In 1998, Subba beat his nearest BJP rival Iswar Prasanna Hazarika by more than 150,000 votes.

---

[34] Subba managed to secure a Congress ticket in 1998 despite his alleged involvement in a lottery scam in the neighbouring State of Nagaland. This is testimony to his clout in the Congress party.

[35] Subba also had a hold in Sikkim, allegedly offering Chief Minister, Pawan Chamling, Rs. 5 crore to help him contest the 1998 Lok Sabha election as a Congress candidate. The arrangement involved payment in three installments, after the ruling Sikkim Democratic Front assured support, inclusion of Subba's name in the voters' list and no objections at the scrutiny stage. Sonia Gandhi too gave him a ticket for Tezpur overriding her own earlier choice. Was this in return for financial support? The same consideration had probably prompted the renomination of Subba.

Table 3.40
Contestants in Tezpur Lok Sabha Constituency (Assam)

Candidate	Party	Votes
	1991	
Swarup Upadhayaya	Indian National Congress	237955
Purna Narayan Sinha	Asom Gana Parishad	131638
Tanka Bahadur Rai	Natun Asom Gana Parishad	61914
Rana Prasad Deouri	United Reservation Movement Council Assam	39823
Jay Narayan Luitel	Bharatiya Janata Party	33968
Golok Nath	Independents	21349
Punu Oraon	Independents	12636
Rabin Deka	Independents	12134
Dilip Kumar Agarwala	Independents	11935
Iswar Dayal Prajapati	Doordasthi Party	4631
	1996	
Iswar Prasanna Hazarika	Indian National Congress	207071
Harsha Bahadur Biswakarma	Asom Gana Parishad	200352
Dhruba Prasad Baishya	Bharatiya Janata Party	82893
Rana Deuri	Independents	40908
Swarup Upadhyay	All India Indira Congress (Tiwari)	39461
Syeda Hasna Begum	Independents	30979
Purna Narayan Singh	Janata Dal	14950
Bhuban Chandra Chutia	Independents	5853
Gopi Chand Shahabadi	Samajwadi Party	4713
Hanuman	Independents	4696
Golok Nath	Independents	3538
Madhab Kalita	Independents	2548
	1998	
Mani Kumar Subba	Indian National Congress	286372
Iswar Prasanna Hazarika	Bharatiya Janata Party	156023
Kartik Hazarika	Asom Gana Parishad	137330
Rana Deori	Independents	17724
Joseph Kandulna	Independents	17345
Bibek Das	Communist Party Of India (Marxist-Leninist) (Liberation)	9292
Purna Narayan Sinha	Independents	6008
Satrughna Roy	Rashtriya Janata Dal	4100

(Contd....)

Candidate	Party	Votes
	1999	
Mani Kumar Subba	**Indian National Congress**	230884
Ram Prasad Sarmah	**Bharatiya Janatha Party**	205178
Dr. Kosheswar Bora	**Asom Gana Parishad**	203141
Joseph Kandulna	**Independents**	17626
Bibek Das	**Communist Party Of India (Marxist-Leninist) (Liberation)**	8855
Kul Bahadur Chetry	**Nationalist Congress Party**	2657
Syed Hussain Ali Shah	**Independents**	1893
Noor Jaman Ahmed	**Independents**	1234
Ilman Tanti	**Independents**	1232
Helena Murmur	**Independents**	1197
Kanak Khaund	**Independents**	891
Mohibullah	**Rashtriya Janata Dal**	882
Purnanarayan Sinha	**Independents**	838
Abul Khayer	**Independents**	694
	2004	
Mani Kumar Subba	**Indian National Congress**	289847
Padma Hazarika	**Asom Gana Parishad**	219402
Ghisa Lal Agarwall	**Bharatiya Janatha Party**	164662
Rubul Sarma	**Communist Party Of India (Marxist-Leninist) (Liberation)**	24595
Dipen Tanti	**Independents**	21262

Source: www.electionnext.com

Seemingly or otherwise, the Tezpur constituency thus has been a winning spree for Mani Kumar Subba.

In the Assembly election of 2001, it was the Congress which won from the constituencies of Gohpur, Barchalla, Sootea, Biswanath and Rangapara. The AGP could register wins in two constituencies, viz, Tezpur and Dhekiajuli. Hence, the Congress did maintain its hold in the Sonitpur district (Tables 3.41 to 3.49).

Although Tezpur constituency has returned a Nepali to the Lok Sabha for the last three successive elections, it does not indicate that ethnicity has been playing a role in the elections. The Nepali community in the constituency is not a unified one under one political symbol. They rally behind

Table 3.41 (A)
Result of Dhekiajuli Constituency

Party Abbreviation	Current Party Status	Percentage of Valid Votes Caste in Favour of Contesting Parties				
		2001	1996	1991	1985	1978
AGP	S	**50.24**	**46.68**	15.07	-	-
AIIC (T)	NE	-	1.19	-	-	-
BJP	N	-	10.63	-	-	-
CPM	N	-	-	-	10.74	-
ICS	NE	-	-	-	1.39	-
ICS (SCS)	NE	-	-	1.89	-	-
INC	N	44.21	33.73	**53.6**	**31.77**	**34.93**
INC (I)	NE	-	-	-	-	0.93
JNP	NE	-	-	-	2.42	29.44
NAGP	NE	-	-	5.06	-	-
NCP	N	0.82	-	-	-	-
PTC	NE	-	-	-	8.93	-

Source: www.eci.gov.in

Table 3.41 (B)

List of winning candidates: Dhekiajuli Constituency

Year	Voters in 1000	Voter Turnout (Percentage)	Winner			Runner-up		
			Candidate Name	Percentage	Party	Candidate Name	Percentage	Party
2001	82.25	75.89	Joseph Toppo	50.24	AGP	Hiranya Bora	44.21	INC
1996	74.99	80.39	Joseph Toppo	46.48	AGP	Hiranya Bora	33.73	INC
1991	68.95	77.74	Hiranya Bora	53.60	INC	Ratul Nath	15.07	AGP
1985	57.37	80.78	Hiranya Bora	31.77	INC	Joseph Toppo	25.03	IND
1978	42.73	76.72	Pratap Kalita	34.93	INC	Indra Kanta Bora	29.44	JNP

Source: www.eci.gov.in

Table 3.42 (A)
Result of Barchalla Constituency

	Percentage of Valid Votes Caste in Favour of Contesting Parties					
Party Abbreviation	**Current Party Status**	**2001**	**1996**	**1991**	**1985**	**1978**
AGP	S	23.51	39.31	16.69	-	-
AIIC (T)	NE	-	1.04	-	-	-
BJP	N	14.92	6.53	-	-	-
CPM	N	11.35	-	-	-	-
ICS	NE	-	-	-	3.33	-
INC	N	35.79	30.02	41.81	20.79	22.39
INC (I)	NE	-	-	-	-	2.11
JD	NE	-	0.95	-	-	-
LKD	NE	-	-	-	3.13	-
NAGP	NE	-	-	13.98	-	-
NCP	N	0.6	-	-	-	-
PTC	NE	-	-	-	20.11	28.57
PTCA	-	-	-	12.09	-	-

Source: www.eci.gov.in

Table 3.42 (B)
List of winning candidates: Barchalla Constituency

Year	Voters in 1000	Voter Turnout (Percentage)	Winner			Runner-up		
			Candidate Name	Percentage	Party	Candidate Name	Percentage	Party
2001	76.59	74.72	Tanka Bahadur Rai	35.79	INC	Prafulla Goswami	23.51	AGP
1996	74.15	81.35	Prafulla Goswami	39.31	AGP		30.02	INC
1991	68.89	78.57	Rudra Parajuli	41.81	INC	Prafulla Goswami	16.69	AGP
1985	60.16	85.96	Prafulla Goswami	43.85	IND	Kshemraj Adhikari	20.79	INC
1978	44.90	73.97	Kamal Chandra Basumatari	28.57	PTC	Prafulla Goswami	25.13	IND

Source: www.eci.gov.in

Table 3.43 (A)
Result of Tezpur Constituency

Party Abbreviation	Current Party Status	Percentage of Valid Votes Caste in Favour of Contesting Parties					
		2001	1996	1991	1985	1983	1978
AGP	S	38.61	44.68	4.16	-	-	-
AIIC (T)	NE	-	2	-	-	-	-
BJP	N	-	10.93	-	-	-	-
INC	N	37.33	42.01	45.02	23.72	93.66	25.08
INC (I)	NE	-	-	-	-	-	6.75
JD	NE	-	-	4.05	-	-	-
JNP	NE	-	-	-	-	-	51.51
NAGP	NE	-	-	27.23	-	-	-
SAP	-	0.49	-	-	-	-	-

Source: www.eci.gov.in

Table 3.43 (B)

List of winning candidates: Tezpur Constituency

Year	Voters in 1000	Voter Turnout (Percentage)	Winner			Runner-up		
			Candidate Name	Percentage	Party	Candidate Name	Percentage	Party
2001	79.18	71.17	Brindaban Goswami	38.61	AGP	Robindra Kumar Goswami	37.33	INC
1996	72.47	75.87	Brindaban Goswami	44.68	AGP	Bijit Saikia	42.01	INC
1991	62.86	71.24	Bijit Saikia	45.02	INC	Brindabon Goswami	27.23	NAGP
1985	59.61	82.20	Brindaban Goswami	59.01	IND	Naren Sarma	23.72	INC
1983	6.21	10.47	Nabin Chandra Kath Hazarika	93.66	INC	Mahammad Ali	6.34	IND
1978	34.99	66.07	Jiban Bora	51.51	JNP	Sreekanta Sarmah	25.08	INC

Source: www.eci.gov.in

Table 3.44 (A)
Result of Rangapara Constituency

Party Abbreviation	Current Party Status	Percentage of Valid Votes Caste in Favour of Contesting Parties					
		2001	1996	1991	1985	1983	1978
AGP	S	-	-	9.9	-	-	-
AIIC (T)	NE	-	5.36	-	-	-	-
AITC	S	2.17	-	-	-	-	-
BJP	N	22.36	8.45	-	-	-	-
CPM	N	16.71	27.02	21.2	19.46	22.47	27.44
ICS	NE	-	1.3	-	1.58	-	-
ICS (SCS)	NE	-	-	0.92	-	-	-
INC	N	51.28	47.67	50.14	34.36	53.89	42.88
JNP	NE	-	-	-	1.94	-	27.14
NAGP	NE	-	-	8.82	-	-	-
NCP	N	1.19	-	-	-	-	-

Source: www.eci.gov.in

Table 3.44 (B)

List of winning candidates: Rangapara Constituency

Year	Voters in 1000	Voter Turnout (Percentage)	Winner			Runner-up		
			Candidate Name	Percentage	Party	Candidate Name	Percentage	Party
2001	80.77	77.75	Bhima Tanti	51.28	INC	Rishilal Upadhyaya	22.36	BJP
1996	74.56	80.29	Bhima Tanti	47.67	INC	Dhaniram Khosla	27.02	CPM
1991	66.84	76.10	Golok Rajbanshi	50.14	INC	Dhaniram Khosla	21.20	CPM
1985	55.91	75.12	Golok Rajbanshi	34.36	INC	Dhaniram Khosla	19.46	CPM
1983	22.64	40.10	Golok Rajbanshi	53.89	INC	Dhaniram Khosla	22.47	CPM
1978	39.40	75.54	Golok Rajbanshi	42.88	INC	Dhaniram Khosla	27.44	CPM

Source: www.eci.gov.in

Table 3.45 (A)
Result of Sootea Constituency

Party Abbreviation	Current Party Status	2001	1996	1991	1985	1978
	Percentage of Valid Votes Caste in Favour of Contesting Parties					
AGP	S	47.82	40.84	11.82	-	-
AIIC (T)	NE	-	10.07	-	-	-
BJP	N	-	1.87	0.86	0.77	-
CPI	N	-	-	2.89	-	-
CPM	N	-	-	-	-	24.7
INC	N	48.67	13.01	35.99	33.78	26.39
INC (I)	NE	-	-	-	-	4.22
JD	NE	-	1.41	3.78	-	-
JNP	NE	-	-	-	3.43	37.19
NAGP	NE	-	-	15.89	-	-
PTC	NE	-	-	-	14.11	-
PTCA	-	-	-	18.08	-	-

Source: www.eci.gov.in

Table 3.45 (B)

List of winning candidates: Sootea Constituency

Year	Voters in 1000	Voter Turnout (Percentage)	Winner Candidate Name	Winner Percentage	Winner Party	Runner-up Candidate Name	Runner-up Percentage	Runner-up Party
2001	90.88	76.78	Praneswar Basumatari	48.67	INC	Padma Hazarika	47.82	AGP
1996	82.14	81.19	Padma Hazarika	40.84	AGP	Praneswar Basumatari	23.36	IND
1991	71.81	71.49	Kushal Sahu	35.99	INC	Nagen Basumatari	18.08	PTCA
1985	66.27	81.02	Robin Saikia	39.17	IND	Dulal Chandra Bhuyan	33.78	INC
1978	38.84	74.43	Golok Kakati	37.19	JNP	Narayan Bhuyan	26.39	INC

Source: www.eci.gov.in

Table 3.46 (A)
Result of Biswanath Constituency

Party Abbreviation	Current Party Status	Percentage of Valid Votes Caste in Favour of Contesting Parties				
		2001	1996	1991	1985	1978
AGP	S	44.3	42.62	17.39	-	-
AIIC (T)	NE	-	9.01	-	-	-
BJP	N	-	15.69	-	-	-
CPM	N	5.2	-	12.29	-	-
INC	NE	48.55	31.76	46.49	20.88	21.58
INC (I)	NE	-	-	-	-	15.23
JD	NE	-	0.49	8.38	-	-
JNP	NE		-	-		57.57
JP	-	-	-	0.79	-	-
MUL	S	0.15	-	-	-	-
NAGP	NE	-	-	6.34	-	-
PTC	NE	-	-	-	2.49	-
SP	S	0.35	-	-	-	-

Source: www.eci.gov.in

Table 3.46 (B)
List of winning candidates: Biswanath Constituency

Year	Voters in 1000	Voter Turnout (Percentage)	Winner			Runner-up		
			Candidate Name	Percentage	Party	Candidate Name	Percentage	Party
2001	82.88	81.46	Nurjamal Sarkar	48.55	INC	Prabin Hazarika	44.30	AGP
1996	74.53	81.58		42.62	AGP	Nurjamal Sarkar	31.76	INC
1991	66.31	79.23	Nurjamal Sarkar	46.49	INC	Prabin Hazarika	17.39	AGP
1985	58.33	79.05	Padmanath Koiri	45.95	IND	Kosheswar Barah	29.66	IND
1978	37.57	75.34	Kosheswar Bora	57.57	JNP	Satya Narayan Ram	21.58	INC

Source: www.eci.gov.in

Table 3.47 (A)
Result of Behali Constituency

		Percentage of Valid Votes Caste in Favour of Contesting Parties				
Party Abbreviation	Current Party Status	2001	1996	1991	1985	1978
AGP	S	-	18.9	4.4	-	-
AIIC (T)	NE	-	9.1	-	-	-
BJP	N	50.65	8.99	-	-	-
CPM (ML) (L)	S	18.65	-	-	-	-
CPM	N	-	-	-	11.29	-
INC	N	30.1	33.43	51.48	40.37	34.18
JD	NE	-	3.87	4.43	-	-
JNP	NE	-	-	-	8.69	22.59
JP	-	-	-	4.71	-	-
NAGP	NE	-	-	2.36	-	-
SAP	-	0.43	-	-	-	-

Source: www.eci.gov.in

Table 3.47 (B)

List of winning candidates: Behali Constituency

Year	Voters in 1000	Voter Turnout (Percentage)	Winner			Runner-up		
			Candidate Name	Percentage	Party	Candidate Name	Percentage	Party
2001	67.84	80.09	Ranjit Dutta	50.65	BJP	Barnabash Tanti	30.10	INC
1996	60.67	79.78	Barnabash Tanti	33.43	INC	Kosheswar Borah	18.90	AGP
1991	54.45	78.26	Barnabash Tanti	51.48	INC	Biswajeet Goswami	9.31	IND
1985	45.76	77.52	Swarup Upadhyaya	40.37	INC	Amarnath Upadhyaya	15.53	IND
1978	32.77	68.52	Bishnulal Upadhaya	34.18	INC	Kamakhya Prasad Tripathi	22.59	JNP

Source: www.eci.gov.in

Table 3.48 (A)
Result of Gohpur Constituency

Party Abbreviation	Current Party Status	Percentage of Valid Votes Caste in Favour of Contesting Parties				
		2001	1996	1991	1985	1978
AGP	S	44.19	36.72	9.36	-	-
AIIC (T)	NE	-	11.63	-	-	-
BJP	N	-	4.22	-	-	-
CPI	N	1.17	-	8.17	6.1	8.59
INC	N	53.23	33.96	20.65	23.37	21.51
INC (I)	NE	-	-	-	-	2.96
JD	NE	-	-	5.32	-	-
JNP	NE	-	-	-	3.93	34.97
NAGP	NE	-	-	2.13	-	-
NCP	N	0.22	-	-	-	-
PTC	NE	-	-	-	16.29	-

Source: www.eci.gov.in

Table 3.48 (B)

List of winning candidates: Gohpur Constituency

Year	Voters in 1000	Voter Turnout (Percentage)	Winner			Runner-up		
			Candidate Name	Percentage	Party	Candidate Name	Percentage	Party
2001	112.01	81.68	Ripun Bora	53.23	INC	Ganesh Kutum	44.19	AGP
1996	96.56	77.05	Ganesh Kutum	36.72	AGP	Ripun Bora	33.96	INC
1991	88.04	75.81	Kosheswar Barua	20.65	INC	Sobharam Goyari	14.40	IND
1985	77.46	79.48	Ganesh Kutum	39.58	IND	Kosheswar Barua	23.37	INC
1978	46.91	67.69	Ram Chandra Sarmah	34.97	JNP	Bipin Kataki	21.51	INC

Source: www.eci.gov.in

Table 3.49 (A)
Result of Bihpuria Constituency

Party Abbreviation	Current Party Status	Percentage of Valid Votes Caste in Favour of Contesting Parties					
		2001	1996	1991	1985	1983	1978
AGP	S	26	39.91	16.15	-	-	-
BJP	N	-	3.5	-	-	-	-
CPI	N	3.61	-	14.36	-	2.52	11.63
CPM	N	0.72	-	-	-	-	-
INC	N	26.04	24.92	21.28	-	97.25	15.98
INC (I)	NE	-	-	-	-	-	5.22
JNP	NE	-	-	-	0.98	-	11.59
NAGP	NE	-	-	2.46	-	-	-
NCP	N	4.85	-	-	-	-	-
PTC	NE	-	-	-	1.13	-	-
SP	S	-	0.62	-	-	-	-

Source: www.eci.gov.in

Table 3.49 (B)

List of winning candidates: Bihpuria Constituency

Year	Voters in 1000	Voter Turnout (Percentage)	Winner			Runner-up		
			Candidate Name	Percentage	Party	Candidate Name	Percentage	Party
2001	76.81	79.01	Premadhar Bora	27.73	IND	Borgoram Deuri	26.04	INC
1996	67.82	77.96	Kesharam Bora	39.91	AGP	Borgoram Deuri	24.92	INC
1991	60.69	72.69	Borgaram Deori	21.28	INC	Kesharam Bora	16.15	AGP
1985	58.42	80.73	Kesharam Bora	58.95	IND	Borgaram Deuri	14.57	IND
1983	0.44	0.69	Borgaram Deori	97.25	INC	Subheswar Phukan	2.52	CPI
1978	41.91	66.20	Premadhar Bora	17.33	IND	Durgeswar Pathak	15.98	INC

Source: www.eci.gov.in

a number of parties, which means that there is division of votes. As alleged, money power does play a role. Newspaper reports and interviews with voters and leading citizens soon after the election corroborate the common understanding of the role of money power. However, a number of factors work together to decide the fate of the candidate. Money power may be one of such factors but undoubtedly not the sole factor.

REFERENCES

Ahmed, Abu Nasar Saied (Forthcoming). "Participation of Muslims in Governance: A Case of the Muslims of Assam" in K.N. Jahangir and M.A. Jawaid (eds) *Minorities in India in the New Millennium.* New Delhi: Manas.

Amar Asom (2004). March 19.

Amar Asom (2004). March 29.

An Educational Study on Voting Behaviour of Electorate and Development Works done in Constituencies of Assam (2001). Guwahati: National Education Foundation.

Bete´ille, Andre´ (2005). *Social Class.* Guwahati: Foundation Day Lecture, OKDISCD.

Brass, Paul R. (1991), *Ethnicity and Nationalism: Theory and Comparison.* New Delhi: Sage Publication.

Chaubey, S. K. (1985). *Electoral Politics in North East India.* Madras: Universities Press. Chapter II, p.63.

Community Information Centre (CIC) Gabharu. District Profile. http://www.cic.nic.in.

Community Information Centre (CIC) Pub Chayduar. Sonitpur District. Assam. www.sonitpur.nic.in.

Das Gupta, Barun (1998). "Assam". *Frontline.* Volume 15, No. 06. March 21 – April 3.

De, Bimal J. and Dilip K. Lahiri (1985). *Assam Muslims: Politics and Cohesion.* New Delhi: Mittal.

Devraj, Ranjit (2003). "Tribal autonomy a step for peace". *Manushi: A Journal about Women and Society.* February. http://www.indiatogether.org.

Election Analysis: Assam (2001). "On Predictable Lines". *Frontline.* Vol.18, Issue 11, May 26-June 8.

Election Commission of India. http://www.eci.gov.in.

ElectionNext. http://www.electionnext.com.

Goswami, Sandhya. (2004). "Mixed Verdict". *Economic and Political Weekly.* Vol XXXIX, No. 51. December 18-24.

Goswami, Kanaka (1999). "Election Politic in Assam: A Study of Elections held in 1983 and 1985". Unpublished PhD Dissertation, Dibrugarh University.

Hussain, Wasbir (2005). "Assam: Truce before the Storm?" *South Asia Intelligence Review,* Weekly Assessments & Briefings. Volume 3, No. 46. May 30.

Kar, M. (1990). *Muslims in Assam Politics.* New Delhi: Omson. p.161.

Kothari, Rajni (1970). "Social Infrastructure" in *Politics in India.* Boston: Little, Brown and Co. Chapter VI.

__________ (1970). "Caste in Indian Politics" in *Caste in Indian Politics.* New Delhi: Orient and Longman

Mishra, Kirti (2005). "Growing Discontent Of Adivasis In Assam". April 12. http://www.countercurrents.org.

North East News Agency (2005). "BJP eyeing for Assam". Special Report. Vol. 3, Issue No. 29. June 7-21. http://www.nenanews.com.

Pathak, Geetartha. "Tea Garden Labour Neglected in Assam". http://www.dayafterindia.com

Prabhakar, M.S. (2002). "The Bodo Question", *Frontline.* Volume 19, Issue 15. July 20 - August 02.

__________. (2003). "Promises and Problems". *Frontline.* Volume 20, Issue 05. March 01 – 14.

Pratidin (2004). April 21.

Profiles of some Constituencies (2004). http://www.cpiml.org.

Rogus, Benjamin O. (2001). "Ethnic Parties and Centre-State Relations: The Case of Assam in Northeast India". San Francisco State University. http://www.bss.sfsu.edu.

Rongphar, Borsing (2005). *Karbi Anglongor Rajnaitik Itihas*. Diphu: Fu Fu Publication. Karbi Anglong.

Sarangi, Prakash (2001). "The Party System in India". *Teaching South Asia: An Internet Journal of Pedagogy*. Volume I, No. 1. Winter. http://www.mssu.edu

Statistical Handbook of Assam (2000). Government of Assam.

Statistical Handbook of Assam (2004). Government of Assam.

Tea workers' movement is gaining momentum in Assam (2002). June. http://www.cpiml.org

The Sentinel (2004). April 7.

The Telegraph (2004). April 16.

Three Member Experts Committee Report (1991). Government of India: Ministry of Home Affairs. Vol. IV, 25th February.

Vedanti: Burning Assam (Earlier Issues). Various Issues. http://www.vedanti.com.

Vinayak, G. (2004). *Rediff Special,* September 24.

Weiner, Myran and John Osgood Field (1975). "How Tribal Constituencies Vote" in *Studies in Electoral Politics in Indian States*. New Delhi: Manohar. Vol. II. Chapter II.

CHAPTER 4

Defining Campaigns

There are countless definitions of democracy. All these define that it is a concept enshrining people's participation, empowerment of the people to ensure social and economic justice and so on. One such definitions state that democracy is "an institutional arrangement for arriving at political decisions in which individuals acquire the power to decide by means of a competitive struggle for people's vote"[1]. This definition identifies campaign as the most intense form of struggle. In other words, efforts to secure vote for electoral victory is the main objective of a campaign in any election. Not all candidates campaign for win, as indicated in Chapter II, as some candidates campaign to register their existence, but most political parties campaign to win the elections. Therefore, campaign can be considered as a process of acquiring and using the political resources that can secure votes[2].

The election campaign in India, as elsewhere in other democracies of the world, is the period when the political parties put forward their candidates and arguments with which they hope to persuade people to vote for their candidates and parties[3]. However, during the campaigning

[1] Joseph A. Schumpeter, *Capitalism, Socialism and Democracy*, third edition (New York: Harper, 1962), p. 269.

[2] For some details see David A. Leuthold, *Electioneering in a Democracy: Campaign for Congress* (New York: John Wiley, 1968) Chapter I, Introduction.

[3] Candidates are given a week's time to put forward their nominations. These are scrutinised by the Returning Officers and if not found in order are rejected

period, the political parties and contesting candidates are expected to abide by a Model Code of Conduct evolved by the Election Commission in the country on the basis of a consensus among political parties[4].

Once an election has been called, parties issue manifestos detailing the programmes they wish to implement if elected to government, the strengths of their leaders, and the failures of other contesting parties and their leaders[5]. Rallies and meetings where the candidates try to persuade, cajole and enthuse supporters, and denigrate opponents, are held throughout the constituencies. Personal appeals and promises of reform are also made.

The Manifestos: *A Reading*

The manifestos of political parties need a careful perusal as...

> they offer several things important in a democracy: one, a standard of performance against which subsequent achievements can be measured; two, a measure of the issuing party's clarity on policy; three, articulation of the popular consensus on major themes – parties that entertain reasonable hope of getting elected to power say what they believe the voters would like them to say rather than what they actually stand for[6].

---

after a summary hearing. Validly nominated candidates can withdraw within two days after nominations have been scrutinised. The official campaign in India lasts at least two weeks from the drawing up of the list of nominated candidates, and officially ends 48 hours before polling closes - *Election Commission of India.*

[4] The model Code lays down broad guidelines as to how the political parties and candidates should conduct themselves during the election campaign. It is intended to maintain the election campaign on healthy lines, avoid clashes and conflicts between political parties or their supporters and to ensure peace and order during the campaign period and thereafter, until the results are declared. The model code also prescribes guidelines for the ruling party either at the Centre or in the State to ensure that a level field is maintained and that no cause is given for any complaint that the ruling party has used its official position for the purposes of its election campaign - *Election Commission of India.*

[5] Generally in India, slogans are used to popularise and identify parties and issues, and pamphlets and posters distributed to the electorate.

[6] 'Polarisation and Consensus', *Economic and Political Weekly,* vol. XXXIV, No. 34-35, August 21– 27/28, September 3, 1999.

The manifestos redeeming the hopes and aspirations of the political parties are supposedly the mirrors of the parties in the battle of electioneering, reflecting not only the image and standing of the party concerned but echoes the views and aspirations of the general masses. A broad look at the manifestos of the major political parties in the State, therefore, can bring to the forefront the real campaigns undertaken by the party stalwarts and the party workers to woo the voters.

The Bharatiya Janata Party

In 1999, the electorate in the 13th Lok Sabha poll, voted the National Democratic Alliance (NDA) to power of which the Bharatiya Janata Party (BJP) was not only the largest constituent but was also the single largest party in the Lok Sabha. For the 13th Lok Sabha, the party had encapsuled its promise to the general masses of the country in the assurance, "Able Leadership, Stable Government", which saw the party through and it came to power at the Centre.

With the clarion call *Shaktishali Bharat ke liye Shaktishali BJP*, the Vision Document which read "An idea whose time has come: India as a Developed Nation and a Great Power", perhaps captures in a nutshell the whole gamut of activities and promises that the BJP had hoped to fulfill, and unfold, if it could once again occupy the Centre winning the 14th Lok Sabha poll. Setting forth, the party's core beliefs, basic commitments and priority agenda for the next term, the BJP manifesto proposed the following to mention a few among many[7]:

1. Making India a Developed Nation and a Great Power by 2020, and creating an unshakable national resolve to achieve this goal.
2. Further strengthening national security both external and internal – to overcome present and future challenges.

[7] *Vision Document 2004*, Bharatiya Janata Party.

3. Further broadening and deepening of economic reforms, based on self-reliant approach, for sustained double-digit GDP growth rate to achieve complete eradication of poverty and unemployment; end of regional and social disparities; and bridging the urban-rural divide.
4. Bringing vibrancy to small-scale industries, cottage enterprises and activities of rural artisans; revitalization of traditional industries like textiles; and giving due recognition and full encouragement to the informal sector of the economy.
5. Dealing with the challenge of water on a war footing with a three-pronged approach: launch the River-Linking Project; massive encouragement for micro-initiatives such as watershed management, check dams, rainwater harvesting, drip irrigation, etc., and cleaning up of rivers and traditional water bodies.
6. Empowerment of the civil society to promote people's participation in development at all levels and for creating effective dispute resolution mechanisms outside the realm of the government and the judiciary.
7. Comprehensive good governance reforms, encompassing administrative reforms, judicial reforms, electoral reforms, devolution of powers to states and effective empowerment of panchayati raj institutions and urban local bodies.

Besides, for the Northeast, consolidating the gains already made, the party especially commited to achieving[8]:

(a) Restoration of peace and normalcy in all the disturbed regions by dialogue with all groups who are willing to give the path of violence, and by firmly dealing with those who continue on this path.

(b) Ensuring that the ethnic identities of all the people in the Northeast are protected.

[8] *ibid.*

(c) Putting an end to infiltration from Bangladesh and vigorously pursuing the 3-D formula—Detect, Delete, and Deport.

(d) Accelerating economic development that provides growth opportunities to all.

(e) Development of the communication infrastructure to overcome the constraints of physical distance.

(f) Making all Indians more aware of the rich history and cultural heritage of the Northeastern states, including Sikkim.

(g) Expanding regional economic cooperation with countries in the eastern neighbourhood and South East Asia.

The BJP also had a "Charge Sheet against Congress Government of Assam" on the eve of the Lok Sabha poll of 2004. The Charge Sheet mentioned that the Congress has pushed Assam to the brink of disaster mainly owing to its wrong policy. The main issue on which the BJP attacked the Congress was the 'foreigners issue'. It mentioned that the BJP is not surprised at the Congress party's projection of Sonia Gandhi as the Prime Ministerial candidate. After all, the Congress in Assam is well known for its policy of supporting the IMDT Act, 1983, which not only gives protection to the foreigners in Assam but also has helped in draining the financial and other resources from the State and has given rise to various social frictions, which threatens the very existence of the State[9].

Besides, the BJP in its *Charge Sheet* also accused the Congress government in the State on several grounds:

- The State government run by the Congress party failed to maintain law and order in North Cachar Hills where ethnic violence claimed 55 lives in Cachar

[9] *Charge Sheet against Congress Government*, Bharatiya Janata Party Assam Pradesh.

and North Cachar Hills, and damaged property worth over Rs.10 crore in the district[10] in 2003.

- The government failed to solve the problem of the tea labourers, inspite of the fact that the Assam Chah Mazdoor Sangha had several Congress leaders at the helm.
- The Congress government in the State was using the police force as party cadres. There had also been several cases of crimes and corruption and highway extortion through unauthorised gate by the police under the Congress government in Assam. Shri Tarun Gogoi mentioned in the Assembly floor on August 4, 2003 that a total of 134 cases had been registered against police persons for various crimes since his government took over in 2001. Here, the police instead of acting as protector was acting as criminal.
- The Congress also failed to make headway in the enquiry of secret killings that were in spree during the last part of the AGP government's regime in the State.
- The government also failed to protect the Adivasi people who had been evicted from the fallow and waste government land. The anti Adivasi stand of the Congress became very clear when the government hoodwinked the Adivasis and killed eight of them on July 25, 2003 at Kachubil bazar under Paneri police station in Darrang district.
- The unemployment scenario further deteriorated with the official figure of unemployed rising by nearly five lakhs from September 2000 to March 2003.

---

[10] *ibid.* It may be mentioned that Rokybul Hussain, Minister of State for Home, quoted the figures in the Assembly.

The Congress

"Unity, Amity, Trust, Growth and Development"[11] (*Aikya, Sampreeti, Bisshakh, Unnayan aru Bikash*), this is what, for which the Congress stood. The Congress Manifesto for the 14th Lok Sabha poll published by the Assam Pradesh Congress Committee mentioned, "The Hand of the Congress is Voice of the People" (*Congressor Haat Raijor Maat*).

The manifesto mentioned that no matter what the BJP and the AGP have in store to accuse the Congress rule in Assam, the history of development of the State for the last fifty years tells in itself that it is for the Congress alone that developments in all directions, be it in the field of socio-economic, education or industries, have been possible in the State. The success of the Guwahati, Bongaigaon, Numaligarh oil refineries, bridges built across the mighty Brahmaputra like the Saraighat, Jogighopa, Kalia Bhumura or even those under construction like that of the Bogibeel bridge, establishment of the North East Frontier Railway's main office at Maligaon, establishments of the Guwahati, Dibrugarh and Silchar Medical Colleges, establishment of the Gauhati and Dibrugarh Universities, and the Assam Agricultural University at Jorhat, to list a few, undoubtedly goes to the credit of the Congress. That the people of Assam still have hope on the Congress has been manifested in its wins in the 1998, 1999 Lok Sabha polls, the 2001 State Assembly election, the Panchayat polls held in December 2001 and the Guwahati Municipal Committee elections of 2003.

The Manifesto further going into accusations and counter accusations of the national parties like the BJP and the regional parties like the AGP brought into focus that the AGP, while it was in power, left the State under a financial loan burden of more than Rs.12 crore. Besides, the public

[11] Mentioned in *The Manifesto of the Assam Pradesh Congress*, 2004 (*Asom Pradesh Congress Committeer Karma Khushi*).

sector in the State virtually was sick and on the verge of closing down. This, the Congress accused, was well supported by the BJP at the Centre who was a mute spectator to the unruly governance of the AGP in the State. The BJP, on the other hand, had been accused of being least interested in Northeast and Assam for that matter. Citing certain examples, the Congress brought to the fore BJP's negligence of Northeast in general and Assam in particular. The eleventh Finance Commission under the BJP rule did injustice to the State and its people by granting an amount of Rs. 110 crore, which was ten times less than what was allotted by the tenth Finance Commission. This speaks volume of the State's deprivation under BJP's rule at the Centre. Another harrowing issue is the perennial floods and erosion occurring in the State. Though Bijoya Chakraborty was the Union Minister of Water Resources, in the BJP tenure at the Centre, the government failed to implement all the 54 schemes put up by the State government to control the menace of floods and erosions. Added to it, despite of repeated demands, the BJP at the centre failed to declare the floods in the State as a "National Problem". The BJP further failed to release more than Rs.400 crore, which was due to the State as sales tax from the Indian Oil Corporation and other oil companies for selling the mineral resources like oil and petroleum products available in the State to these companies.

The Congress, on the other hand, promised the following:

1. It would solve the problem of unemployment and to give a one step push to industrialization in the State, the Assam Gas Cracker Project at Lepetakota would be given a thrust to start functioning at the earliest by putting all kinds of pressure on the Central government to restart the Project at once.
2. The party would also pressurize the Centre to build two

bridges over the Brahmaputra connecting Jorhat, Majuli and Lakhimpur, and the other connecting Gohpur and Bokakhat.

3. It would demand the Centre to transform the entire metre gauge lines of the railways into broad gauge in the State.
4. The Congress would try and implement the Employment Guarantee Scheme in the State.
5. The Congress would pressurize the power at the Centre to work for the solution of the insurgency problem in the State.
6. The party would also try to uplift the living standard of the tea community by bringing changes in the Assam Tea Labour Plantation Act, 1951.
7. It would continue its fight to safeguard the minorities in the State and also continue fighting against the repeal of the IMDT Act.

The Asom Gana Parishad

The Asom Gana Parishad, the regional party from the State, stressed mainly on the following issues in its party manifesto released ahead of the 2004 Lok Sabha poll[12]:

1. It pledged to fight for greater autonomy, and therefore, struggle for decentralisation and devolution of more power to the states.
2. The party also renewed its call for creation of a separate economic zone to facilitate growth of trade and commerce between the Northeastern states and the South East Asian nations.
3. For the unemployed, the party promised to put up a tough fight for 100 per cent job reservation for locals in grade

[12] *Election Manifesto*, Asom Gana Parishad, 14th Lok Sabha Polls, (*Nirbashani Istahaar*, Asom Gana Parishad, *Chatur Daksh Loka Sabha Nirbashan*), 2004

III and grade IV sections of all public sector industries in the State.

4. It would also go all its way to put pressure on the Centre for shifting of the Tea Head Office (Corporate Office) from Kolkata to Guwahati. The party also realises in depth the problems of the small tea growers and would take up necessary steps to solve the same.
5. It would try and play a decisive role in converting the loan component from the Centre for flood control in the State to a 100 per cent grant.

The manifesto further read, "We firmly believe that Assam can catch up with other states of the country if the Centre keeps with itself only defence, external affairs, communications and currency while decentralising the other subjects". According to the party manifesto, the aspirations of all the ethnic tribes inhabiting the states could only be achieved by giving them rights over their natural resources. Demanding rights over natural resources, the AGP manifesto, therefore, further pointed out that since 1974, the Centre had been collecting oil development cess on the crude oil extracted from Assam at the rate of Rs.1,800 per metric tonne[13]. The Asom Gana Parishad (AGP), therefore, iterated its demand for a federal structure of governance in the country and creation of a separate economic zone for the Northeast. "Greater autonomy[14]" for the states was the only way to ensure better and more judicious utilisation of natural resources for the benefit of the people.

---

[13] "In this way every year, the Centre is collecting nearly Rs 850 crore but instead of spending it for the development of Assam, the whole amount is transferred to the Centre's consolidated fund. We want that out of this whopping amount, at least 50 per cent should be returned to the oil-producing states," Brindaban Goswami said. *India News on Line,* North East Scenario, 2004, www.indiamart.news.com.

[14] Playing the regional card, Brindaban Goswami, while unveiling the party manifesto said that without ensuring equal rights and respect for all ethnic communities, a State like Assam can never prosper and regional autonomy is the only answer to it. *The Telegraph,* 4th April 2004.

The Left Parties

The Left parties like the Communist Party of India and the Communist Party of India (M) also did come out with their manifestos', which also went on to highlight the failures on the part of the BJP and the Congress in the country and in the State of Assam as well. Their manifestos could be read together as their political objectives were more or less similar. However, the Left parties spearheaded their attack more on the BJP than the Congress, and therefore, were more vocal in pointing out the failures of the NDA government led by Atal Behari Vajpayee at the Centre.

The manifestos of the Left parties were clear about their objectives[15]:

1. To defeat the Bharatiya Janata Party and its allies who worked against the development of Assam.
2. To increase the strength of the CPI and other left parties.
3. To give Assam the status of a "special category State".
4. To request the masses to vote for the formation of a secular government at the Centre.

The Left parties criticized Vajpayee-led government for calling an early election in 2004 and dissolving the Lok Sabha. They alleged that in its six years reign, BJP's mass discrimination, deception and deprivation continued towards Assam and hurt tremendously the sentiments of the Assamese people. In following a general economic and political policy, the Vajpayee led government had only followed a liberal economic policy grossly supporting the capitalists, and, a political ideology with a mass support to the United States' led sectarian and communal policies.

[15] *Manifesto of the Communist Party of India (M)*, Assam State Committee, 14th Lok Sabha Polls, 2004, (*Bharator Communist Party (Marxbadi), Asom Raizik Committee, Nirbashani Gushona Patra, Chaturdaksh Loka Sabha Nirbashan, 2004)*; Communist Part of India (CPI), Assam State Council, *Election Manifesto*, 14th Lok Sabha, 2004 (*Bharator Communist Partyr Asom Raizik Parishad, Nirbashani Istahaar, Chaturdaksh Loka Sabha, 2004)*.

Defining BJP's rule, the Left parties in their manifestos' highlighted the following failures on the part of BJP during its regime:

- Attacking in a planned manner the non-Hindus and liberal believers of Hinduism.
- Giving top priority to economic sovereignty by emphasizing a liberal economic policy in support of the capitalists.
- Creating mass unemployment among the general people by adopting a capitalists' economic policy.
- Deterioration in the fiscal power of the states in the country during the rule of the Vajpayee led government.
- Adoption of a draconian law like the POTA discarding TADA.
- Failure in generating 'literacy for all' in the country.
- Corruption reaching new heights during the tenure of the BJP government.

The age long injustice and deprivation against economically stagnant and backward Northeast, and more specifically Assam, became prominent during BJP's rule at the centre. Too powerful a centre virtually dealt a blow to the federal democratic structure of the country which later even went on to impinge upon decentralized powers of the states. Though Atal Behari Vajpayee announced a special package of Rs. 10,271 crore for development of Northeast in Shillong, he failed to keep his promise. The formation of the Department of Development of the North Eastern Region (DoNER) only seemed to be a farce. In the face of these accusations, the glaring failures of the BJP government were:

- There was a reduction in the grant from the Planning Commission through the NEC from Rs. 750 crore to Rs. 395.29 crore.

- The Centre failed to go ahead with the Gas Cracker Project.
- Fencing along the Indo-Bangladesh border in Assam, which was supposed to be taken up by the Vajpayee government did not take off.
- A few announcements like building of the Bogibeel Bridge on the river Brahmaputra and connecting of the East-West corridor were made without the sanction of any economic packages.
- Floods in Assam were never declared a national problem.
- The BJP failed to allot any of the six AIIMS hospitals newly announced to be opened all over India in Assam or for that matter in India Northeast.
- The "River Linking" project was taken up all over the country. This project also included the River Brahmaputra, Sankosh and Manash. But the government did not think of consulting the people of Assam before going ahead with the plan.
- Insurgency and ethnicity related violence mounted in the Sate during Vajpayee's tenure.

Even the AGP in Assam showed its inability and unwillingness to fight against the anti-secular policies of the BJP and instead was hand in gloves with the BJP and was planning to tie up with the State unit of the BJP to fight the polls jointly.

It was Narasimha Rao-led Congress that introduced the concepts of privatization and liberalisation. The ideology of the free market economy of the Congress was also no alternative to that of the BJP and the AGP. Instead, the policies of the Congress backing the United State's ideology in the economic and political fields only helped the BJP to come out stronger in the country.

In the case of Assam the Congress failed miserably, the Left parties alleged. With mounting unemployment, rising fiscal debt, deteriorating health and education scenario in the State, the Congress also had to deal with insurgency and ethnic violence. Hence the Left contemplated putting up its candidates in its stronghold constituencies to realise an increase in the strength of the Left forces at the Centre so as to form a government and remove the ills of present policies and rules, and – (i) to support and hold secularism and democracy of the country, (ii) to fight for social and economic justice for all, and (iii) to work for the initiation of a democratic movement to uplift the weak states like Assam.

The Left forces hence put up their candidates in Silchar, Barpeta, Diphu, Tezpur, Dibrugarh and Lakhimpur in Assam with the promises of:

1. Taking steps to reinvest 50 per cent of the annual turnout from the natural resources in the State like tea, oil, gas, wood, coal, etc., in the State itself.
2. Transferring the main office of the tea industry to Assam.
3. Regenerating the sick industries in the public and cooperative sectors in Assam.
4. Declaring the floods and erosion in Assam as national problems.
5. Pressurising the Centre to bear the financial burden of the expenditure of the State in dealing with the insurgents and their outfits.
6. Deciding the boundaries of the Northeastern states by taking up a project called the "Survey of India".
7. Giving preference to the scheme of supplying identity cards to the genuine citizens of the State and to legally detect and deport the illegal immigrants in the State who have come over to the State after March 25, 1971.
8. Safeguarding the ethnic tribes, to upgrade the lives of

the farmers, to solve the problems of women and last but not the least to bring to some settlement the problems of the minorities in the State.

Campaigns: *A Foresee of Elections*

It is a common practice among the political parties to make tall promises in their election manifestos but on most occasions than not, the promises made in the manifestos are really meant to remain within the manifestos only. It has been found that the local issues get preference during the poll campaigns, more than those published in the manifestos, more so in the rural areas. The promises in the manifestos are mostly meant to woo the urban middle class who really seem to understand the issues raised in the manifestos as these issues find a place in their daily lives. Moreover, very rarely the issues which are dealt with in the election manifestos are uttered in public by the candidates and their supporters to woo the voters, both rural as well as urban. The promises made in the manifestos' of the parties in Assam and the campaigns that actually took place on field prior to the 14th Lok Sabha poll, were perhaps on this line of thought and also perhaps ways apart. This can be judged if a few cases of real campaigns, which were undertaken by the parties, are read into.

Observing Campaigns

In glaring contrast to the summer loathsomeness in Assam, there was a surge of activity all around on the eve of the 14th Lok Sabha poll as political parties, their leaders and workers in the State geared up for a tough poll battle. The principal constituencies wore festive looks with rows of party festoons, banners and flags. Multi-coloured graffiti outdid one another in art and imagination, the objective being to woo the voters. Public meetings and street-corner lectures rattled the air in most constituencies. Appeals, both rhythmic and prosaic, sentimental and emotional, filled the poll firmament. Ethnic issues like autonomy to the different communities under the Sixth Schedule, SC status to the Koch Rajbangshis, clashes between different groups in Karbi Anglong and NC Hills districts and formation of the BTAD were likely to dominate the poll campaigns in Assam, particularly in the tribal belt.

(i) Local Issues: The Heartline of Campaigns

The local issues, as usually desired, were at the centre stage of the campaigns of the candidates in the State. The candidates while addressing the rallies raised the issues like development of basic amenities in the different constituencies, including medical facilities and supply of potable drinking water facilities[16] and other infrastructural facilities like roads, bridges, and the supply of electricity. In the two constituencies of Dibrugarh and Jorhat, certain specific local issues were raised in the campaigns.

Dibrugarh Constituency

Irrespective of the party in this constituency, the candidates fought the election on the following issues:

(i) To solve the problems of tea-garden workers.
(ii) Improvement of roads in the Dibrugarh district.
(iii) Infrastructural development of Assam Medical College, Dibrugarh.
(iv) Establishment of the Gas Cracker Plant.

Nonetheless, certain national issues such as the unemployment problem, preventing the river linking project and repeal of the IMDT Act also figured in the campaigns. Focussing on these issues, the BJP candidate Kamakhya Prasad Tasa's mode of campaign in the district was both

[16] Whereas 62.3 per cent of households across the country have access to drinking water, only 45.86 per cent of households in relatively water rich Assam have access to this basic amenity. These figures indicate the abysmal condition of drinking water in the State.

door to door and campaigns through public meetings[17]. Tasa also received the support of the national figures like L.K. Advani, Susma Swaraj, Shatrughna Sinha, and Venkiah Naidu in his campaigns.

The Congress candidate Pawan Singh Ghatowar[18] too toed Tasa in the mode of campaigns led. On April 10, 2004, Ghatowar addressing a public meeting in Assam Chah Mazdoor Sangha, Panitola Branch, Tinsukia, cited the issues of tea gardens that needed immediate attention. In this rally, the likes of Rameswar Dhanowar and Sarat Borkotoky also shared the platform.

While Sarbananda Sonowal from the AGP, leading the campaigns from door to door, and also addressing the mass gatherings at the public meetings, defended the causes for which he stood in the elections. Addressing a party rally at Bokel in Dibrugarh district on April 22, 2004, Sonowal said that if elected, he would ventilate the grievances of the Assamese people and the exploitation perpetuated by the Central government for the last fifty-seven years.

Mostly, the three candidates seemed to echo the local issues like removing the grievances of the tea-community and improvement of roads and infrastructure in their campaigns. However, the momentum of campaign was vitiated when posters calling upon the Assamese community to choose between a coolie (a derogatory term used by the British to mean the tea garden workers) and a native appeared at several places in the constituency. The posters meant that the Assamese community should cast vote only in favour of an Assamese candidate, i.e. Sarbananda Sonowal from the AGP.

[17] It was also noted that the leaders and members of ATTSA campaigned actively for Tasa. Even the Assam Chah Mazdoor Sangh supported him in the campaigns.

[18] Ghatowar in an interview mentioned that if elected, he would look into the issues of unemployment, higher education and the establishment of the Gas Cracker at Tengaghat at the earliest.

Jorhat Constituency

The local issues highlighted in the constituency were:

(i) The socio-economic and cultural upliftment of the downtrodden people.

(ii) The linking of East-West Corridor upto Kunming through Stilwell road.

(iii) National Highway status for Dhodar Ali.

(iv) Giving the status of a world heritage site to Sibsagar district.

Bijoy Krishna Handique, while campaigning from the Congress, addressed a meeting near Jorhat town on March 28, 2004, attended by Shri Tarun Gogoi and Hemoprabha Saikai as well. Mainly focussing on the works done by the Congress in the district, Handique appealed to the public to vote for the Congress for further development of the State[19].

The BJP candidate, Dayananda Borgohain from the constituency campaigned along with the party leaders like Susma Swaraj and Venkiah Naidu. In their campaigns, Borgohain and the senior party leaders mainly focused on three issues – 'Bizli', 'Sadak' and 'Pani' and appealed to the voters to vote the BJP for the development of Assam.

Dulal Baruah, an AGP candidate from the district concentrated only on door to door campaigns[20]. The CPI candidate, Dhrupad Borgohain, on the other hand attended only public meetings. The issues raised in these campaigns were mostly the local problems of lack of infrastructural development and upliftment of the district in the economic front.

(ii) Bouquets and Brickbats: A Part of Campaigns

In Assam, the campaigns were set forth in the right

[19] Significantly enough, Brindaban Goswami, President, AGP and Dulal Baruah, candidate of AGP for the Jorhat Constituency also attended the meeting.

[20] It was essential because people might get confused about his party affiliation, as most of them were not aware of his joining the AGP.

earnest. In Barpeta, the issue of the IMDT was to determine the fate of the candidates. Kick starting its election campaign without even finalising the party candidate from the constituency, the leaders of the Congress in Barpeta strongly criticised the AGP and BJP and urged the people to elect the Congress in the polls. Interestingly, the Congress veteran, Gulam Osmani, was ignored in the Congress campaigns and was also avoided by the party leaders in the campaigns[21]. The Youth Congress went ahead with the 'cleaning campaign' to attract the voters in Barpeta and Barpeta road. They did it to attack the policies of NDA government leading to unemployment[22].

In Dibrugarh, Pawan Singh Ghatowar, faced strong challenge from Kamakhya Prasad Tasa. His former organisation, the ATTSA, blamed that the Congress government failed to fulfill even a single demand among the many demands that were put forward for the development of the tea tribe community. Meanwhile, Sarbananda Sonowal and Kamakhya Prasad's popularity ended all possibilities of Pawan Singh Ghatowar's win. Ghatowar lost the mass support as his meetings were attended by a very few people. It was also noticed that while Ghatowar was silent about the cases of police firing on Bajalani Tea Garden, Sonowal took a positive stand on these matters. Kamakhya Prasad, the candidate of the BJP also had a considerable hold on the tea garden areas. But he failed to command full support from the ATTSA as most of the ATTSA people were members of the AGP and the Congress.

While in the Kaliabor constituency, the AGP took a very strong position in campaigning and posed a very strong challenge to the Congress candidate Deep Gogoi. The Congress failed to gather support in favour of Deep Gogoi by

---

[21] *Amar Asom*, 2004.
[22] *Amar Asom*, 18th February 2004.

its all traditional means – wine and money, and the party was also accused of taking the help of the State machinery in all its illegal activities. Violence occurred in many places where AGP workers were the victims of Congress mafias and muscle men[23].

In Kokrajhar, the Sanmilita Janagosthiya Sangram Samiti (SJSS) candidate Sabda Ram Rabha campaigned in a huge election meeting in Sri Rampur organised by the All Assam Adivasi Students' Union. In a rare display of unity, the United Minority Front (UMF) President, Hafiz Rashid Ahmed Choudhury also urged the people to vote for Rabha. Approximately fifteen thousand people gathered in one of the meetings, including some Congress workers[24]. Restoration of the political rights of the non-Bodos in the BTAD was announced as one of the main poll planks of the Sanmilita Janagosthiya Sangram Samity. While the All Bodo Students' Union and the Co-ordination Committee for Bodoland Peoples' Organisation (CCBPO) supported candidate, S.K. Bwiswmuthiary, in a press conference held said that the BTC was created with the supreme sacrifice of the people of Bodoland region and he promised to work for the people in the BTC region belonging to all communities. Laying stress on peace, growth and development of the BTC, Bwiswmuthiary said that if voted to power, he would pressurise the Central government to implement the remaining clauses of the BTC Accord.

In Mangaldoi, Narayan Borkotoky appealed to the people to vote for him for development and reduction of poverty in Assam. He claimed that BJP had performed better in its five year term compared to the 45 years rule of the Congress and 10 years of AGP rule in Assam.

In Nowgong, the AGP leader Atul Medhi discovered some

---

[23] *Pratidin,* 24th April 2004.
[24] *ibid,* 19th April 2004.

bottles of "Desi Wine" which were distributed in the tribal areas of Raha amidst campaigns. These bottles were labelled with the picture of Vajpayee and the symbol of BJP. On the other hand, BJP accusing the AGP and Congress went on to say that both the parties were playing fowl and they were doing this in the name of BJP's Rajen Gohain[25].

(iii) Central Party Leaders and the Onset of Electioneering in the State

Expectedly the campaign for the 2004 election developed into two major components dealing with a mix of national and regional issues. The kind of national visibility of the campaigns led by the BJP led NDA and the Congress Party that was seen this time was something new in the sense that the campaigns of the other all-India parties and regional parties was confined to the issues of the concerned states and the regions.

The projection of a strong leadership was the critical electoral theme for the BJP and its allies. For that reason, the NDA campaign was almost entirely dominated by the personalities of Atal Behari Vajpayee and Lal Krishna Advani, the then sitting Prime Minister and Deputy Prime Minister of India respectively. Despite his advanced age and faltering health, the former addressed over 100 meetings spread over a month-and-a-half all over the country. The latter undertook a nationwide march, colourfully, called the Bharat Uday Yatra (India Shining Drive). The Prime Minister, Atal Behari Vajpayee who was on a countrywide mission to campaign for his party (BJP) and the ruling National Democratic Alliance (NDA) reached Guwahati on April 6, 2004. In his thirty-minutes speech, addressing an election rally at Guwahati, he called upon the electorate to vote for the BJP so as to enable him to solve problems of the region. Highlighting the need for repeal of the IMDT Act, an

[25] *Amar Asom & Pratidin,* 26th April 2004.

issue which has been also a potent weapon of the ruling Congress and the Opposition Asom Gana Parishad (AGP), Vajpayee warned Bangladesh against continuous infiltration from that country. The Prime Minister expressed apprehension that the Assamese would be reduced to a minority if the border with Bangladesh is not protected to check infiltration[26].

Citing the accord signed with the disbanded Bodo Liberation Tigers (BLT), and the creation of a territorial council as an example of a militant outfit giving up violence and realising the need of resolving their problem through peaceful means, the Prime Minister offered to hold talks with such outfits as the United Liberation Front of Asom (ULFA) provided they give up violence[27]. Introducing the party's candidate for the Gauhati Lok Sabha constituency, Dr. Bhupen Hazarika, the Prime Minister expressed his happiness at Hazarika's decision to join the BJP.

"It has become a global pattern to deal with militants with an iron hand. As a member of the committee of nations, we will toe a similar line," Advani kicked off his day with the statement on militancy in the region at a meeting at Dibrugarh, where he addressed a gathering of over 2,000 people. This was Advani's first rally in the State for the 2004 Lok Sabha poll. The Deputy Prime Minister who had a

---

[26] However, Vajpayee failed to explain why his government tabled a Bill to repeal the IMDT only toward the end of the 13th Lok Sabha. He was silent on the Centre's apparent lack of drive on completing the fencing along the Indo-Bangla border. The reality is that the people of Assam are weary of political promises on infiltration and the IMDT. *The Sentinel*, 7th April 2004.

[27] Observers point out that all parties have overlooked the violence and tension between Karbi and Kuki tribes in Karbi Anglong hill district despite the loss of over 40 lives in conflicts there, in the run-up to the polls. The parties have failed to realise the Kukis' determination for a separate regional council. It is a demand which has the capacity to set fire to the entire hill district. The situation appears to be turning for the worse with many forces trying to meddle to gain mileage. The Karbis and Kukis appear to be pawns in a much bigger game plan involving other militant groups as well as security agencies.

whirlwind tour of the State on April 24, 2005 campaigned at Dibrugarh, Diphu[28] and Nagaon. In Dibrugarh, he appealed to the masses to vote for BJP for the development of Assam. In Nagaon, despite the minorities having a decisive presence, Advani went on to declare that if the NDA returns to power, it would declare the Illegal Migrants (Determination by Tribunals) Act null and void. "We failed to do this as we do not have a majority in the Rajya Sabha, and this will be taken care of this time," reiterated Advani.

Leading the Congress campaigns, the AICC Secretary and APYC in charge, Chandan Bagshi, while addressing a rally at the Sonaram High School Field, Guwahati, in a vitriolic speech laced with criticism of the NDA government's policies, criticised BJP's attempts to bring in Sonia Gandhi's foreign origin issue in its campaigns[29]. Sonia Gandhi, too, visited the State for campaigning. She attended party meetings at Golaghat, Diphu and Guwahati. Delivering a lecture on Women's Day celebration in Guwahati in March 2004, Sonia Gandhi urged the people of Assam to wipe out the AGP and the BJP from Assam in the forthcoming Lok Sabha poll of 2004.

(iv) State Party Leaders and the Onset of Campaigns in the State

The Congress

The Chief Minister Tarun Gogoi who had also been touring the State campaigning for his party, the ruling Congress, blasted the BJP for bringing up the issue of Sonia Gandhi's foreign origin before the Lok Sabha poll. "Earlier it was Ram Janmabhoomi and now it is Sonia Janmabhoomi," he added. Criticizing the Asom Gana

---

[28] The United People's Democratic Solidarity (UPDS) had called an 11-hour Karbi Anglong and North Cachar Hills bandh to foil Advani's visit to Diphu. However, Advani successfully addressed a mass gathering of 10,000 at Diphu.
[29] *The Sentinel*, 15th February 2004.

Parishad (AGP), on the other hand, Shri Gogoi said that the State had witnessed killing of innocent people during the AGP's rule. "Peace has descended upon the State. Now people can stay out late at night without any fear. We have succeeded in bringing back peace to the State," he claimed.

Enraged and annoyed with the opposition, particularly the Asom Gana Parishad (AGP), for creating uproar in the concluding session of the State Assembly over criminalization of politics, Tarun Gogoi attacked the regional party leaders for keeping mum over "the Centre's step-motherly treatment" towards Assam[30]. The Chief Minister accused Delhi of a discriminatory attitude towards the State, which he said, had stymied growth at the grassroots level[31]. Addressing another election rally, launching a strong attack on the BJP, Gogoi charged that Vajpayee and Advani were the RSS regulars. "It is a known fact now that the BJP is communal and it runs its governments at the behest of the RSS. If it was not so, it would not have required another Rath Yatra to collect votes", he accused. Attacking the BJP for its "communal face," Gogoi said, "As Hindus, we, too, believe in harmony, but Hinduism had never believed in communal violence, like the one unleashed at the behest of the Sangh Parivar (RSS family)". The Chief Minister also slammed those opposition parties which had been blaming the Congress for "doing nothing" during its almost four-decade-long rule in the State after Independence. Claiming that the Congress was a party for the downtrodden, the Chief Minister termed the BJP, a party, which only cared for the capitalists. That was why they had hiked the prices of kerosene and

---

[30] Shri Gogoi went on to question that, "People like Sarbananda Sonowal and Brindaban Goswami can only show their 'red eyes' to me. Why can't they say anything to Atal Behari Vajpayee on the Gas Cracker issue? Because, they have a secret understanding with the BJP."

[31] *The Telegraph*, 2nd February 2004. The development of the villages being the top priority of the Congress, Gogoi also highlighted the *Gaon Yatra* of his party in the State in one of his campaigns in Dibrugarh.

LPGs but slashed plane fares and the prices of cars, he pointed out.

The State Congress unit chief and candidate for the Dibrugarh Lok Sabha seat, Paban Singh Ghatowar, attacked the AGP and the BJP, terming both parties opportunists and anti-people. The AGP, the so-called torch bearers of regionalism, had completely failed on all fronts during its ten-year tenure.

Kirip Chaliha from the Congress while addressing a Press Meet at Guwahati reiterated that he would raise the issues of the State at the Parliament if elected.

The Bharatiya Janata Party

Bhupen Hazarika, who attended the rally addressed by the Prime Minister, Vajpayee, at Guwahati, in his short speech, described Vajpayee as a worshipper of peace. Hazarika promised to become a torch bearer of Vajpayee's vision and lift up the darkness engulfing Assam, which he attributed to the abject negligence towards the State by the Congress during its five-decade long rule. In yet another rally, Dr. Hazarika promised that he would do everything to complete the development activities of his 'sister' Bijoya Chakrabarty. Dr. Hazarika also claimed that he joined the BJP as he regarded it to be a humanist party. Arguing that the label of communalism imposed on the BJP was unjust, he said that Atal Bihari Vajpayee, as the Prime Minister of the country was leading it to a desired goal. So, he urged the people to vote for the BJP. Hazarika in his 25 minutes lecture also sang a few songs to impress the people[32].

---

[32] It was alleged that Bhupen Hazarika requested the higher authorities of Prasar Bharati to approve his own programmes only for telecast. As a member of Prasar Bharati his action generated high discontentment among the cultural sections of the society. *Pratidin,* 30th March 2004. There were allegations that Hazarika had a deal with Sushma Swaraj to hush up a financial mismanagement in the Sangeet Natak Academy of which Hazarika was the Chairman.

At Mirza and Chaygaon in Kamrup, despite the tons of promises[33] made, Hazarika's campaigns failed to attract the general voters, as he lacked a political image. In these campaigns, he was accompanied by Goenka and the surrendered ULFA (SULFA) Jugal Kishore Mahanta[34].

The sitting MLA, Dinesh Sarkar, kicking off BJP's campaign in Dhubri, said that Tarun Gogoi and his party's rule have brought Assam nothing but a chaotic situation.

Asom Gana Parishad

AGP's candidate Afzalur Rahman delivering a campaign speech in an election meeting on March 10, 2004 where above 20 thousand people were present, claimed that the AGP always stood with the general people. It is reported that though this was the largest gathering of people in an electioneering meeting of the AGP, it was argued that the people attended the meeting not because of the party (which lacked popularity among the immigrant Muslims) but because of the candidate who had a base among them.

More than 6,000 people attended an election rally addressed by the AGP President, Brindaban Goswami, at Bihutoli, in Duliajan. Addressing the rally, Goswami appealed to the people to help the party to create an *Asthar Asom* and to strengthen the regional party by electing young leaders of the party. Mr. Goswami also criticised the BJP

---

[33] Bhupen Hazarika promised that he would open the doors of Northeast and connect it to the South East Asia. In a number of election meetings he made contradictory statements as he tried to mix up his progressive image as an artist once associated with the IPTA, with a rightist party he had joined just before the election.

[34] Hazarika's actions during the poll campaigns generated a lot of controversies. Hazarika's intimacy with the SULFA leader Jugal Kishore Mahanta and some others created uproar among the general masses. Dr Hazarika's singing though swayed generations of listeners in Assam, his political speeches as the BJP candidate from the Gauhati constituency did strike many discordant notes. In fact, a stray comment made in one of his campaigns threatened to snowball into a major controversy. Putting one of his logics forward to establish the fact that the BJP as a party was devoid of communal colour, he argued that it just could never be communal since it had made a member of the minority community, Dr APJ Abdul Kalam, the country's President. *In http://www.tribuneindia.com.*

led NDA Government for its proposed projects like interlinking of rivers. Commenting on the decision of the BJP to nominate, Dr. Hazarika, to fight the election in BJP ticket, Goswami reiterated that the BJP has made a futile attempt to sweep the election with the glamour of Dr. Hazarika[35]. The Vajpayee Government at the Centre, according to Goswami, was ever neglecting the interests of Assam and treating it as a "garbage dump". In yet another campaign, Goswami accused the Congress of becoming a party of the criminals. It is interesting to note that the AGP maintained a distance from the IMDT issue, as it needed the support of the immigrant Muslims who constituted majority in three Lok Sabha constituencies covering more than 23 Assembly segments.

Trinamool Gana Parishad

Deben Dutta, from the Trinamool Gana Parishad, promised that he would play a major role in the parliament for the cause of Assam in a "Meet the Press" ceremony held in Guwahati. Dutta also promised to take the State problems to the parliament as and when needed.

(v) A Few Major Issues in the Campaigns

Insurgency, ULFA and Peace

As the BJP's poll-campaign moved into gear in Assam, the NDA Government's 'peace-efforts' were what the party was trying to cash in on in the militancy-hit region. The campaigns highlighted the peace-deal with the Bodo Liberation Tigers (BLT), which was said to be one of the major achievements of Atal Behari Vajpayee's government in Assam[36]. But, ahead of the Lok Sabha (LS) poll, the crackdown in Bhutan was what the BJP leaders and the

---

[35] *Vedanti Back Issues.*

[36] "The Congress was in power in Delhi for nearly five decades since independence. This was the period, when most of the insurgencies in Northeast India were born, obviously due to the wrong policies of the ruling Congress. The BJP-led NDA Government in the last few years made sincere efforts to bring peace in the region, by holding dialogues with the militant outfits," said the President of the BJP unit in Assam, Indramoni Bora. *Deccan Herald, Friday, 9th April 2004.*

party's candidates were most reluctant to talk about[37]. Perhaps, the party was voicing one of the promises mentioned in its manifesto i.e. to strengthen national security both external and internal – to overcome present and future challenges. Obviously, the BJP, desperate to gain more ground in Assam did not want to hurt the peoples' sentiments ahead of the Lok Śabha poll. The BJP had refrained from taking credit for the crackdown on militants in Bhutan.

However, the NDA Government was criticised by both the Congress and Asom Gana Parishad for pursuing different policies to deal with the rebels of Assam and Nagaland in their campaigns. Pawan Singh Ghjatowar, the Congress MP from the Dibrugarh Parliamentary constituency in his campaign alleging the NDA government said, "The NDA Government made no effort to find a political solution of the problem of insurgency in Assam"[38]. On the other hand, Apurba Bhattacharya, the AGP's candidate from Mangaldoi Lok Sabha constituency questioned, "If Mr. Vajpayee's Government could hold talks with the NSCN (IM), why couldn't it do the same with the ULFA? It made efforts to bring peace in Nagaland through talks, but tried to end insurgency in Assam by coercive measures"[39].

---

[37] What the BJP seemed to have deliberately dropped from the list of NDA Government's 'achievements' was its success in making the monarch of neighbouring Bhutan launch a military operation to flush out the ULFA and other outfits from the kingdom's southern region. The soldiers of the Royal Bhutan Army (RBA) not only destroyed all the camps, which the militant outfits had been using for hit-and-run guerrilla-strikes in Assam but also nabbed and handed over to the Indian Army a number of extremists, including some top leaders. It was for New Delhi's persistent pressure that Thimphu, the king of Bhutan, had to launch the 'Operation All Clear' in December 2003. The crackdown hit the ULFA hard and hundreds of militants were either killed or apprehended or made to surrender. Anirban Bhaumik, *Deccan Herald, Friday,* 9th April 2004.

[38] In "BJP Silent on ULFA Crackdown in Bhutan for Poll Reasons", Anirban Bhaumik, *Deccan Herald, Friday,* 9th April 2004.

[39] *Ibid.*

Illegal Migrants (Determination by Tribunals) Act

Launching the poll campaign of the Congress party at Prabhat Chandra Barua Playground, Dhubri, on April 4, 2004, Tarun Gogoi severely criticizing both the BJP and AGP for continuously opposing the IMDT Act in both Houses of the Parliament and outside and dismissing all speculations over scrapping of the IMDT Act, announced that the Act will be in its place forever in its present form[40].

On April 4, 2004 in a desperate move to woo the minority voters, Jayashree Goswami Mahanta, wife of former Assam Chief Minister, Prafulla Kumar Mahanta, while addressing a gathering at Bilasipara made a comment in favour of the retention of the IM DT Act. She lambasted Mr. Sarbananda Sonowal for filling a petition in the Supreme Court praying for the repeal of the IMDT Act. On the other hand, the AGP candidate for the Gauhati Lok Sabha seat Bhrigu Kumar Phukan on April 7, 2004 blamed the Centre for its inaction in solving the migration issue.

(vi) Campaigns and Cine Stars

With mass participation from the top names in the Assamese film industry to folk theatre and humour groups, campaigning for the Lok Sabha elections in the State was more than its usual share of colour. All the major political parties, the AGP, the BJP and the Congress tightened up their campaign strategies with a liberal dose of cultural events and glamour, both home-grown as well as national, to lend a colourful touch to the campaigns in the different constituencies.

Celebrated film actress and Rajya Sabha M.P., Hema Malini, visited the State on April 18, 2004 and reiterated that the BJP was serious about curbing illegal influx in the Northeast, while revealing that if voted to power again, the party would undertake all steps to find a solution to the

---

[40] *Vedanti*, Various Issues.

thorny issue. The actress also claimed that Dr. Bhupen Hazarika had greater chances of winning the coming Lok Sabha election from the Gauhati constituency. Dara Singh, yet another cine personality of yester years campaigned for the BJP candidate, Dr. Bhupen Hazarika, in Guwahati. In the campaigns, Singh argued that only a bold leader had the capabilities to bring forward the country which was lacking in the Congress.

It was Jaya Prada and Tarun Gogoi who jointly campaigned for the Congress candidate Gulam Osmani in Barpeta.

(vii) Inaugurations and Major Grants amidst Campaigns

It was a sop story all the way as the National Democratic Alliance's pre-poll gravy train ran its course in Assam with the announcements and inauguration of infrastructure projects. The other political parties in the State were also not way behind.

- Accompanied by George Fernandes and Sharad Yadav, Nitish Kumar[41] flagged off work on two rail projects – restoration and gauge conversion from Haibargaon to Moirabari and Senchowa to Silghat on February 8, 2004 in Nowgong district.
- There was a declaration by Nitish Kumar of 40 per cent reservation of jobs in the railways for the resident candidates in the State.
- Inaugurating a riverbank erosion control project at Sonapur, S.M. Dev criticised the AGP government to be indifferent towards the Barak Valley during its reign. Further, he added that though the Congress was under financial constraint, nevertheless, it performed for the people in the Barak Valley.
- Public Health Engineering Minister, Dinesh Prasad

[41] Railway Minister, NDA Government.

Gowala, inaugurated the Eid Milonutsob at Baskandi. The meeting was attended by the Divisional Forest Officer, Salman Choudhury. Gowala also inaugurated the Lalang Bridge built at a cost of Rs. 12 Lakh to enhance the development in the area.

- The congress MLA from Ratabari in Karimganj district, Kripalnath Mala laid the foundation for a school and college at Ramkrishnanagar worth Rs. 10 lakh.
- The Chief Minister Tarun Gogoi and other Congress stalwarts with Santosh Mohan Dev inaugurated the bridge at Ranighat and named it as Altaf Setu.
- The Chief Minister laid the foundation of Malinibil IIDC, an Infrastructural Development Project worth Rs. 5.10 crore at Malinibil.
- Gautam Roy granted Rs. 5 lakh for Chorgola Higher Secondary School at Karimganj.
- Tarun Gogoi assured a sanction of Rs.10 lakh for Kabugange Janata College, Silchar.
- North Karimganj MLA from the BJP, Mishon Ranjan Das, had said in an Atal Sandesh Yatra that he had granted Rs.10 lakh for various projects in North Karimganj. He also laid the foundations of the 545 Raimoni L.P. School and 319 Chorrekuri Junior Basic School and granted Rs. 1,50,000 for the schools.
- The Finance Minister, Yashwant Singh, performed the Bhumi Pujan and laid the foundation of the Silchar to Balacherra section of NH 54 on East-West Corridor from Silchar to Porbandar. He lamented at the dilapidated condition of the roads in Silchar.
- Parimal Suklabaidya, the MLA, granted Rs.1 lakh to the Shri Shri Hari Sabha Mandir Community Hall at Natun Bazar, Dholai, and laid the foundation and gave assurance to extend more monetary help.

Table 4.1
Party wise number of candidates nominated for 2004 Lok Sabha poll

Party	No. of Candidates	Names of the Candidates
AGP	**12**	
Autonomous District	1	Sailendra Hasnu
Barpeta	1	Kumar Deepak Das
Dhubri	1	Afzalur Rahman
Dibrugarh	1	Sarbananda Sonowal
Gauhati	1	Bhrigu Kumar Phukan
Jorhat	1	Dulal Chandra Baruah
Kaliabor	1	Keshab Mahanta
Karimganj	1	Nepal Chandra Das
Kokrajhar	-	-
Lakhimpur	1	Arun Kumar Sarma
Mangaldoi	1	Apurba Bhattacharjee
Nowgong	1	Dhruba Kumar Saikia
Silchar	-	-
Tezpur	1	Padma Hazarika
BJP	**12**	
Autonomous District	1	Ratan Teron
Barpeta	1	Ranjit Thakuria
Dhubri	1	Jabeen Borbhuyan
Dibrugarh	1	Kamakhya Prasad Tasa
Gauhati	1	Bhupen Hazarika
Jorhat	1	Dayananda Borgohain
Kaliabor	-	-

(Contd...)

Party	No. of Candidates	Names of the Candidates
Karimganj	1	Parimal Sukla Baidya
Kokrajhar	-	-
Lakhimpur	1	Uday Shankar Hazarika
Mangaldoi	1	Narayan Chandra Barkataky
Nowgong	1	Rajen Gohain
Silchar	1	Kabindra Purkayastha
Tezpur	1	Ghisa Lal Agarwal
Congress	**14**	
Autonomous District	1	Biren Singh Engti
Barpeta	1	A.F. Golam Osmani
Dhubri	1	Anowar Hussain
Dibrugarh	1	Paban Singh Ghatowar
Gauhati	1	Kirip Chaliha
Jorhat	1	Bijoy Krishna Handique
Kaliabor	1	Dip Gogoi
Karimganj	1	Lalit Mohan Suklabaidya
Kokrajhar	1	Derhagra Mochahary
Lakhimpur	1	Ranee Narah
Mangaldoi	1	Madhab Rajbangshi
Nowgong	1	Bisnu Prasad
Silchar	1	Santosh Mohan Dev
Tezpur	1	Mani Kumar Subba

(Contd...)

Party	No. of Candidates	Names of the Candidates
Left	**6**	
Autonomous District	1	Dr. Jayanta Rongpi
Barpeta	1	Manoranjan Talukdar
Dhubri	-	-
Dibrugarh	1	Subhas Sen
Gauhati	-	-
Jorhat	1	Drupad Borgohain
Kaliabor	-	-
Karimganj	-	-
Kokrajhar	-	-
Lakhimpur	-	-
Mangaldoi	-	-
Nowgong	-	-
Silchar	1	Noorul Huda
Tezpur	1	Rubul Sarma
Independents	**47**	
Autonomous District	2	(i) Chember G. Momin (ii) Sanmoni Kemprai
Barpeta	2	(i) Jilane Haque Laskar (ii) Dr. Tara Prasad Das
Dhubri	7	(i) Gandhi Nath (ii) Jayasree Goswami Mahanta (iii) Dr. Motiur Rahman Mondal

(Contd...)

Party	No. of Candidates	Names of the Candidates
		(iv) Minhar Ali Mandal
		(v) Listi Rabha
		(vi) Radha Ballav Adhikary
		(vii) Shajahan Sheikh
Dibrugarh	2	(i) Amrit Borgohain
		(ii) Badhram Rajgarh
Gauhati	6	(i) Bhabani Bodo
		(ii) Dhwajen Brahma
		(iii) Kazi Nekib Ahmed
		(iv) Rajat Chandra Rabha
		(v) Sumitra Das
		(vi) Umesh Chandra Das
Jorhat	-	-
Kaliabor	5	(i) Binod Gogoi
		(ii) Bikash Tanti
		(iii) Jiten Gogoi
		(iv) Jitu Sarmah
		(v) Juren Rajkhowa
Karimganj	5	(i) Babul Ram Das
		(ii) Babul Roy
		(iii) Lukendra Roy
		(iv) Radha Kanta Tanti
		(v) Sushil Kumar Das

(Contd...)

Party	No. of Candidates	Names of the Candidates
Kokrajhar	3	(i) Rajendra Mushahary (ii) Sabda Ram Rabha (iii) Sansuma Khunggur Bwiswmuthiary
Lakhimpur	5	(i) Biju Narah (ii) Ghanashyam Bhattarai (iii) Rabin Deka (iv) Hekjal Wood (v) Isak Korkoria
Mangaldoi	3	(i) Aroon Baruah (ii) Bhupendra Nath Kakati (iii) Tridip Pati Singha
Nowgong	-	-
Silchar	6	(i) Ashutosh Das (ii) Benu Bhushan Nath (iii) Kantimoy Deb (iv) Kshitindra Sarkar (v) Manoranjan Das (vi) Samarendra Ghosh
Tezpur	1	Dipen Tanti

Source: www.electionnext.com

REFERENCES

"Polarisation and Consensus".(1999) *Economic and Political Weekly*. Vol. XXXIV, No. 34-35. August 21– 27/28, Sept. 3.

Amar Asom (2004).

Amar Asom (2004). February18.

Amar Asom (2004). April 26.

Asom Pradesh Congress Committeer Karma Khushi (2004). The Manifesto of the Assam Pradesh Congress.

Bharator Communist Party (Marxbadi). Asom Raizik Committee. Nirbashani Gushona Patra. Chaturdaksh Loka Sabha Nirbashan, 2004.

Bharator Communist Partyr Asom Raizik Parishad. Nirbashani Istahaar. Chaturdaksh Loka Sabha, 2004.

Bhaumik, Anirban (2004). "BJP Silent on ULFA Crackdown in Bhutan for Poll Reasons". *Deccan Herald*.

Brindaban Goswami (2004). *India News on Line*, North East Scenario. http://www.indiamart.news.com.

Charge Sheet against Congress Government (2004). Bharatiya Janata Party Assam Pradesh.

Deccan Herald (2004). April 9.

Election Commission of India. http://www.eci.gov.in.

Leuthold, David A. (1968). *Electioneering in a Democracy: Campaign for Congress*. New York: John Wiley. Chapter I. Introduction.

Nirbashani Istahaar, Asom Gana Parishad. (2004). *Chatur Daksh Loka Sabha Nirbashan*. Election Manifesto, Asom Gana Parishad, 14th Lok Sabha Polls.

Pratidin (2004). March 30.

Pratidin (2004). April 19.

Pratidin (2004). April 24.

Pratidin (2004). April 26.

Schumpeter, Joseph A. (1962). *Capitalism, Socialism and Democracy*. New York: Harper. Third edition. p. 269.

The Sentinel (2004). February 15.

The Sentinel (2004). April 17.

The Telegraph (2004). February 2.

The Telegraph (2004). April 4.

Tribune India. http://www.tribuneindia.com.

Vedanti - Burning Assam (Earlier Issues). Various Issues. http://www.vedanti.com.

Vision Document (2004). Bharatiya Janata Party.

CHAPTER 5

Role of Media

Prologue: Election *sans* Issues

Two of the most significant aspects of the 14th Lok Sabha election in Assam were that, first, there was no single major issue for the State as whole, which could become a deciding factor, so far the election results were concerned; and second, it seemed that media had accepted the peoples' verdict with the opinion that the result was due to "sharing of votes" rather than the peoples' confidence over the political parties. This, however, was not unique to Assam alone, but was reflected even at the national level as well. The fragmented character of the Indian politics and its consequent pre and post poll political alliances in different forms and degrees has become a reality of the Indian democracy for quite some time[1]. Although the BJP led "India Shining" slogan and a few others like anti-incumbency factor and Gujarat riots were gaining importance among a particular section of the

[1] K K Katyal, "Issues and Trends in Indian Elections", *South Asian Journal*, Vol. July-September, 2004, No. 5. An Electronic version of the article was available at the following website when accessed on August 16, 2005. http://www.southasianmedia.net/Magazine/Journal/issues_trends.htm. In this article Katyal tries to view this fragmentation from two diverse perspectives; one, the number of seats going to the political parties; and two, the poll percentages. This (fragmentation) was, according to him, due to "the combined result of the multiplicity of political parties and the peculiar electoral system, under which the first past the poll if the winner."

electorate, these had, however, hardly reached those who mattered most in the actual electoral process in the Indian democracy – the rural poor and the marginalised. The 14th Lok Sabha election clearly reveals the decisive role that the Dalits and the Adivasis played in determining the poll results. Similarly, other important issues like terrorism and war with Pakistan, Ayodhya and Hindutva, which occupied centre stage in the earlier elections were on the wane and failed to appeal the Indian voters. The same tendency was also evident in the case of Assam. The poll wining issues like the Assam Accord, the IMDT (Illegal Migrants Determination by Tribunals) Act and Illegal Foreigners Act could not deliver the usual result that they used to do in the couple of previous elections. This, perhaps, was the reason why it became so difficult to predict the poll results this time and the results confounded most pre-election analyses and expectations. Interestingly and quite intriguingly enough, media, particularly the regional media in Assam, on the average, showed a favourable bend towards the regional parties while results were just the opposite. This, together with the terrible failure of many pre-poll analyses, most of which were conducted under the aegis of various media organisations and houses, in itself, raises several issues and questions as to the role of media in the election processes in particular and, also, as to the reaction of the public towards it in general.

Media, Democracy and Public Opinion: *A Theoretical Construct*

One frequently offered argument is that the free media is a *sine qua non* of successful and functional democracy. Essentially, this view embeds the argument that access and right to information, and freedoms of expression and of the press are necessary for the success of democracy.

There may be several lines of reasoning in support of this argument. In a recent technical paper, the US Agency for International Democracy (USAID) points out two functions of media that ensures a fully functional democracy. First, by guaranteeing access to information, media ensures that citizens make "responsible and informed choices rather than acting out of ignorance or misinformation"; and second, this information often serves a "checking function" by making it sure that "elected representatives uphold their oaths of office and carry out the wishes of the electorate"[2]. McConnell and Becker add two more 'functions' of media to these. Firstly, they posit that an independent media helps strengthening the rule of law; and secondly, it contributes to "transparent elections" by giving candidates access to and by reporting on the relevant issues in timely and objective manner[3]. While the USAID's technical paper admits media to be a sub set of the civil society space, it also notes that in many cases the 'space' and scope of media overlaps "other functional areas of democracy and governance". Interestingly, it also goes on to describe:

> In some societies, an antagonistic relationship between media and government represents a vital and healthy element of fully functioning democracies. In post conflict or ethnically homogenous societies, such a conflictual, tension ridden relationship may not be appropriate, but the role of the press to disseminate information as a way of mediating between the State and all facets of civil society remains critical[4].

The idea of "responsible and informed choices", as described by the USAID, assumes greater significance when

---

[2] USAID, "The Role of Media in Democracy: A Strategic Approach", *Centre for Democracy and Governance, Bureau of Global Programs, Field Support, and Research*, Washington, D.C., June, 1999.

[3] McConnell Patrick J and Becker Lee B, "The Role of Media in Democratization", A paper presented at the Political Communication Section of the International Association for Media and Communication Research at the Barcelona Conference, July, 2002.
Accessed at the website: http://www.portalcomunicacion.com/bcn2002/n_eng/programme/prod_id/asp4.asp?id_pro=1461

[4] USAID, n. 2, p. 3.

it is applied to the actual election process under democracy. Technically speaking, the election process and voting by an individual is nothing but a matter of rational choice on the part of the individual voters. Given a number of candidates, an individual constructs a relative preference schedule of his or her own for all the candidates at his or her disposal and finally, by exercising the power of franchise, a rational choice is arrived at in favour of a particular candidate depending on those preferences. The ultimate rationality of the individual voter is, in fact, conditioned by his or her own set of preferences. The rationality, thus obtained, is, therefore, justifiable on grounds of righteousness of those sets of individual preferences. It is, generally, argued that lack of information and/or misinformation put a limit to this righteousness.

Here in comes the role of media. Ideally, media is expected to provide at least two sets of information. At the first place, it should try bringing the real issues of the contemporary society to the fore; and secondly, it should also try to provide information about the candidates' ability and credentials vis-à-vis those real issues.

At the collective level, however, the role of media can be perceived in a slightly different way. Just like the individuals' economic preferences, in the case of electoral preferences also, people usually confront with different and often conflicting and mutually competing individual preferences. This makes it difficult to obtain a consensus social electoral choice. Although, democracy relies mostly on the rule of majority, even then, such a social consensus may prove to be useful for a successful democracy.

Nobel Laureate and a widely acclaimed authority of the social choice theory, Professor Amartya Sen, in one of his recently given television interviews, has explained how such a consensus can be reached through a process, which he calls "public reasoning". The problem with the popular reasoning, he argues, is that relatively lower category issues mostly guide it. The real issues like those of health, education, employment, quality of life and security are pushed to the corner and take a backseat in the whole process, albeit, these are common issues and affect all sections of the society almost equally. To bring those issues of health, education and employment back to the core of the public discourses, it is extremely important that there exists a domain where an objective and appropriate public reasoning can have its course. The media, as he finds it, has the rare ability to provide such a public reasoning domain. The need of the media, therefore, when considered as a public reasoning domain, is to identify the real issues, pick them up, collate them and politically articulate them in a way so that these come to the 'centre' from the 'margin'. The process by which such a shift can be imagined, he said, may be termed as the process of public reasoning. The so-called failure of the Indian democracy, according to him, is due to "the absence of such a public reasoning domain".

Professor Sen's construction of media as a domain of public reasoning, in a sense, is a liberal attempt at theorising the role of media for it not only extends the scope of media in the process of democratisation, but also liberates it from its certain inherent limiting factors. There is a tendency to equate media with civil society. This role of media either as a "civil society space" where issues are to be discussed, debated and contested, or as an interface between the State and the civil society might appear to be a "media supremist position"[5] as some would argue, but there is another issue, which has generated some lively debates among the media professionals and political scientists. Is it always the case that media freedom and/or other communication freedoms lead to successful and functional democracies? In the words of Jakubowicz "the issue of whether mass media lead or

[5] McConnell and Becker (2002), n. 3, p. 1.

follow, whether they mirror or mould society, and whether they should be conceptualised as agents of change or the status quo is yet to be resolved"[6]. In fact, there are sections of people who would feel that media freedom should be viewed as an indicant of democratic reforms, rather than an independent determinant of it. It is also quite possible that the media freedom may slow down or even hinder the process of democratization. Or would the media play no role at all, with democracy emerging quite independent of press and other communication freedom?

The fear that media might come in the way of democratisation, when it is conceived as a part of the civil society space, which characteristically rules out the possibility of 'exclusion', stems from the fact that in a society, where literacy rate is very much low, especially in countries like India where it remains at just above sixty per cent, there is always a danger that media, particularly the print media, becomes a sounding board of the handful of 'elites' – the 'literates', thereby 'excluding' a large part of the participant population. How many of Indians do read newspapers or watch television? As per the National Readership Study (NRS)[7], released on June 17, 2002 by the National Readership Studies Council (NRSC), mapping media trends in India, has revealed that about 248 million adults are 'literate' but do not read any publications. According to the NRS, readership base for the newspapers and dailies in India has been 156 million in the year 2002. A look at the newspaper circulation data would depict the same story. The Ministry of Information and Broadcasting, Government of India record reveals that in the year 2003-2004, total

---

[6] Jakubowicz, Karl, "Media in Transition: The Case of Poland", in *Media Reform: Democratizing the Media, Democratizing the State,* M E Price, B Rozumilowicz and S G Verhulst (eds.), (London: Routledge, 2002). As quoted in McConnel and Becker (2002), n. 3, p. 2.

[7] The detailed results are available at the website:
http://www.indianprinterpublisher.com/aug/archive-i.../
newspaper%20readership%20in%20indian.htm.

circulation of registered newspapers, including the weeklies and monthlies, in the country stood at 133.09 million. In Assam, the figure stood at 781,409 with 32 newspapers and periodicals.

The spread of audio-visual media is, again, very limited. The NRS has recorded that the television is mostly confined to urban viewers and the average viewing time of television programmes has come down from 85 minutes per person in 1999 to 82 minutes per person in 2002. There is another way to look at the scenario. In India, as per the Census 2001, only 31.6 per cent of the total household owns a television, coloured or black-and-white, out of which only 18.9 per cent is rural household. In Assam, these figures are 18.3 and 12 per cent respectively. Similarly, only 35.1 per cent household has radio/transistors in the country out of which 31.5 per cent is rural household. For Assam, the figures are found to be just 30.2 and 28.6 respectively.

The liberalists adhere to the fact that civil society is a property of democratic states. Privileging the civil society as the sphere where democratic politics can be constructed has a few significant implications. Ideally, a civil society space is imagined as a space of common and/or shared concerns and interest, which brings together individual and groups otherwise located in private discourses, on the basis of those shared and common interests. The space is imagined as a domain of public reasoning lying outside the "officially prescribed channels of communication provided by the State" and desirably having peoples' full access to it[8]. Thus, democratic political theory privileges civil society because it assumes that existence is inextricably bound up with that of civil society.

Chandhoke, in a different place, argues that though the

[8] Chandhoke N, *State and Civil Society- Explorations in Political Theory* (New Delhi: Sage Publications, 2000), p. 163.

emergence of civil society is historically bound up with that of democracy, this does not by any means indicate that the domain will be by that fact alone, democratic. When it is lowered from the "theoretical heights" and relocated in its constitutive material and social setting, the sphere is found to be "not only exclusive but also exclusionary"[9]. It is, she goes on to argue, bound to be so because differential power relation stamp it, just like they do other domains of human action. To quote her:

> Therefore, it is not surprising that when marginalised groups determine that they should be heard in the sphere, when they resolve that civil society should register their condition and hear their demands, they have to battle enormous obstacles. They have to rend asunder dense and overlapping complexities of power. They have to weave their way through un-hearing, uninterested, and perhaps uncaring public. And they have to storm the linguistic and conceptual ramparts that protect the domain.[10]

This leads to the fact that the stylised notions that civil society is inherently civil and receptive to all the inhabitants of the sphere may prove to be an ultimate illusion in the process. The only way to get rid of this illusion is to exclude the marginalised, which makes the civil society exclusionary and exclusive. The best part of it, however, according to her, is that it can be re-appropriated by the marginalised as a result of which the space itself becomes "unstable, precarious and only ambiguous source of democracy". This, what she calls, is the "paradox of democracy"[11].

Taking the exclusionary and exclusive character of the civil society space, we may, perhaps look at the media as a

---

[9] Chandhoke N, *The Conceits of Civil Society* (New Delhi: Oxford University Press, 2003), p. 206.
[10] *ibid*, p. 207.
[11] *ibid*, p. 238.

domain of public reasoning. In our case, this exclusiveness and exclusionary character of the hypothesised domain is further confirmed by realities like literacy rates and ownership of television and radio, simply leaving aside most of the general public outside the domain. Their voices go unrecorded in the conventional public discourses and debates most of which are determined by the power relations that dominate the centre of the domain. These power relations form a nexus with the political power brokers and the ideals of democracy is, thus, distanced.

In the subsequent sections, the role of media in the last Lok Sabha election, more particularly in Assam, will be discussed in greater detail to prove this point and also to highlight the need for a shift in the whole process to fulfil the political aspirations of the majority of people lying at the periphery of the domain of public reasoning.

Brief Analyses of the Issues: *Mapping Local on to the National*

In this section, an attempt has been made to analyse the issues that surfaced during the 14th Lok Sabha election at two different levels – at the national level and at the regional or state level. Often, the regional parties are moved by the assumption that the national parties, generally speaking, fail to appreciate the regional aspirations of people, and, therefore, turn a black eye on the regional issues. This 'allegation' is examined by mapping the regional voices on to the national discourses taking Assam as a case. For analytical conveniences, it is, basically, intended to focus on three national 'allies', of course, with some tangential references to others at times i.e. the NDA led by the BJP, Congress and its allies, and the Left Front. As for the regional parties, the main concentration is on the AGP for the obvious reason that it is the single most important regional party of the State that enjoyed unprecedented peoples' confidence in couple of earlier elections.

Issues of the recently concluded general election, like any other elections in the past, surfaced in two spheres – in the party manifestos (as discussed in Chapter 4), and in the public rhetoric. The party manifestos embodies the major thrusts and issues of the parties and are important document for the analysts. These testify the commitments and concerns of the political parties, which may be seen and contextualised against the contemporary social realities. To have a general idea of the national issues, the NDA's manifesto has been considered first, as the party in power then, focus then is shifted on the Congress and its allies manifesto and finally the manifestos of the Left Front has been taken into account.

Interestingly, just before the election, the BJP, the then ruling party at the centre, released its Vision Document (2004) with a pledge to make India a "developed nation and a great power" by 2020. The document, as it stated, embodied "core beliefs, basic commitments and the party's priority agenda for next five years and beyond". Through it, the BJP, along with the partners of the National Democratic Alliance (NDA), sought a "renewed mandate from people" with the usual promise of a *Shaktisali Bharat* (powerful India). It criticized the Congress party's "wrong policies and long misrule" for India's underdevelopment. The document virtually talked of everything, right from national security to food security, from removal of poverty to work guarantee, from industrial and economic progress to creating of the state of the art of infrastructure, from rural development to ideal Indian cities, and from quality of life to empowerment of civil society. More importantly, it also reiterated, quite categorically, its "commitment to construction of a *magnificent* Ram Mandir at Ayodhya; amicable resolution of the issue through dialogue for starting a new chapter in Hindu-Muslim relations". This was, probably, an indication of the non-shifting internal balance of the NDA where the forces like VHP and Sangh Parivar continued to occupy a potent place of importance. The imperative was, later on, felt even more forcefully when the party had to declare that "efforts will be made to evolve a consensus for passing central legislation for protection of the cow and her progeny".

One of the most striking features of the BJP's Vision Document was the ambiguity and conceptual vagueness of certain issues and ideas, which the party was trying hard to drive home. For instance, it talked of "cultural nationalism" declaring that "Indian nationhood stems from a deep cultural bonding of the people that overrides differences of caste, region, religion and language" (Clause 4.4 of the document). On the other hand, it also stated that "we (BJP) believe that Cultural Nationalism for which Indianness, Bharatiyata and Hindutva are synonymous – is the basis of our identity" (same Clause). It also idealised "Maryada Purushottam Ram" as the "inspiring cultural symbol of India" (Clause 4.5 of the document). What was remarkable about this document was that this Hindu-centric construction of Indian nation was presented in a more accommodative way, perhaps to shed away the popular "communal image" of the party. It argued that the Hindutva is not a "religious or exclusivist" concept. It is "inclusive, integrative and abhors any kind of discrimination against any section of the people of India on the basis of their faith" (Clause 4.4). It also provided its understanding of secularism as *Sarva Pantha Samabhava* (treating all faiths with respect). The document also declared religious freedom as its (BJP's) core value (Clause 4.6). The same clause promised removal of the distinctions between the 'minorities' and 'majorities' without having any clear definitions of these two politically sensitive terms. Placing them under a Clause, which dealt with the "religious freedom" and, which is preceded by Clauses describing the *Hinduness* of the Indian nation, the terms like 'minority' (the *Muslims?*) and 'majority' (the *Hindus?*) might well be interpreted in religious lines.

Similarly, the party failed to take a clear stand on the issues of globalisation and economic reforms. On one hand, it chanted the 'Swadeshi' *mantra,* and on the other it admitted that "a big shift is taking place in the global economy, and India should be prepared to take advantage of it" (Clause 4.9). It tried to reconcile both these ideas in a way, which appeared to be rather precarious. It talked of further economic reforms to place the country's predominantly young population in an advantageous position. This was, the document claimed, "the Swadeshi approach to turning globalisation into an opportunity for India in the 21st century" (Clause 4.9). Even in the case of hot issues like Ayodhya, the party's position was found to be equivocal. The Clause 4.5 said that the BJP remained committed to its stand that the judiciary's verdict in this matter should be accepted by all. In the same document, it also expressed its belief that a negotiable settlement of the issue was possible through mutual dialogue. All these lost their significances when the party announced building of a "magnificent Ram Mandir".

How does one explain such evident "positional dilemma" of the BJP, or for that reason, of the NDA, which was at the helm of affairs at that time? Clearly, the BJP's 'position' in most of the cases was conditioned by two things – one, political compulsion of the coalition politics and, two, populist tactics to win the confidence of the general masses. For instance, the idea of the BJP's Hindu-centric India was necessitated by the existent pressure within the coalition of the NDA. The rise of the BJP as a strong force in the political sphere of the Indian democracy was, in fact, associated with the emergence and political articulation of the concept of Hindutva. However, as the party in power, BJP's imperative was to take people on board for a renewed mandate in the ensuing election. The BJP's goal, therefore, was clear and definite – the party had to maintain the existing power balance within the coalition and it had to expand its political support base by being more 'accommodative' in its approach. Given this political compulsion, the party had to adopt a "middle path" dispensing with any categorical standing.

Next, it will be worthwhile to see how it had responded to the regional issues and aspirations. Two regions namely Jammu and Kashmir and Northeast India figured explicitly in the BJP's agenda for next "five years and beyond". The issues and problems of these two regions, however, had become more national than regional in intensity and interest. The BJP proposed Autonomous Regional Councils for Jammu and Ladakh with adequate financial and administrative powers. Development and peace were the two most important ingredients of the agenda for the Northeast. Putting an end to the infiltration from Bangladesh and vigorously pursuing the 3 D formula – Detect, Delete and Deport was also mentioned. The party, however, remained silent on the issue of controversial Illegal Migrants Determination (and Deportation) by Tribunals (IMDT) Act.

The Assam State unit of the BJP released its election manifesto, which proudly recorded the successes and achievements of the Vajpayee government during its tenure. The document released by the unit had no special mention of any specific regional issues as such; it only echoed and reflected the party's general agenda.

On the contrary, the election manifesto of the Assam Pradesh Congress Committee (APCC) was more comprehensive and elaborate, which documented both local and national issues. It started with the glorious history of Congress and ended with a candid note of further progress and prosperity. As the ruling party in the State, it took pride in enlisting its successes in the State. It took a strong and critical stand in describing the failure of the AGP for its "anti-people activities".

It was clear from the Congress manifesto that the BJP was perceived as a "threat to Indian secularism" and Indian nation. As opposed to the Hindu-centric Indian nation of the BJP, the Congress tried to glorify the "unity in diversity" aspect of the Indian nation. The issue of governance received a tacit focus in the Congress manifesto, and it elaborated various scams and scandals of the BJP regime.

The issue of good governance, however, appeared in the BJP's manifesto as well, as a priority agenda for next five years. It talked of various reforms, which also included the strengthening of panchayati raj institutions. The BJP has spelt out, very categorically, its idea of governance. According to the BJP,

> The principal aspect of the Congress misrule was its failure to transform India's hard-won *Swaraj* (self-governance) to *Su-raj* (good governance). It caused the government to enter every sphere of our national life, excessively enlarging the ordinary citizen's interface with the public authority. The overload of the government has led to inefficiency, harassment and corruption.

The party also reaffirmed its commitment to making the role of the government more focused and effective by initiating a set of reforms for good governance with the same priority as allotted to economic reforms. It promised to make the government's interaction with citizens more "people friendly and service-oriented".

In passing, it may be mentioned that some analysts observe a relation between anti-incumbency factor and the issue of 'governance' in explaining election results. In the popular parlance, the average quantity and quality of public services provided by the government to its citizen, normally, is equated with the notion of "good governance". Just as in the case of private goods and services, public has a tendency to identify deterioration of quantity and quality of public goods and services with the failure of government machinery and such negative experience of government performance accentuates with the increasing deterioration of the delivery system of the public utilities. The BJP's idea of good governance talked more of reforms and liberalisation than improvement of the quantitative and qualitative aspects of the public services and their delivery mechanisms. The Congress, however, tacitly stuck to the "popular idea" of governance and attacked BJP on the ground of "deterioration of the delivery of public services" to make it appear as a "failure of the government" before the general public and to make a case for anti-incumbency factor. This provided the rationale for exposing the scams and scandals of the BJP government in "plain and clear language" in the Congress manifesto.

Creation of better infrastructure, problem of flood, insurgency, illegal immigration, fiscal management were some other major issues that got focus in the Congress's manifesto. The party sympathetically considered the problems of tea and ex-tea garden labourers and of various ethnic groups. There were separate sections to deal with the specific development issues of Barak Valley and Hills and Border areas. Issues of employment and social security were also highlighted. It also stressed on adopting a new forest policy and special packages for the welfare of the underprivileged and youths. On the issue of proposed scraping of the IMDT Act, the party maintained its earlier stand and pledged to continue with the Act for the "protection of the religious minorities" from "unnecessary harassments". On the average, the election manifesto of the Congress was found to be a populist but a politically matured and meaningful one. Notable feature of the whole document was that the party tried not only to capitalise on its existing strengths but also, at the same time, tried to expand its support base among all section of the society.

The Left parties, namely the CPI (Communist Party of India) and the CPI (M) (Communist Party of India –Marxists) also released their election manifestos. The CPI State wing, in its election manifesto, highlighted "a few significant issues" of the State within the broad framework of the national agenda of the party. The basic thrust of the national agenda of the party, it seemed, were to "search for an alternative road to internal prosperity" and "to follow an anti-imperialist foreign policy". The State specific issues spelt out in the manifesto were viewed as only "complementary" to those of national ones, nevertheless, all those adequately reflected some of the important regional concerns as well. It raised a few very critical and, in a sense severe, issues like providing special status to Assam under the provisions of the Articles 370 and 371 of the Indian Constitution, to operationalise full federalism in the country, to resolve the border disputes permanently and to declare Assam a tribal State through appropriate legislations. Regarding the issue of IMDT and illegal migration into the State, the manifesto stressed upon detection and deportation of illegal migrants by judicial means. It also talked about photo identity cards for the genuine citizens and renewal of the national citizens list. However, the party categorically mentioned that "controversial clauses of the IMDT act should be amended as per the country's Citizenship Act". Apart from these the issues of insurgency and development also figured in the CPI's manifesto.

The party took a critical stand against both the BJP and the Congress. It emphasised on the need and importance of consolidating the Left forces to fight against the forces of communalism and stagnation. The Left was idealised as an alternative against the status quo and the party promised a just and progressive State.

The critical stand against the BJP was reiterated, even more emphatically, in the manifesto of the CPI (M). The CPI

(M) declared four basic objectives of the party in its manifesto - first, to defeat the BJP and its allies; second, to strengthen the Left force in the politics; third, to give special category status to Assam; and fourth, to form a secular government at the centre. The party had criticised the BJP government at the centre for its failures in various social fronts. The fundamental criticism, however, was the BJP's attempt to create a Hindu State, which the party perceived as a threat to composite Indian nationality and culture. The BJP's economic policies were severely attacked by the party in its manifesto on obvious ideological grounds. The most important aspect of the party's manifesto was that although, the BJP was projected as the main enemy of the party, the party also had maintained some amount of disagreements with the Congress policy as well. In fact, it necessitated the significance of the Left forces for real economic and political liberalisations. Among the major issues, which got prominence in the manifesto of the party, improvement of infrastructure, problem of flood and insurgency, creation of employment for local people and improving the status of various social groups and ethnic communities, including the *char* areas, were important. The basic thrust of the whole document lied in advocating the supremacy of the secular forces over communal forces. Politically, this made the party more aligned towards the Congress than the BJP, which, perhaps, enabled the party to become a partner in the United Progressive Alliance (UPA) led by the Congress.

Can we, then, draw a broad canvas that would eventually capture the basic issues and thrusts of these three major political forces? Loosely speaking, the issues, so surfaced, may be clubbed under four broad heads – security, development, welfare and governance (SDWG). These four, however, are related in some way or other, each having different and complex interconnections with other socio-political issues. Nevertheless, the four dimensional domain, so obtained, may be useful in mapping the regional issues onto it and to examine how far the regional parties are *regional* in reflecting the *regionality* of the political aspirations. The Asom Gana Parishad (AGP), the most important regional party in the State, can be studied carefully for the purpose.

Historically, the AGP emerged out of two supposedly apolitical organisations – All Assam Students' Union (ASSU) and All Assam Gana Sangram Parishad (AAGSP) with its constituents (e.g. AJD and PLP) as a result of the historic Assam Accord way back in 1985, mid October. The central issue, which held together – the organisations, Assam Accord and consequently formation of a regional political party, the AGP – was the illegal foreigners' issue, especially those coming from Bangladesh. The party occupied the seats of power with an overwhelming majority in 1985 Assembly election and ironically lost the very next election held in 1991. It regained power in 1996 and lost again in 2001. Obviously, the cyclical success and failure of the party itself remains an interesting issue for discussion.

The manifesto of the AGP enlisted twelve major issues, viz. federalism and autonomy, development of ethnic communities, creation of a northeast economic zones, rights to state's resources, Assam Accord and IMDT, industrialisation, employment, flood, erosion and river linking, women's right and empowerment, insurgency, tea, and social sector development. Apparently, it is quite possible to map these issues onto the broad national canvas - SDWG with little or no manipulations. Where does then, the *regionality* get reflected?

The answer lies in understanding the "basis of our political society". Renowned economic historian Amalendu Guha writes:

> The functioning of political parties – some of them originating in the colonial days – is much influenced by the geographical factors (such as country's size, cultural plurality etc) as well as its past history. All these work together to create a feeling of unity in diversity. In course of the protected united struggle of the Indian people against the British rule, national consciousness in India developed mainly on a dual basis; simultaneously, at the pan-Indian level, as well as, at the regional levels. These two streams of nationalism, intertwined and dovetailed, provide the basis of our political society today.....
>
> Nonetheless, ours is a bourgeois multi-party system, based on the Western model, functioning in a class divided society. In such a society, the parties, essentially and severally, represent different class interests. While mobilising mass support they make their respective programmes and election manifestos as attractive and inclusive as possible through consensus, compromises and alliances. While the all-India parties generally represent bourgeois landlord interests (as led by monopoly capital) or the worker-peasant interests in essence, the regional parties represent regional middle and small bourgeois as well as the petty bourgeoisie classes (including rich peasants and landlords). However, these class interests, more often than not, are concealed in the declared objectives under camouflage of other labels[12].

The idea of dual nationalism and similarity of dominant class' interests are, in deed, remarkable theoretical formulations. At the time of freedom struggle, the immediate aim of the nationalists was to get rid of the British Raj, all other problems that confronted within the country were to

[12] In the Preface to the book *Class, Ideology and Political Parties in India*, Arun K Jana & Bhupen Sarmah (eds.), (New Delhi: South Asian Publishers Pvt. Ltd., 2002).

be solved later[13]. Hence, the Congress was able to dominate the early periods of independent India's politics. However, successive failure of the party to address those internal conflicts has aggravated the situation and, consequently, the idea of nationality permeated and trickled down – from state to region and from region to community levels. This has led to the feeling that each lower level is being exploited by the higher levels, just like the colonial rule, and things have gradually become more serious and complicated. The very introduction of the election manifesto, released by the AGP, testifies to this fact. It tried to justify the existence of the AGP as a regional party and rejected national parties for the simple reason that they had "exploited the State" over the years in various forms and means. The one-to-one or many-to-one mapping of the regional domain over the national domain is possible under such a situation. The interests of the dominant class rule the mapping or the functional properties and laws between these two domains. Since the power relations remain more or less same in both the domains, which are, in turn, determined by the class relations, inclusiveness of the regional agenda also accommodates the national agenda and vice versa. The regionalism, when seen from this perspective, explains many of the features of the election manifestos discussed above.

Visiting the Public Rhetoric: *Much Ado about Nothing*

The second sphere of issues – issues generated in the public rhetoric – again is an interesting subject of observation and analysis. Apart from mud-slinging and character assassinations, these also surface a few important questions, which invites academic enquiry. Remarkable aspect, as it may appear of it, is the fact that there lies a gulf between

---

[13] Pai Sudha (2002), "Parliamentary Elections in Contemporary India – Breakdown of Dominant Party System and Ascendancy of Regional Parties", in *Class, Ideology and Political Parties in India,* Arun K Jana & Bhupen Sarmah (eds.), (New Delhi: South Asian Publishers Pvt. Ltd., 2002) , P. 68.

the two spheres – one declared (manifestos) and the other one generated (public rhetoric); first one is hardly taken seriously by the people, and the second one is guided by popular perceptions and trends.

Looking at the media reports of the 14th Lok Sabha election in the State, one would see a few dominant topics that occurred and reoccurred in the public discourses during that period. One of them was the speculated AGP-BJP alliance. Both the AGP and BJP were targeting the Congress and such an alliance was thought of as a poll-tactic. There were even views that the proposed alliance from all reckoning could give the "AGP-BJP combine a definite edge" to keep the Congress at bay. Failure to forge such an alliance was termed as "political expediency playing over political wisdom" by a section of media[14].

Uncertainty and confusion about the proposed alliance continued and media kept coming with different versions of interpretations and arguments. The news about the proposed alliance appeared in early February. Reportedly, at the initial phases, the parties were not very keen to forge an alliance. Jagadish Bhuyan, an AGP spokesman, told media that "the AGP will not rely on support from any of the national political parties to send some of its members to parliament". The party, he said would never compromise on the issues, concerning the protection of land, people and resources of Assam[15]. The BJP's position was clear – such an alliance was tried in the assembly election and people rejected that, therefore, there was no reason to go for similar kind of alliances. Wasbir Hussain, in a column, reflects on the issue and talked of BJP's confidence in the party in overthrowing the Congress from the power[16].

The AGP, however, found it difficult to completely do

---

[14] *The Sentinel*, 27th March 2004.
[15] *The Assam Tribune*, 2nd February 2004.
[16] *The Sentinel*, 6th March 2004

away with the idea of an alliance. This was because of the internal dynamics of the party. The faction led by the former Chief Minister Prafulla Kumar Mahanta was all in favour of such an alliance least they feared that non-Congress vote bank would split, which would benefit the Congress. Former AGP top guns like Bhrigu Phukan commented that a regional party should also have a national outlook as well, which might compel it to forge an alliance with national parties[17]. After the initial hick-ups, the AGP thought of "seat sharing arrangements" with the BJP and both the leaderships tried to work out an agreeable formula. There were speculations in the media about an agreeable formula. A section of newspapers flashed the news that seat sharing arrangement had failed for both parties were uncompromising about the Mangaldoi constituency[18].

Amidst much confusion, there was news that the AGP entered a poll-alliance with the newly constituted North East People's Forum (NEPF). The report said that both the parties were keen on forming an alliance to "strengthen the forces of regionalism" in the region, but there were "some differences over certain fundamental issues", which hindered the process. The major issue, as per the report, was the support to NDA government at the Centre. The AGP made it clear that the party was not ready to support the BJP led NDA under any circumstances[19]. Under this backdrop media predicted a BJP-AGP alliance within a very short span of time[20]. Then came the news that the AGP dropped its veil of ambiguity on its strategy for the Lok Sabha election and declared that it was working towards "seat adjustments with the like minded parties for preventing a split in non-Congress votes"[21]. The report went on to explain that the term 'non-

---

[17] *The Sentinel*, 17th February 2004.

[18] *Amar Asom*, 15th February 2004.

[19] *The Sentinel*, 22nd February 2004.

[20] *Dainik Janambhumi*, 4th March 2004.

[21] *The Telegraph*, 7th March 2004.

Congress' could be read as the BJP and they share a common vote base and were keen to keep it intact to prevent the Congress from gaining a leeway.

The prospective alliance came under severe criticism at the hands of the Congress. In a rally held in Guwahati on February 14, the AICC Secretary, Chandan Bagchi, said "BJP is now allying with AGP in Assam, just like they had allied with Trinamool Congress in West Bengal in the previous elections. Like the alliance in West Bengal, they will be wiped out in Assam in the coming elections as well"[22].

Clearly, for the AGP, the 14th Lok Sabha election was a comeback opportunity. The internal crisis and conflicts had already created problems for the party. The internal rift between Prafulla Mahanta, former party President and Chief Minister, and Brindaban Goswami was again becoming a threat for the party. Hence, the leadership issue became so important for the party and the party top brass felt that the success of the party lies in resolving the evident internal crisis. This was revealed in an interview by the AGP Vice-President, Dilip Saikia. He said that in order to keep the AGP alive as a strong regional party, it is imperative that all differences are resolved and the party reinforced confidence in the people's mind[23]. However, the internal rift within the party widened and the factional fight dominated the proceedings of the executive meet of the party held on January 22, 2004, which was supposed to give final shape to the party agenda[24]. The rift continued and Goswami was given the responsibility to head the party in the Tezpur conclave of the party. Unfortunately, he began a cleansing operation against the Mahanta loyalists within the party instead of bridging the gap. Positional security prevailed over political security of the party and the media reacted sharply.

---

[22] *The Sentinel*, 15th February 2004.
[23] *The Sentinel*, 8th January 2004.
[24] *The Sentinel*, 23rd January 2004.

It was reported that a number of powerful AGP leaders had to lose their "otherwise sure berths" in the new executive committee[25].

The AGP was reported to play the "regional card", when it announced its election manifesto[26]. The media had played a conspicuous role in "redefining this regionalism", so to say. There was a kind of "resurgent regionalism" as the media tried to focus during sudden outburst against the Hindi-speaking communities. Similar trend could be observed in certain phenomena like emergence of Asom Sena similar to that of Shivsena in Maharashtra. The media predicted that this attempt at redefining regionalism in Assam would weigh heavily in the AGP's agenda under the stewardship of Mr. Goswami. Noted journalist Gauri Shaṇkar Kalita, in a column, wrote: "one can only wish that Mr. Goswami's wishes were fulfilled – that the AGP will again ride crest of resurgent waves of Assamese regionalism, which will keep all other national parties and players at bay and, which will give every Assamese the identity and sense of belonging unlike today, when the people of Assam feel lost in the pell-mell of the national politics and issues[27]. He also pointed out the changing compulsions of the present political scenario - a strong Bangladeshi lobby with an enormous political influence, centrifugal tendency of the plains tribes to part with the Assamese identity and the depredation by the ULFA – all these was to be taken into consideration in making a political choice. In his words:

> "The concept of regionalism, as it has developed in the mid 1970s, has always been a nebulous one, meaning many things to many people, but essentially aimed at putting the entire blame for the various ills plaguing Assam, on the Centre. ....One can only

[25] *The Sentinel*, 8th February 2004.
[26] *The Telegraph*, 4th April 2004.
[27] *The Sentinel*, 8th February 2004.

wish that Mr. Goswami will come up with a clearer definition of regionalism for Assam before he could expect to believe that it is a new resurgent of regionalism in Assam today….." [28]

The Assam Accord, as always, figured this time too, albeit in a different way. Normally, the IMDT and the issue of illegal migration occupy the centre-stage whenever Assam Accord comes for scrutiny. Both the AGP and BJP tried to use these two cards this time. Both the parties stressed on scrapping the allegedly illegal Act. Launching the party's campaign, BJP leader and the then Prime Minister, Vajpayee, used these two cards. Even the BJP claimed that the AGP has hijacked the IMDT issue from the saffron party[29].

The AGP and the ASSU, on the other hand, tried to capitalise on another issue –the issue of the Gas Cracker. Opposing the centre's decision to go for a fresh viability study regarding the proposed Gas Cracker project, Sarbananda Sonowal, an AGP top liner and the Chief Convenor of the Gas Cracker Sangram Samiti warned about launching a mass agitation, which would rock both "Dispur and Delhi"[30]. Earlier, the AASU had reiterated its uncompromising stand on the issue[31]. The Congress, though, had nothing to say about the issue, the Youth Congress lambasted AASU saying that the AASU had no moral right to blame others on the issue for AASU itself was silent over the issue when the AGP was in power[32].

Another issue that attracted overwhelming media reaction was Bhupen Hazarika joining the BJP. The media immediately got divided into two sides –one supporting Hazarika's move and the other taking a critical stand over

---

[28] *The Sentinel*, 8th February 2004.
[29] *The Sentinel*, 6th April 2004.
[30] *The Telegraph*, 7th March 2004.
[31] *The Assam Tribune*, 7th February 2004.
[32] *The Telegraph*, 13th February 2004.

the issue. Even much before he joined BJP formally, there were speculations in media about Hazarika's joining active politics. It was reported that he might file nomination from Tezpur constituency under the AGP banner[33]. Many viewed his joining BJP as a political move for forging an alliance with the AGP. These speculations were so powerful that Hazarika himself had to offer a clarification regarding his joining the BJP[34].

The tribal population was reported to play a determining role in the forthcoming election. In a newspaper report it was reported that while the Karbis might vote for different parties, most of the Mising population was expected to support the Congress. The Takam Mising Porin Kebang (TMPK) and the Mising Mimag Kebang (MMK) said that they were satisfied with the State government's initiative to form a Mising Autonomous Council under the provision of the Sixth Schedule. A section of the Nepali community, who did not get a proper platform to raise their voices earlier, had announced its support to the AGP[35]. In Karbi Anglong the ASDC and AGP tie was broken due to "betrayal of the ASDC" during the time of Rajya Sabha elections.

Last but not the least, there were two more issues about which much of the media hype could be related. These were "feel good factor" of the BJP and its "India Shining" slogan. Majority of the media reacted to these as pro-urban and pro-rich propaganda. The Congress came down heavily on the BJP alleging that the feel good factor was only for the rich class and the BJP cared only for the rich[36].

It is worth mentioning here that despite all these electoral pell-mell, media also carried a kind of cynicism about the political leadership of the State. The issue of "silent

---

[33] *Dainik Janambhumi*, 25th February 2004.
[34] *Dainik Janambhumi*, 3th March 2004.
[35] *The Sentinel*, 7th April 2004.
[36] *The Telegraph*, 2nd February 2004.

MPs" came into focus on several occasions and the media took a very severe stand on the issue. Inability of the State MPs to handle issues and raise their voices for the sake and interest of the State were publicly criticised[37]. The Sentinel even carried an editorial entitled "Where are our MPs" on February 10, 2004.

Epilogue: *Shifting Political Base*

What is evident then from the foregoing analysis? What can be concluded? The media, as it was observed, picks up, articulates and highlights those issues, which float on the surface. It does not try to penetrate the surface to bring the hardcore, real issues, which lie beneath the surface. As such, media follows a populist trend and serves the purpose of the dominant power and interest groups. The voices of the masses are, often, sidelined and media turns out to be a sounding board of the dominant class. Under such a situation, media fails to be a public reasoning domain, where the issues can be debated, discussed and contested. So long media remains with the dominant power and interest groups, it cannot lead but only follows dominant trends.

There have been signs of shifting social basis of political power in the recent years. In the last decade, starting with the 1990s, there has been increased participation and more intense politicisation of the marginalised social groups. To use the words of Yogendra Yadav "while the urban middle classes were busy bashing the politics and politicians, the democratic space provided by the electoral politics was being used by the socially and politically marginalised"[38]. The meaningful role of the media in forming a public reasoning domain lies in realising the changing political environment of our country and shifting social basis of its political power.

---

[37] *The Sentinel*, 18th January 2004.

[38] Yadav Y, "Elusive Mandate of 2004", *Economic and Political Weekly*, Vol. 39, No. 51, December 18, 2004, p. 5394.

REFERENCES

Amar Asom (2004). February 15.

Chandhoke, N (2000). *State and Civil Society- Explorations in Political Theory*. New Delhi: Sage Publications. p. 163.

__________ (2003). *The Conceits of Civil Society*. New Delhi: Oxford University Press. p. 206.

Dainik Janambhumi (2004). February 25.

Dainik Janambhumi (2004). March 3.

Dainik Janambhumi (2004). March 4.

Indian Printer Publisher. http:/www.indianprinterpublisher.com/aug/archive-i.../ newspaper%20readership%20in%20indian.htm.

Jakubowicz, Karl (2002). "Media in Transition: The Case of Poland" *in* M E Price, B Rozumilowicz and S G Verhulst (eds.) *Media Reform: Democratizing the Media, Democratizing the State*. London: Routledge.

Katyal K K (2004). "Issues and Trends in Indian Elections". *South Asian Journal*. Vol. July-September, No. 5.

McConnell Patrick J and Becker Lee B (2002). "The Role of Media in Democratization". A paper presented at the Political Communication Section of the International Association for Media and Communication Research at the Barcelona Conference, July. Accessed at the website: http://www.portalcomunicacion.com/bcn2002/n_eng/programme/prod_id/asp4.asp?id_pro=1461

Pai, Sudha (2002). "Parliamentary Elections in Contemporary India –Breakdown of Dominant Party System and Ascendancy of Regional Parties" in Arun K Jana & Bhupen Sarmah (eds.) *Class, Ideology and Political Parties in India*. New Delhi: South Asian Publishers Pvt. Ltd. p. 68.

The Assam Tribune (2004). February 2.

The Assam Tribune (2004). February 7.

The Sentinel (2004). January 8.

The Sentinel (2004). January 23.

The Sentinel (2004). February 8.

The Sentinel (2004). February 15.

The Sentinel (2004). February 17.

The Sentinel (2004). February 22.

The Sentinel (2004). March 6.

The Sentinel (2004). March 27.

The Sentinel (2004). April 6.

The Sentinel (2004). April 7.

The Telegraph (2004). January 18.

The Telegraph (2004). February 2.

The Telegraph (2004). February 13.

The Telegraph (2004). March 7.

The Telegraph (2004). April 4.

USAID (1999). "The Role of Media in Democracy: A Strategic Approach", *Centre for Democracy and Governance, Bureau of Global Programs, Field Support, and Research,* Washington, D.C., June.

__________. (2002). n. 2, p. 3.

__________. (2002). n. 3, p. 1.

Yadav, Y (2004). "Elusive Mandate of 2004". *Economic and Political Weekly*. Vol. 39. No. 51, December 18. p. 5394.

CHAPTER 6

The Verdict

Election results are conspicuous and revealing aspects of a political system that is essentially rooted in a democracy. They constitute the climax of the highly dramatized concluding chapter of the entire process of elections bringing sharp relief, insights into the political system and introspection. That is why the act of voting and its consequences are frequently studied. Voting has become more or less a ritual rather than a conscious, informed participants' political action or rational exercise of political choice. It is more so in India in recent times when booth capturing, violent incidents stifling the process of free elections, use of money and muscle power to ensure victory have shaken the very foundation of democracy. Viewed from this angle and induced inputs on poll results floated by the media on the basis of faulty pre-poll surveys, the common voters face the predicament of unending confusion and apprehension till the results are formally announced. The academic community is at bay as the act of voting is no longer a responsible exercise. Nonetheless, the act of voting on the final day of the whole process remains as the central foci of attention for not only those who are real stakeholders but also for the academic community. It is important to see what is the voting turnout, how the voters collectively vote, who wins and why, and what message is thrown to the people which remains valid for a considerable period of time. Voting, after all, is the final act and the dramatic climax of the electoral process, which is multi-staged and highly complex mechanism in a political system. That is why long back Maurice Duverger, in a seminal article, wrote:

> It is obvious that the electoral system must influence political life. The radical changes brought about in the structure of various states by the adoption of universal suffrage or the machinery of arranged elections, for instance, sufficiently indicate the importance of this factor. It is, however, extremely difficult to analyze that influence scientifically. The factors conditioning the political life of a country are closely interrelated, so that any study on the effects of one of those factors considered in isolation is necessarily artificial. All such a study can do is to define tendencies, likely to be influenced by the operation of the other factors.[1]

In the Indian context, as in the case of any democratic country elsewhere, the major premises of an election study is that all national elections are significant and meaningful as they are likely to bring about a major policy change at least at the domestic level. The empirical evidence that is presented in a study to confirm the degree of influence impacted on the political system by election leads one to conclude whether the political system is degenerating towards decay or rejuvenating to development.

The 2004 Lok Sabha election in India, thus, represented elements of continuity as well as change in the Indian electoral behaviour – (i) continuities, exemplified by an unwillingness on the part of the system to force an exit from yet another coalition government at the Centre thereby maintaining the importance of regional parties allied with a major national party, and, (ii) changes, marked by a critical electoral verdict that unseated the BJP led National Democratic Alliance and facilitated the formation of a

[1] Maurice Duverger, "The Influence of the Electoral System on Political Life", *International Social Science Bulletin* II (Summer 1971), p. 314.

Congress led coalition with the parliamentary support of the largest ever contingent of communist parties elected to the Parliament.

The success of the Congress in the 2004 Lok Sabha election, resulting in the return of the Nehru-Indira and Rajiv Gandhi era, seemed a welcome trend for the democratic and secular forces in the country, as observed by the political forces opposed to the BJP-led NDA. However, the results of the 2004 general election proved to be a surprise as the Indian National Congress (INC) obtained the largest share of seats in the Lok Sabha, something beyond expectations and predictions. The INC was able to form a government by securing 35.07 per cent of the vote, winning 145 seats[2], and its main contender, the BJP, obtained 22.94 per cent of the vote, winning138 seats. It is obvious that the new coalition gains and losses, which the Congress and the BJP had in their bags in 2004 compared to 1999 (shown in Table 1) reveals blatant blize that the new coalitions were a Congress gain in totality as it could gain 46 seats more from the new coalition compared to 1999.

Table 6.1

Performance of UPA and NDA (Plus-Minus Alliances)

	Congress and allies (UPA)		***BJP and allies (NDA)***	
	Seats	**Vote per cent**	**Seats**	**Vote per cent**
New allies added in 2004	49	6.32	4	2.53
Alliances of 1999 dropped	3	2.80	31	3.96
Net gain	+46	3.52	-27	-1.43

Source: "Coalition Politics in India: Dynamics of a Winning Combination", Focus on Regional Issues, Vol XXIV, No. 1, 2005, Institute of Regional Studies, Islamabad

[2] The INC did secure the cooperation of several regional and Leftist parties in forming the coalition ministry of minority government called the United Progressive Alliance (UPA).

Observations: State Poll Verdict

BJP'S Inroad into Assam: *From Strength to Strength*

The 1999 Lok Sabha elections in the country, which pronounced the worst debacle for the Congress party in decades, and a more than comprehensive victory for the National Democratic Alliance (NDA), managed to pronounce an unambiguous verdict. In the process, the 13th Lok Sabha elections proved that regional parties, which emerged the ultimate winners in these elections, would determine national politics, in the foreseeable future. It was a matter of fact that it was the composition of the NDA itself that charted the emergence of regional parties as a major force in the country. It was also interesting to find that the largest component of NDA's alliance, the Bharatiya Janata Party, enhanced its character as a national party in some unexpected pockets across the country[3].

In Assam, however, though contrary to the national scenario, the Lok Sabha poll of 1999 sounded the death knell for its regional voice, the Asom Gana Parishad (AGP), the BJP, an admittedly growing party in the region succeeded in drawing the Assamese voters. The BJP gained control of the two most prestigious seats in the State, Nagaon and Guwahati, one an ULFA stronghold, the other, the State capital comprising not only the urban, upper and middle class Assamese and other linguistic groups from across India but the labour class as well.

With this spectacular, albeit marginal inroad that the BJP made into Assam, the party was supposed do well in the region perhaps now looking beyond its North India centric stakes. The BJP's vote percentage in Assam did grow from an unimpressive 15.92 per cent in 1996 to a whopping 29.84 per cent in 1999, securing next to the Congress position

---

[3] The BJP for one was slowly but surely making its presence felt in Northeast India.

of capturing 38 per cent. The winds of change were thus quietly sweeping the beleaguered State. The reasons were well grounded.

(i) Erstwhile urban Assam drenched in regionalism since the late 70s was fast shedding its regional coat. Regional chauvinism, which expressed itself dangerously in anti-Indian sentiments during the Assam agitation, disdained into thin air. Hence enough space, that which was preoccupied with regional chauvinism amidst the masses, was emptied. The BJP with its new vigour succeeded in occupying this empty space.

(ii) The national politics which till yesterday was anathema to the Assamese middle class today has turned into a boon. The disappointed voices of regional chauvinism and as well as the enlightened ones in the State were turning to the BJP[4]. It saw its future and destiny in the national voice articulated by the BJP.

(iii) Having wallowed in the Centre's neglect of its interests for the past two decades, though a late realisation, the "educated Assam" definitely was feeling the lack of representations in that very Centre. This very growing faith on the Centre had been written into the text of the BJP's performance in the State.

(iv) Despite the fact that a substantial immigrant Muslim population dominates the State, BJP's inroad into the State inspite of its "fundamentalist" tag as an alternative national force to the Congress was perhaps because of its stability at the Centre.

---

[4] The ULFA hotbed Nagaon dared to openly vote in favour of this widely acknowledged "nationalist" party the BJP, in the 1999 Lok Sabha poll.

It was but natural that the on the eve of the 2004 Lok Sabha poll, many political observers, therefore, predicted that the Congress and Asom Gana Parishad bastion –Assam, was never under so much threat especially from a national party. Rising strength of the BJP in Assam also made the central committee of the party see gain in the region.

Assam: *The Poll Verdicts*

Table 6.2

Comparative View of the Poll Results of the 13th and the 14th Lok Sabha Polls (Assam)

2004 vs 1999			
Party	***2004***	***1999***	***Gain***
AGP	2	0	2
BJP	2	2	0
CPI (ML)	0	1	-1
INC	9	10	-1
Ind	1	1	0

Source: electionnext.com

In Assam, the Congress won 9 seats, followed by the BJP and the AGP at two each. The BJP repeated its tally of 1999, while the AGP recovered from its 1999 debacle when it won no seats. Amidst these gains and losses of the parties, one constituency of Kokrajhar did stand out where an independent candidate won[5] (Table 3).

[5] However, Sansuma Khunggur Bwiswmuthiary, the independent candidate winning from the constituency with a vote percentage of 71 (6, 89,620), was supported by the Bharatiya Janata Party (BJP). He is credited with the highest victory margin in the State of 4, 84,129 votes. Though the Congress had its candidate contesting from this constituency, the AGP did not field any candidate in the constituency.

Table 6.3
Winners, 2004 Lok Sabha Poll (Assam)

Candidate	*Assembly*	*Electorate Polled*	*Valid Votes Obtained*	*Votes*	*Percentage of Valid Votes*
Bharatiya Janata Party (Assam)					
Rajen Gohain	Nowgong	11,49,244	7,86,069	3,42,704	43.6
Narayan Chandra Borkataky	Mangaldoi	12,09,839	8,48,938	3,45,863	40.74
Asom Gana Parishad (Assam)					
Sarbananda Sonowal	Dibrugarh	9,69,905	6,31,240	2,20,944	35
Arun Kumar Sarma	Lakhimpur	11,26,632	8,00,020	3,00,865	37.61
Indian National Congress (Assam)					
Kirip Chaliha	Gauhati	14,41,360	8,81,775	3,53,250	40.06
Moni Kumar Subba	Tezpur	10,06,389	7,19,768	2,89,847	40.27
Bijoy Krishna Handique	Jorhat	10,78,149	6,66,835	2,23,624	33.54
Santosh Mohan Dev	Silchar	8,79,243	6,08,233	2,46,215	40.48
Biren Singh Engti	Autonomous District	5,79,284	4,01,377	1,25,937	31.38
Anowar Hussain	Dhubri	11,49,939	8,63,592	3,76,588	43.61
A. F. Golam Osmani	Barpeta	10,75,749	7,62,681	2,66,972	35
Dip Gogoi	Kaliabor	11,53,483	7,63,083	3,01,893	39.56
Lalit Mohan Suklabaidya	Karimganj	9,79,105	6,71,491	3,21,059	47.81
Independents (Assam)					
Sansuma Khunggur Bwiswmuthiary	Kokrajhar	12,16,553	9,66,987	6,89,620	71.32

Source: electionnext.com

The Congress' victory was mainly due to a divided opposition, which led to triangular contests in the State. The party's victory, however, was not without its share of defeats. The Congress' evident victory, therefore, has an underlying story. Though the Congress won a majority of the seats, it could secure only 35.07 per cent of votes as compared to 38.42 per cent in 1999. The fall of support by 3.35 per cent went in favour of the AGP in Lakhimpur and Dibrugarh constituencies, where the Congress suffered defeats. The Congress' position among the Hindu upper castes[6] is even worse which comes in third after the AGP. Then, there is a definite erosion of its social base as well, more so the erosion of its support base amongst its traditional supporters, the Dalits and the tribals. The Dibrugarh constituency dominated by the tea garden labourers, a traditional support base of the Congress, where it did not see defeat since the first general elections held in the State in 1952, for the first time lost to the AGP. The AGP succeeded in wresting the seat from the Congress by defeating Paban Singh Ghatowar, the State party President of the Congress. The party's vote share also declined in Assembly segments with substantial numbers of tea garden workers and represented by Ministers such as Sarat Barkataki, Hemoprabha Saikia, Rameswar Dhanowar and Hem Prakash Narayan and Assembly Speaker Prithvi Majhi. Even the Chief Minister, Tarun Gogoi, admitted that the party has failed to realise the erosion of its support base among the tea garden workers and that it has taken for granted its influence among this section of people[7]. The victory margin of the party in the Jorhat constituency, where Bijoy Krishna Handique from

[6] But then this is not much of a surprise, as the Hindu upper castes had long been alienated from the Congress.

[7] The by election necessitated by the death of Congress MLA and Minister Rupam Kurmi, in the Mariani Assembly constituency, yet another constituency dominated by the tea garden workers, where the Congress lost to the NTC shows further erosion of its support base among the tea garden labourers.

the party went on to win was also a low one. It also lost the Mangaldoi constituency, despite the fact that there was increase in the votes in absolute number captured by the Congress candidate. The Congress attributed its defeat in Mangaldoi to the All Bodo Students' Union (ABSU) lending support to the BJP[8]. As the ABSU did not put up a candidate in the constituency in order to extend moral support to the BJP, the division of non-Congress votes was on a smaller scale thus ensuring victory for the BJP. But for these upsets, the Congress was not without its share of successes. The Congress also won the Autonomous District constituency defeating long time MP Dr. Jayanta Rongpi. But the most spectacular victory that stood out for the Congress was its success in defeating Dr. Bhupen Hazarika, the BJP candidate and a popular cultural icon of the State.

The Muslims, officially constituting 31.9 per cent (2001 census) of the State's population, is the only community, which overwhelmingly backs the Congress[9]. The Congress' support base among the minorities remained intact as indicated by the party's victory in the Muslim-dominated seats of Barpeta and Dhubri in lower Assam. In Barpeta, it was A. F. Golam Osmani who won with a vote percentage of 35 and Anowar Hussain from Dhubri won with a vote percentage of 44.

So far the AGP goes, with Brindaban Goswami being elected as the leader of the party, it was deemed that the alliance could have been reviewed and revived in the fast changing political equations in the entire North East. Brindaban Goswami, with his clean image, had been trying to refurbish the party and by being BJP's helping hand at this juncture, it was thought, could strengthen the base for

[8] There is a substance in the assertion of the Congress because the then Union Home Minister L.K. Advani on a number of occasions had been extending the party's support to the idea of a territorial council for the Bodos.

[9] About 66 per cent of the Muslims in Assam support the Congress. Among all other communities, it is the new entrant BJP, which seems to lead the Congress.

a joint strategy and fight to regain the lost ground. The formation of North East People's Forum (NEPF)[10] by Purno A. Sangma had already created the platform for consolidation of anti-Congress and anti Left forces[11] in the region. The AGP[12] dropped the veil of ambiguity on its strategy for the Lok Sabha election and declared that it was working towards seat adjustments with like-minded parties for preventing a split in non-Congress votes. The term "non-Congress" could be read as BJP in political circles as both parties were known to be working behind the scenes. The parties sharing a common vote base were keen to keep it intact to prevent the Congress from gaining any leeway. By sharing pre-poll seat sharing adjustment, it was well thought the AGP-BJP combine could take splintered groups like the ASDC, the NCP and the Samata Party with them to prevent anti-Congress votes split. It was also reported that the Muslims, who count for 35 per cent of the total electorate in the State and preferred Congress in 1999, "are having a second thought this time"[13]. The alliance from the reckoning naturally could give the AGP-BJP combine a definite edge to keep Congress at bay.

Political expediency, however, seemed to have played over political wisdom. The marriage of convenience did not click. The NEPF did not take off at all. The internal bickering within the AGP crippled its strategy. The BJP's choice in Guwahati and Tezpur proved to be wrong. Although the AGP could wrest two seats from the Congress in Lakhimpur and Dibrugarh, its overall performance was still poor with a vote

---

[10] NEPF is a platform, which encompasses the regional parties of Nagaland, Manipur, Meghalaya and Mizoram.

[11] *The Sentinel*, 27th March 2004. Common minimum agenda with burning issues like the IM (DT) Act, infiltration, border fencing, special financial packages for the development of Assam as well as welfare incentives could tilt the balance in favour of the alliance, it was thought.

[12] The Party President, Brindaban Goswami, said that, "We are against joining any national front, but to prevent any split in non-Congress votes we are in favour of fielding combined Opposition candidates against the Congress nominees in as many Lok Sabha seats as possible". *The Telegraph*, 8th March 2005.

[13] *The Sentinel*, 27th March 2004.

share of 20 per cent. Nevertheless, it improved its position. The party, which was completely routed out in the previous two Lok Sabha elections of 1998 and 1999, had reasons to be upbeat with its performance, as it won two important seats by defeating two seating Congress MPs and remaining in the second lead in four other constituencies. The AGP pulled off a surprise when its candidate Sarbananda Sonowal, a former President of the All Assam Students' Union (AASU), won the Dibrugarh seat. On the other hand, the squabbles within the Congress helped the AGP wrest the Lakhimpur seat where its candidate Arun Sarma defeated the sitting Congress MP, Ranee Narah. Therefore, it was happy to show signs of a resurgence of regionalism in the State[14]. This revival of the AGP may be credited to the change in leadership and the return of dissident leaders to its fold. Former minister Dulal Baruah[15] and two-time Congress MP from Karimganj Nepal Das[16] were miffed on being denied tickets to contest Lok Sabha seats from their respective parties. Both joined AGP. A trade union leader, Amarjyoti

---

[14] While the AGP's victory did help party President, Brindaban Goswami, to consolidate his position in the party, it dashed the hopes of Goswami's archrival and former Chief Minister, Prafulla Kumar Mahanta, to stage a comeback. Mahanta's supporters had planned to blame Goswami in the event of the party's defeat in the Lok Sabha poll.

[15] "To them (the BJP Central leadership), we are all ULFA activists or sympathisers of the group. That is the perception they have about us," Baruah, denied a BJP ticket for the Jorhat seat, said. He claimed "outsiders" call the shots in the state unit of the BJP, while local leaders and grassroots-level workers are systematically sidelined. "Many sincere and dedicated BJP functionaries like Union minister of state for water resources, Bijoya Chakrabarty, and senior leaders R.P. Sarma and Romen Deka were deprived of party tickets because money played the crucial role in ticket-distribution." Baruah said the only way to survive in the BJP was to be a "sycophant" and he could not be one. He claimed BJP leaders disliked him because of his"strong voice." *The Sentinel*, 28th March 2004.

[16] Das, who was from the Congress, said corrupt members had shot into prominence in the party at the expense of the honest ones. Singling out social welfare minister Gautam Roy, he said the leader misappropriated funds released by Delhi but was not penalised. He claimed to have personally complained about this to the Chief Minister on several occasions. "Assam does not get its legitimate share of Central funds because of misappropriation of money and lack of initiative on the part of the State government," Das said. *The Sentinel*, 30th March 2004

Tanti, joined the AGP along with them, saying he was "responding to the call by party President, Brindaban Goswami, to all ethnic communities"[17].

The BJP, which banked heavily on the 'Vajpayee factor' and on the music maestro Bhupen Hazarika, failed to achieve anything substantial. Unlike the AGP, the BJP did not succeed in increasing its vote share significantly. Instead its vote share decreased from 29.84 per cent in 1999 to 22.94 per cent in 2004, along with its allies the JD (U) and one independent. It could win only two seats. The party retained the Nagaon seat where its former State president, Rajen Gohain, defeated his nearest rival, the Congress' Bishnu Prasad, and wrested from the Congress the Mangaldoi seat where its candidate Narayan Barkataki, a former State President of the party, defeated the sitting MP Madhab Rajbangshi. But it was a major setback for the party in Guwahati where its candidate Dr. Hazarika, who replaced the sitting MP and Union Minister of State for Water Resources, Bijoya Chakrabarty, was defeated. While Chakrabarty won the seat in 1999 by a margin of 75,238 votes, Hazarika lost to the Congress candidate Kirip Chaliha by 72,849 votes. The results of the polls belied not only the hopes of the party high command of the BJP but also falsified the predictions made by the political observers in the State. There were very little or no gain at all for the BJP in the State in these polls. The party, which was expected to share the honors with the ruling Congress in Assam, thus could win only two seats in the State out of 14. What went wrong for the BJP?

1. BJP's failure in Assam is mainly attributed to the fact that its top leaders misjudged the ground situation. As complacency ventured into the party, the leaders became more relaxed and ignored the popular opinion both in

[17] Newspaper Reports.

the selection of candidates and in campaigning as well. Surprising many, BJP won the prestigious Gauhati Lok Sabha seat in 1999. Bijoya Chakrabarty, the BJP nominee from this constituency was even made a minister in the Vajpayee Ministry. As stated already in Chapter II, to deny the sitting MP with a ministerial berth of the party ticket from the constituency and to nominate eminent singer Dr. Bhupen Hazarika, who joined the BJP only days before the election, was shocking not only to the party workers but also to political observers. The party workers too felt the mood of the electorate who wanted to see Bhupen Hazarika as a singer and a cultural icon, and not as a politician. This not only helped to alienate the general masses in particular but also created faction in the BJP unit of the State.

2. Besides, the common men's verdict did not go with Dr. Hazarika joining a political party. On the eve of joining the party, the balladeer-turned-politician was caught on the wrong foot when he tried to clarify that the BJP had not picked up his name for nomination to the Rajya Sabha at any point of time in the past. Therefore, there was no question of the party having humiliated him by denying him a seat in the Upper House of the Parliament. He sought to dismiss the Rajya Sabha episode as a 'speculation by the media'[18]. But the fact remained that on being denied a place in the Rajya Sabha[19], all the political parties in the Sate came with a proposal of making him a consensus candidate for the next Rajya Sabha election. At that time, Dr. Hazarika however, rejected the proposal, which remained a hard reality.

---

[18] *Political Marriages, Divorce and Patch-ups,* Wasbir Hussain in *The Sentinel,* 6th March 2004.

[19] Dr. Hazarika's name being short-listed for a berth in the Rajya Sabha still seems to be a mystery. Perhaps only Dr. Hazarika and he alone could unveil the reality.

Therefore, it would have been a gain for the BJP, had it utilised the services of Dr. Hazarika in campaigning rather than confining him to Guwahati only and making him a party to some unnecessary controversies.

3. The nomination of Dr. Bhupen Hazarika as the party candidate revealed that the BJP did not realise that Assam was different from mainland India. As seen, in mainland India popular names from other walks of life normally become instant success in the electoral battles. But same is not the case in North East India. Here the electorate is rational enough to weigh the various options before casting their votes. It was not surprising, therefore, that the politically conscious set of minds in Assam failed to realise the rationale behind selecting Dr. Hazarika as the BJP nominee. The candidate who was denied the Rajya Sabha berth from the constituency (of nominated members) a couple of months before the general election, was given the ticket to fight the Lok Sabha poll. This sudden trust of BJP on this noted singer from the region thus roused doubts in the Assamese psyche. Also the BJP made a mistake by overlooking the rightful claim of Bijoya Chakrabarty, as she was most vocal among the BJP leaders in the State against the Tarun Gogoi Government. More aptly than not, therefore, because of the wrong assessment of BJP Central leadership of the situation, Chakrabarty got all the sympathy of the voters and Bhupen Hazarika was left to fight a lost battle from the very beginning.

4. BJP leadership was to be blamed for this fiasco. Beyond doubt, the entry of Dr. Hazarika was a shot in the arm for the party. But the party could not get maximum dividends because of its faulty policies. The factor, which went against the BJP, was its failure to observe the coalition mantra. It's a fact that the coalition era will continue in India for sometime. The BJP's rise to power

is also because of coalition politics. But strangely, the BJP, the major partner of National Democratic Alliance (NDA) did not show any respect to people's opinion in Assam before the election. It overlooked the suggestions of electoral ties with the Asom Gana Parishad (AGP) as well.

5. The party did not enter into any electoral understanding with Purno Sangma-led North East People's Forum (NEPF). The BJP's decision not to have an understanding with the NEPF is perplexing to say the least. Despite being a member of the said forum, the BJP backed out at the eleventh hour. P.A. Sangma through that forum tried to bring all non-Congress parties under one umbrella. But because of BJP's stubbornness Sangma's dream remained unfulfilled.
6. The BJP committed another grave mistake by nominating G.L. Agarwal for the Tezpur constituency, and thereby deprived Ram Prasad Sharma, a local person having grassroots connections. Agarwal, an outsider, had no local base and proved to be a very weak candidate against the sitting MP Mani Kumar Subba. It was quite evident that the BJP lost the support of the local grassroots workers who were with Sharma. It was almost a carbon copy mistake that the party committed in Guwahati and Tezpur.

Elections and Other Voices: *Heat and Misses*

In a democracy, on a decisive plane, where the voice of the majority always counts, the minorities too who at most times than not are banked for a concrete result cannot be completely sidelined. These voices of the majority and minorities generating heat, at times have their way but at many times there are misses too.

The students' organisations in Assam, as elsewhere in the country, have been a force which has time and again since the late 70s raised its voice in all fields, politics being one of them. The growth of a regional society in Assam ending in a more encompassing and liberal one, has all throughout, seen the growth of a vociferous All Assam Students' Union (AASU). The AASU has been representing the general masses of the State as the 'other voice', a non-political voice of the general people in the political arena. The AASU was not a silent spectator for the 14th Lok Sabha poll either. On the eve of the poll, the All Assam Students' Union (AASU) set forth a questionnaire[20] for political parties and candidates in the State to spell out how they would tackle the burning issues confronting the State.

1. The student body asked all political parties to clarify their plan of action for the implementation of the Assam Accord signed in 1985 and sealing of the Indo-Bangladesh border to check infiltration.
2. Besides, the parties were also asked to say where they stood on the issue of 100 per cent reservation of seats in elected bodies like panchayats, local bodies, the State Assembly and Parliament and jobs for the indigenous Assamese.

The questionnaire, however, did not receive the desired response from the political arena of the State. Parties like the Congress, the BJP and the AGP refused answering the questions on having already spelled out their stand on these issues in their election manifestos.

The State unit of the Jamiat Ulema-e-Hind, 'other voice' of the minority Muslims in the State too had its role cut out in the elections. But the role cut out, though for a short period, seemed to move in a new direction for the first time in the

---

[20] The AASU President, Prabin Boro, and adviser, Samujjal Kumar Bhattacharyya, who released an 18-point questionnaire detailing the issues, said that the student body would launch a massive campaign throughout the State to publicise it.

State. It had discussions for pre-poll negotiations both with the AGP and the Congress in the State. Although no serious differences were listed between the Jamiat and the AGP even on the IM (DT) issue[21], it is a different issue altogether that both failed to come to a settlement. Maintaing its tradition[22], it then went on to support the Congress (I) candidates after a discussion with Gogoi, and, the All India Congress Committee (I) observer for Assam and former Madhya Pradesh Chief Minister, Digvijay Singh. The Jamiat's support worked to the Congress (I)'s advantage, as the former was influential with a large section of Muslim voters, particularly the immigrant settlers of the Chars of Brahmaputra.

No wonder that the Jamiat went with the Congress but the fact remains that there was a drift, a drift away from Congress to support AGP in the Lok Sabha poll. Why was this sudden volte-face after decades of friendship with the Congress?

1. For one, the Assam State Congress refused to give nomination to Mahmud Madani, General Secretary of Jamiat Ulema, for the Rajya Sabha seat.

---

[21] A Jamiat spokesman made it clear that, they have no obsession with the IM (DT) issue and if the Act is amended in a "perfect manner", safeguarding the rights of the minority citizens, then there would be nothing to complain about. In the detection of the foreigners' the judicial procedure should be adopted, he asserted. The Jamiat even went a step further and declared that it had no objection on 1971 as the cut-off year for detection of the foreigners in Assam, which the AGP also agreed with, and also agreed that identity cards could be distributed to start with in order to hammer out the controversy. *The Sentinel*, 27th March 2004.

[22] Congress leadership, a Hindutva mouthpiece alleged, is a slave to Muslim vote bank. This is more true in the context of Assam. Congress has been at the citadel of power in the state since Independence except for a decade, due mainly to its brazen appeasement policy towards the religious minority. And behind this consolidation of Muslim votes, Jamiat Ulema-e-Hind has played an influential role to ensure the victory of Congress in the Assembly and Parliamentary elections. As observed by Jyoti Lal Chowdhury in *Statescan*, "Assam: Why is Jamiat Ulema Sore with Congress?", Organiser, April 11th 2004, http://www.organiser.org.

2. Two, Tarun Gogoi did not buckle under constant pressure of Jamiat to induct more ministers out of the 24 Muslim community MLAs in the State out of which 2 are from AGP and 21 from the Congress. In spite of the fact that there are three cabinet rank and five ministers of State in Gogoi's ministry from the Muslim minority community, Jamiat accused Tarun Gogoi of not giving sufficient representation to the Muslim community in the State. Jamiat also regretted that Tarun Gogoi had not taken any effective steps to fulfill its pressing and pending demands which included constitution of a Minority Commission of Assam as well as a Wakf Tribunal, giving rights and pattas to the inhabitants of Char areas and allotment of four per cent of the State plan fund for the development, streamlining the functioning of the Assam Minority Development and Finance Corporation, release of adequate funds for modernisation of madrassas, and, expeditious implementation of the relief and rehabilitation packages for the victims of ethnic violence of Kokrajhar and Bongaigaon.
3. Three, a representation of twenty four Muslim representatives in the Assam Assembly is supposedly more than enough to give the Jamiat the voice to declare that the Congress is alive in the State on the strength and support of the Muslims in 35 Assembly seats. Based on this demographic structure, Jamiat Ulema went on to demand Congress tickets for Muslim candidates in all the 35 Muslim majority constituencies for the next Assembly poll. The Congress knowing well the ramification of this demand preferred to sideline it.

The raptures, therefore, being evident, leave space for new settlements in future polls.

Post 2004 Lok Sabha Polls and Ensuing Assembly Election 2006: *The Equations*

Down the years, despite diverse patterns of Panchayat

elections and a certain conflict among various levels of representation, the entire system from Parliament down to panchayats in India has been one from the point of view of the ruling classes' attempt at legitimising and strengthening their class rule. One must strictly maintain the principle of keeping parliamentary practice subservient to extra-parliamentary politics. It is said elections are about numbers. Just as the BJP and the AGP cannot take its numerical losses in the 2004 poll casually, they may not like to ignore the symbolic gains that these elections have provided the parties with to recast its policies, agendas and coalitions. Though on a winning spree with an eroding social base among the tea-garden workers and with a shaky Muslim vote bank, the Congress too needs to revise its policies.

The motto that one sees so far is "cross the bridge when it comes". The tea tribes having over 52 lakh population and capable of determining the outcome in at least 35 Assembly seats are unhappy with the Congress because of the growing number of sick tea gardens, poor pay package and related deteriorating health care system, and, also on the non-fulfillment of their demand of allotting the Schedule Tribe status. Not to be left far behind, therefore, this strong support base of the Congress is all out to shift its allegiance from the Congress to others or form a new regional party of its own[23]. The powerful Jamiat-Ulema-e-Hind national President, Maulana Asad Madani, also has threatened to overthrow the Tarun Gogoi-led Congress government if its 18-point demands, including the reservation in jobs for Muslims and the reservation of seats for Assembly and Lok Sabha polls, are not fulfilled[24]. As over 80 lakh Muslims in the State are capable of determining the outcome in at least 30 of the total 126 Assembly seats, the Congress needs to think hard. The

---

[23] The All Assam Tea Tribes Students Association has already decided to float a regional party.

[24] *The Assam Tribune*, 4th April 2005.

latest development in the Muslim politics in the State appears to be uncomfortable for the Congress. After the Supreme Court had declared the IM(DT) Act unconstitutional, the Jamiat leadership started its vociferous campaign against the Tarun Gogoi Government accusing its complacency in the court case on the IM(DT) and thereby indirectly allowing the case to be easily won by the petitioner. With a strong feeling of being betrayed, the Jamiat has not only decided to discontinue supporting the Congress but has also launched a new regional party called the United Democratic Front (UDF) headed by Badaruddin Ajmal. The new development is likely to cause heavy erosion in the Congress. The United Minority Front also has decided to join the new political entrant. As for the present, though the new Front is not likely to extend any support to the BJP but its formation itself might draw the Hindu sentiments strongly towards the BJP.

Another powerful tribal outfit, the All Bodo Students' Union, has also floated a regional outfit the Bodoland Peoples Progressive Front (BPPF). The Bodos are decisive in at least 12 Assembly seats in the State. The Koch-Rajbangshi, another ethnic group, is also in a mood to form its own outfit. Does this signal towards formation of new regional forces divided on ethnic lines and, therefore, the re-emergence of regionalism in a new plane in Assam?

On its part, the AGP has already organised conventions involving the Muslims and the tea tribes. But which one is the real AGP? The split in the party posed uncomfortable questions among the sympathizers and grassroots workers. While the Brindaban fraction claims to be the real one, the Mahanta fraction known as AGP (Progressive) leaves no stone unturned to call it the origin AGP and claims the election symbol. The BJP too is making inroads into the tea tribe vote bank of the Congress.

The battle lines for next Assembly election are yet to be

drawn, but the political parties in Assam have already unleashed a verbal battle. With the Assembly election, 2006 round the corner, it seems that while the BJP and the Congress will fight the election on their own strength without forging any alliance with the regional or the national parties, however, the two factions of the AGP led by Brindaban Goswami and Prafulla Kumar Mahanta have no option but to go for alliances with regional and national parties considering their fragile positions after the vertical split. Infact, both seem to be eyeing to having it with the United Democratic Front, which has been formed recently comprising mostly leaders of Jamiat and immigrant Muslims. It appears that the Congress too is going to face a tough challenge in the 2006 election, neither because that the BJP is stronger than before nor because any regional outfit is challenging its strongholds, but because of the possibility of erosion in its support base among the immigrant Muslim community and the tea garden community. Analysts say the Bangladeshi immigration issue invariably gathers momentum ahead of polls in Assam - an emotive issue that political parties try to cash in on. But with the IM(DT) Act being done away with, the forthcoming Assembly poll can be altogether a different game. Elections are after all a game of all possibilities and uncertainties. The last minute equation and strategy can upset any foreseen trend and predictions of psephologists.

REFERENCES

Chowdhury, Jyoti Lal (2004). "Assam: Why is Jamiat Ulema Sore with Congress?". *Statescan,* Organiser. April 11. http://www.organiser.org.

Duverger, Maurice (1971). "The Influence of the Electoral System on Political Life". *International Social Science Bulletin* II. Summer. p. 314.

Hussain, Wasbir (2004). "Political Marriages, Divorce and Patch-ups". *The Sentinel,* March 6.

Institute of Regional Studies (2005). "Coalition Politics in India: Dynamics of a Winning Combination". *Focus on Regional Issues.* Vol XXIV, No. 1. Islamabad. www.irs.org.pk.

The Assam Tribune (2005). April 4.

The Sentinel (2004). March 27.

The Telegraph (2005). March 8.

Appendix 1.A
Assam Parliamentary Constituencies

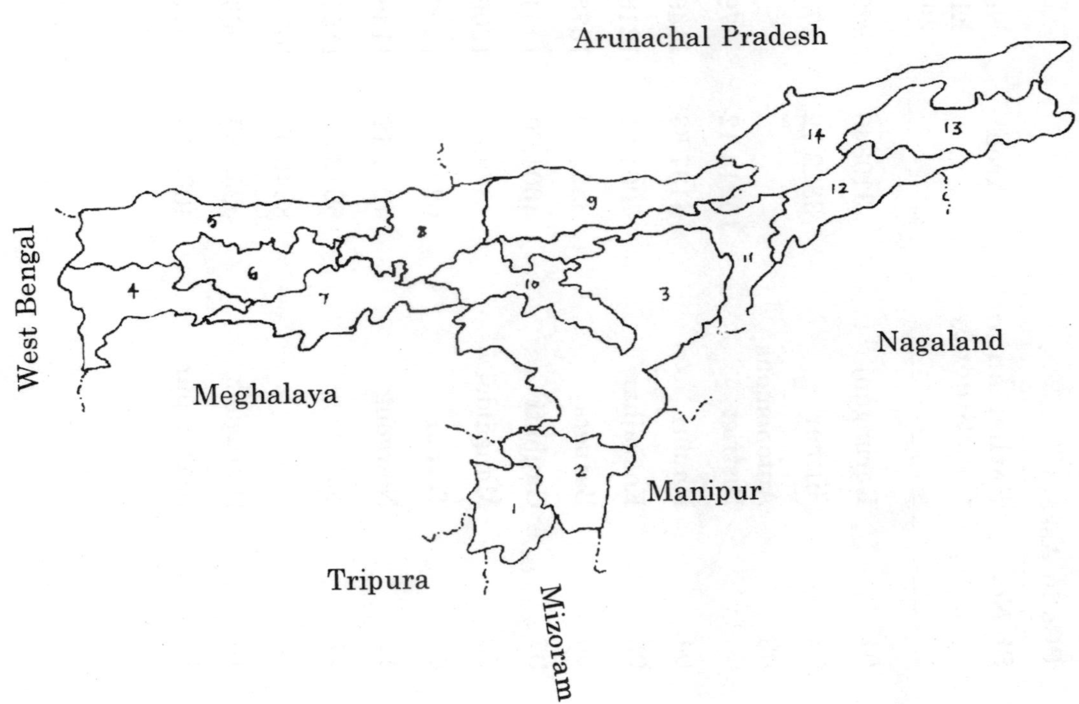

Appendix 1.B

PCs in Assam

Sl. No.	Parliamentary Constituency	Area	No. of Electors 2004
01	Karimganj	319840	979105
02	Silchar	3822.72	879243
03	Autonomous District	15214.12	579284
04	Dhubri	4137.83	1149939
05	Kokrajhar	7061.81	1216553
06	Barpeta	3593.39	1075749
07	Gauhati	4601.26	1441360
08	Mangaldoi	4329.65	1209839
09	Tezpur	6235.83	1006389
10	Nowgong	4064.12	1149244
11	Kaliabor	5012.53	1153483
12	Jorhat	8346.93	1078149
13	Dibrugarh	5259.89	969905
14	Lakhimpur	4003.16	11266.32

Appendix 2.A
Assam Parliamentary Constituencies, 2004

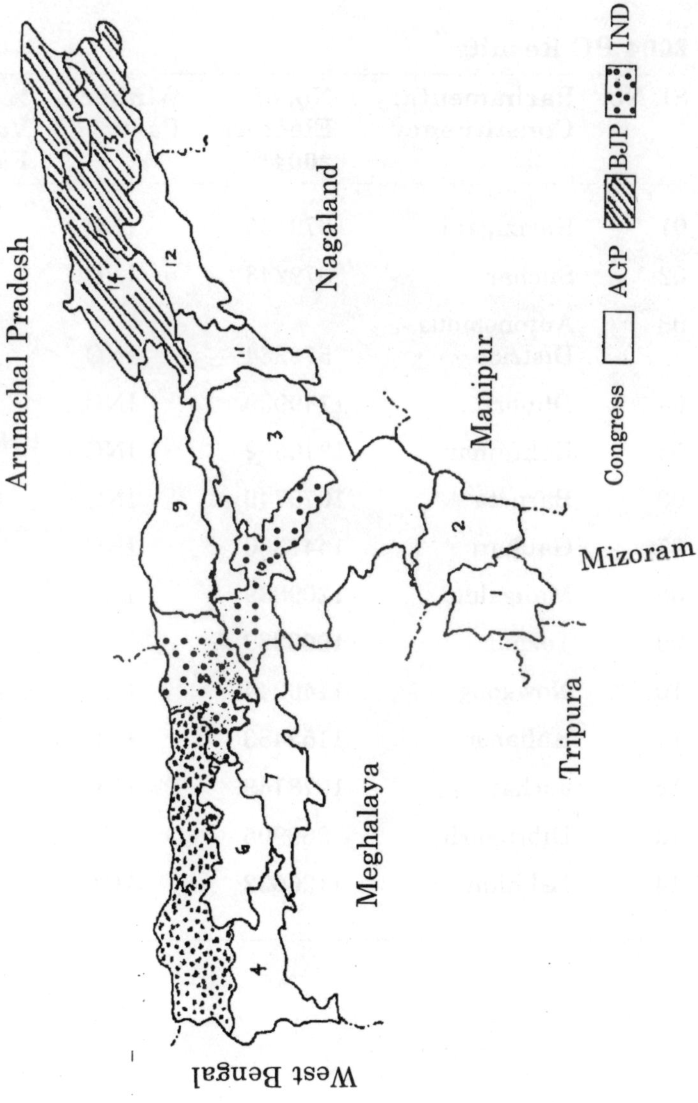

Appendix 2.B

2004 PC Results

Sl. No.	Parliamentary Constituency	No. of Electors 2004	Winner Party	% of Votes in Favour
01	Karimganj	979105	INC	47.81
02	Silchar	879243	INC	55.54
03	Autonomous District	579284	INC	31.38
04	Dhubri	1149939	INC	43.61
05	Kokrajhar	1216553	INC	71.32
06	Barpeta	1075749	INC	35.00
07	Gauhati	1441360	INC	40.06
08	Mangaldoi	1209839	BJP	40.74
09	Tezpur	1006389	INC	40.27
10	Nowgong	1149244	INC	43.6
11	Kaliabor	1153483	INC	39.56
12	Jorhat	1078149	INC	33.54
13	Dibrugarh	969905	AGP	35.00
14	Lakhimpur	1126632	AGP	37.61

Appendix 3.A
Assam Parliamentary Constituencies, 1999

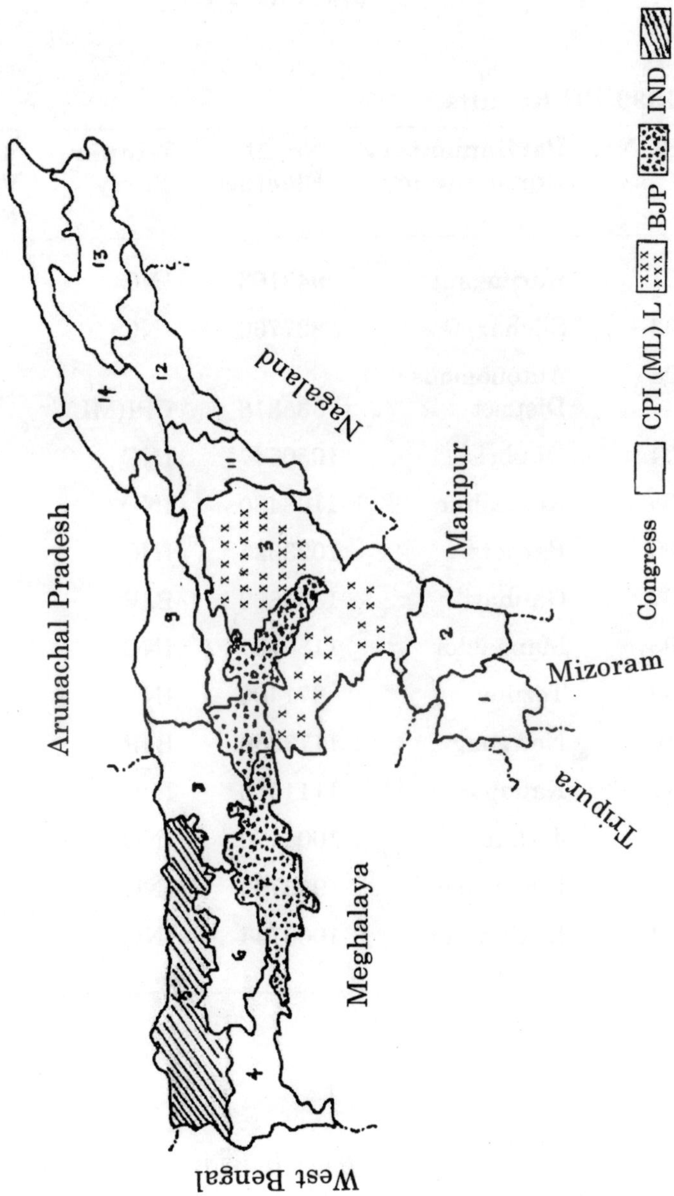

Appendix 3.B

1999 PC Results

Sl. No.	Parliamentary Constituency	No. of Electors	Winner Party	% of Votes in Favour
01	Karimganj	943163	INC	49.55
02	Silchar	827760	INC	40.48
03	Autonomous District	535818	CPI(ML)	53.98
04	Dhubri	1050547	INC	34.58
05	Kokrajhar	1168480	IND	37.57
06	Barpeta	1023625	INC	43.20
07	Gauhati	1354869	BJP	45.95
08	Mangaldoi	1180131	INC	34.09
09	Tezpur	971406	INC	34.09
10	Nowgong	1113339	BJP	43.17
11	Kaliabor	1111536	INC	49.23
12	Jorhat	1003470	INC	48.31
13	Dibrugarh	945785	INC	48.57
14	Lakhimpur	1060744	INC	34.41

Appendix 4
Assam Assembly Constituencies

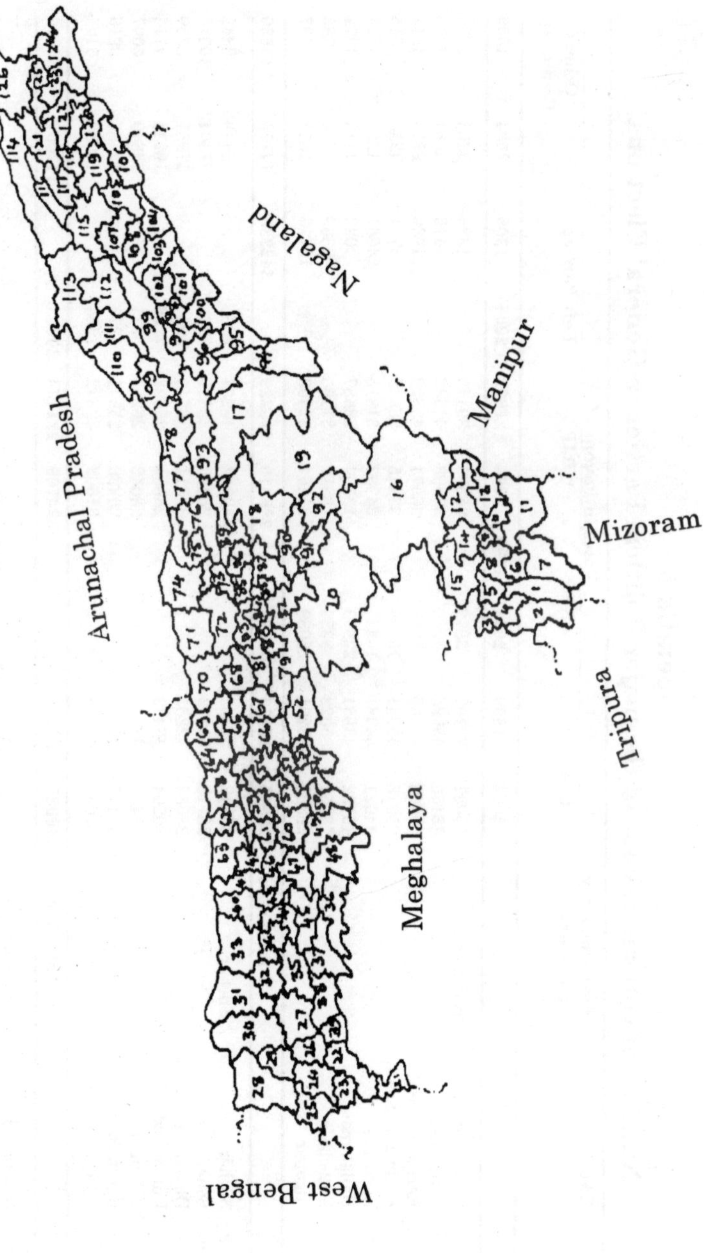

Appendix 5

Number of votes in favour of the major Political Parties in General Elections

Sl.No.	LAC Name	Parliamentary Constituency	Votes in Favour of: Congress		AGP		BJP		Left Parties		Others Combined	
			2004	**1999**	**2004**	**1999**	**2004**	**1999**	**2004**	**1999**	**2004**	**1999**
1	Ratabari(SC)	Karimganj	25087	28197	3976		36568	39119		1486	2303	3234
2	Patharkandi		43155	48098	4900		37898	41532		1416	3284	1268
3	Karimganj(North)		39662	48165	7856		36974	49829		1782	2115	1611
4	Karimganj(South)		25878	45641	19920		33815	36649		4751	1253	3515
5	Badarpur		34921	34381	10347		24983	31815		4681	1285	1321
6	Hailakandi		45782	43931	22993		18804	33687		4022	1112	1371
7	Katlichera		78052	55022	8393		18317	31195		2380	1604	763
8	Algapur		28308	33201	28089		21451	32403		13718	1814	797
		Total Votes	**320845**	**336636**	**106474**		**228810**	**296229**		**342236**	**14770**	**13880**
9	Silchar	Silchar	35112	51562			49032	46267	2855		15439	3842
10	Sonai		36713	51672			25449	26830	2072		27364	10315
11	Dholai		28083	42861			38011	36711	3086		17987	6016
12	Udharbond		30204	46449			28884	26622	2299		16233	4716
13	Lakhipur		41481	48212			26042	26251	3831		13649	6007
14	Barkhola		32447	41026			25429	25811	3277		14485	6016
15	Katigora		42045	47199			31862	32642	2583		11930	5164
		Total Votes	**246085**	**328981**			**224709**	**221134**	**20003**		**117087**	**42076**
16	Halflong(ST)	Autonomous District (ST)	25063	32614	582		14888		8005	25619	25149	6587
17	Bokajan(ST)		19772	23992	733		6893		19409	40016	20563	5092

(Contd...)

			2004	1999	2004	1999	2004	1999	2004	1999	2004	1999
18	Howraghat(ST)		23547	24610	508		8808		15766	42305	20126	1587
19	Diphu(ST)		28527	34452	903		12688		20932	48191	29388	7183
20	Baithalangsho(ST)		28963	33173	1020		14168		10253	52599	44356	8598
		Total Votes	**125872**	**148841**	**3746**		**57445**		**74365**	**208730**	**139582**	**290478**
21	Mankachar	Dhubri	37847	19744	22261		4122	10687		22253	34267	34864
22	Salmara South		43386	35638	26139		618	5255		1590	12302	28077
23	Dhubri		44679	41859	19040		11952	34428		3254	11599	4765
24	Gauripur		41634	39466	40829		5975	41263		2095	8411	6527
25	Golakganj		41785	31093	9098		28572	47347		8302	14136	2076
26	Bilasipara(West)		37821	24407	16515		2301	18243		5235	15477	26132
27	Bilasipara(East)		47735	27811	38250		7427	38752		8285	6249	19313
37	Goalpara(East)		40319	33741	17939		18059	42916		4463	13092	15274
38	Goalpara(West)		18108	11198	32210		7756	19747		1157	16257	38451
39	Jaleswar		23229	14849	37653		3414	9727		1098	5000	37561
		Total Votes	**376543**	**279806**	**259934**		**90196**	**268365**		**57732**	**136790**	**213040**
28	Gossaingaon	Kokrajhar	3812	10230							110543	93078
29	Kokrajhar(West)		2432	5434							107875	96850
30	Kokrajhar(East)		926	4851							116283	97420
31	Sidli(ST)		5411	11149							112172	109348
33	Bijni		4621	4228							72842	65986
40	Sorbhog		17422	10178							72056	76729
41	Bhabanipur		12213	3997							54821	58899
58	Tamulpur		4746	7266							98605	91128
62	Barama		7824	647							69121	64273
63	Chapaguri(ST)		1971	1441							91199	82207
		Total Votes	**61398**	**65231**							**905517***	**835918****

(Contd...)

			2004	1999	2004	1999	2004	1999	2004	1999	2004	1999
32	Bongaigaon	Barpeta	15975	9849	40759		20586	37611	4833	29692	4262	2442
34	Abhayapuri(North)		28075	28772	28315		8274	10705	5018	31446	9148	4037
35	Abhayapuri(South)		30511	32823	26790		18564	28412	1641	17715	11267	7052
42	Patacharkuchi		7343	6647	15939		22180	42067	5427	9554	7356	1878
43	Barpeta		33783	41533	21384		12348	43885	2898	4103	22623	8949
44	Jania		37250	62136	5689		2618	4970	9283	6081	27081	6420
45	Baghbor		37290	46052	7619		1206	2076	3251	3264	15288	11116
46	Sarukhetri		23607	41286	8456		11732	31033	11088	12263	30978	3691
47	Chenga		27386	37306	15618		6139	14646	3443	5751	7232	4325
61	Dharmapur		25740	19390	28266		7381	20959	1723	21346	1951	823
		Total Votes	**266960**	**325794**	**198835**		**111028**	**236364**	**48605**	**141215**	**137186**	**50733**
56	Kamalpur	Mangaldoi	23740	24183	13254	7980	37032	41693			2597	2453
57	Rangiya		26312	26137	17396	13188	40270	35258			3374	14516
59	Nalbari		26677	23158	21427	17605	33087	41646			3480	2355
64	Paneri		22179	18344	5866	4858	42368	17977			4425	31614
65	Kalaigaon		27330	24439	19053	14664	34372	27531			4752	18348
66	Sipajhar		31925	30829	24203	34661	21870	18012			3277	873
67	Mangaldoi(ST)		47111	42403	24017	23831	29353	30395			5379	4046
68	Dalgaon		63474	38255	6988	29562	24669	17425			4429	9915
69	Udalguri(ST)		20527	28746	5737	2278	53091	16623			3858	29211
70	Majbat		26652	27200	8113	6016	29677	20652			5400	13282
		Total Votes	**315927**	**283694**	**146054**	**154643**	**345789**	**267212**			**40971**	**126613**
36	Dudhnoi(ST)	Gauhati	36287	28790	6262	7758	32291	37530			11986	9827
48	Boko(SC)		48105	48153	22085	19660	17377	17390			7977	4320
49	Chaygaon		39068	39402	34525	25534	5805	9680			3709	1962
50	Palasbari		23698	19656	25515	23487	16315	24366			4073	803
51	Jalukbari		46107	25248	15596	3503	25637	50039			2570	969

(Contd...)

			2004	1999	2004	1999	2004	1999	2004	1999	2004	1999
52	Dispur		32603	28085	14338	8427	53657	69980			10205	2239
53	Gauhati(East)		21771	17252	12257	4588	48815	56853			3372	1130
54	Gauhati(West)		25883	20848	19503	10484	46447	54501			4244	1148
55	Hajo		24851	30853	22741	13083	24316	31220			2946	666
60	Barkhetri		54859	51191	8025	2483	21391	32927			4484	1018
		Total Votes	**353232**	**309478**	**180847**	**119007**	**292051**	**384486**			**55566**	**24082**
79	Jagiroad	Nowgong	36754	29668	15139	16378	43344	47507			3553	4543
80	Morigaon		30225	25560	4943	9177	44869	37069			2629	8020
81	Laharighat		42955	42848	4554	6496	27164	23185			2510	2487
86	Nowgong		30805	30480	12997	10624	36869	34835			2573	2088
87	Barhampur		24140	22856	12904	17113	38235	36327			2939	2050
90	Jamunamukh		38564	37219	23030	23028	13729	12744			2872	3338
91	Hojai		38903	36469	8577	9685	55638	56238			4657	2551
92	Lumding		29968	31033	9673	3459	39712	36813			2720	5983
		Total Votes	**272314**	**256133**	**91817**	**95960**	**299560**	**284718**			**24453**	**31060**
71	Dhekiajuli	Tezpur	27856	26829	21517	15099	24866	27413	1836		2912	6597
72	Barchalla		30851	21914	20667	14356	20317	30757	1579		1946	3517
73	Tezpur		28427	21104	27607	10302	20332	35238	1261		1253	2265
74	Rangapara		33083	32688	16666	15852	23269	22816	2938		2884	4755
75	Sootea		40263	24511	39350	47013	5798	11650	2006		2159	2230
76	Biswanath		35414	27367	30317	33980	11851	14117	2003		2792	2762
77	Behali		20740	19030	7742	13687	23047	17489	8777		3558	9797
78	Gohpur		47681	39494	31230	32589	16041	18015	3192		2671	4635
109	Bihpuria		25444	17914	24194	20201	19091	27600	1001		1077	1435
		Total Votes	**289759**	**230851**	**219290**	**203079**	**164612**	**205095**	**24593**		**21252**	**37993**

(Contd...)

			2004	1999	2004	1999	2004	1999	2004	1999	2004	1999
83	Dhing	Kaliabor	40632	69098	11026	10255		5012			38331	2169
84	Batadroba		27912	38451	16163	11092		20476			28912	1144
85	Rupohihat		29494	52233	12235	19331		9437			43026	1695
88	Samaguri		36986	32717	22893	17226		21619			18039	702
89	Kaliabor		18026	20286	37100	27443		18313			12107	986
93	Bokakhat		25212	30693	14215	19992		12678			22742	842
94	Sarupathar		34325	40320	43071	34722		26177			27853	1270
95	Golaghat		38080	34606	25650	26006		19899			12798	697
96	Khumtai		20833	24624	19104	17047		14518			11846	1078
97	Dergaon		30331	30490	33166	23024		19177			10823	1103
		Total Votes	**301831**	**373518**	**234623**	**206138**		**167306**			**226477**	**11686**
99	Majuli	Lakhimpur	27311	18564	33914	20020	7178	15688			1850	14608
110	Naoboicha		34277	46036	28934	18406	24452	23560			6601	3913
111	Lakhimpur		25940	25356	34366	23279	17952	24240			4919	10434
112	Dhakuakhana(ST)		43342	25877	30637	22838	20480	21166			5226	22656
113	Dhemaji(ST)		33610	25053	47767	33996	20990	27169			8265	14668
114	Jonai(ST)		56897	18713	51117	29895	14529	26474			5153	28705
121	Chabua		15104	32138	25898	24246	23219	12601			7129	1393
125	Doomdooma		15349	37340	13975	6752	25383	17153			10000	1275
126	Sadiya		20804	26808	34119	22616	14879	16374			8150	4304
		Total Votes	**272634**	**255885**	**300727**	**202048**	**169062**	**184425**			**57293**	**101956**
115	Moran	Dibrugarh	21241	32211	29449	12288	13256	13166	549	326	2457	96
116	Dibrugarh		14141	20570	18308	3840	28757	32822	556	371	1590	143
117	Lahowal		12838	34350	27605	5678	19391	14842	2235	309	4014	195
118	Duliajan		17441	29420	28500	7268	23367	25571	778	235	3089	480
119	Tingkhong		18823	28542	38455	11488	13645	18439	1129	1003	3045	120

(Contd...)

			2004	1999	2004	1999	2004	1999	2004	1999	2004	1999
120	Naharkatia		18147	28517	28955	12279	16790	20703	917	482	2674	215
122	Tinsukia		19067	27116	15036	6970	32637	30734	1581	717	3288	310
123	Digboi		19489	28836	14700	4801	22637	23055	1011	888	3193	233
124	Margherita		29394	41279	19870	11311	31881	24374	1086	688	4123	330
		Total Votes	**170581**	**270841**	**220878**	**75923**	**202361**	**203706**	**9842**	**5019**	**27473**	**2122**
98	Jorhat	Jorhat	24780	18541	21355	14030	17482	36451	11199		1416	515
100	Titabor		23982	26811	14124	25223	9384	13676	16390		3321	172
101	Mariani		15481	27317	6520	9279	18284	21157	17801		4224	236
102	Teok		22462	24288	8275	10690	12915	20312	13896		2183	177
103	Amguri		25442	30346	20266	17233	7267	12155	13123		2220	113
104	Nazira		17134	36493	1758	7019	8763	15185	35245		2549	301
105	Mahmara		20255	34360	8482	9159	16591	18381	15766		2854	177
106	Sonari		33978	52148	3412	5170	30695	27609	11040		5400	247
107	Thowra		15169	26544	5296	11178	17086	13459	12960		2256	175
108	Sibsagar		24917	27731	3834	9159	11315	26687	24873		1283	412
		Total Votes	**223600**	**304579**	**93322**	**118140**	**149782**	**205072**	**172293**		**27706**	**2525**

Includes 689597 votes of Sansuma Khunggur Bwiswmuthiary (winner contestant)

Appendix 6
Share of votes in favour of the major Political Parties in General Elections,1999 and 2004 (LAC wise)

Sl.No.	LAC Name	Parliamentary Constituency	Votes in Favour of									
			Congress		AGP		BJP		Left Parties		Others Combined	
			2004	1999	2004	1999	2004	1999	2004	1999	2004	1999
1	Ratabari(SC)	Karimganj	36.93	39.14	5.85		53.83	54.30		2.06	3.39	4.49
2	Patharkandi		48.36	52.10	5.49		42.47	44.99		1.53	3.68	1.37
3	Karimganj(North)		45.80	47.51	9.07		42.69	49.15		1.76	2.44	1.59
4	Karimganj(South)		32.00	50.40	24.63		41.82	40.47		5.25	1.55	3.88
5	Badarpur		48.82	47.62	14.46		34.92	44.07		6.48	1.80	1.83
6	Hailakandi		51.62	52.92	25.92		21.20	40.58		4.85	1.25	1.65
7	Katlichera		73.38	61.57	7.89		17.22	34.91		2.66	1.51	0.85
8	Algapur		35.54	41.44	35.26		26.93	40.44		17.12	2.28	0.99
		Total Votes	**47.82**	**49.43**	**15.87**		**34.10**	**43.50**		**5.03**	**2.20**	**2.04**
9	Silchar	Silchar	34.28	50.71			47.87	45.51	2.79	0.00	15.07	3.78
10	Sonai		40.08	58.18			27.78	30.21	2.26	0.00	29.87	11.61
11	Dholai		32.22	50.08			43.61	42.89	3.54	0.00	20.64	7.03
12	Udharbond		38.91	59.71			37.21	34.22	2.96	0.00	20.91	6.06
13	Lakhipur		48.80	59.91			30.64	32.62	4.51	0.00	16.06	7.46
14	Barkhola		42.90	56.31			33.62	35.43	4.33	0.00	19.15	8.26
15	Katigora		47.55	55.52			36.03	38.40	2.92	0.00	13.49	6.07
		Total Votes	**40.48**	**55.55**			**36.97**	**37.34**	**3.29**	**0.00**	**19.26**	**7.11**

(Contd...)

			2004	1999	2004	1999	2004	1999	2004	1999	2004	1999
16	Halflong (ST)	Autonomous District (ST)	34.01	50.31	0.79		20.20	0.00	10.86	39.52	34.13	10.16
17	Bokajan (ST)		29.35	34.72	1.09		10.23	0.00	28.81	57.91	30.52	7.37
18	Howraghat (ST)		34.25	35.93	0.74		12.81	0.00	22.93	61.76	29.27	2.32
19	Diphu (ST)		30.86	38.35	0.98		13.73	0.00	22.64	53.65	31.79	8.00
20	Baithalangsho (ST)		29.33	35.15	1.03		14.35	0.00	10.38	55.74	44.91	9.11
		Total Votes	**31.39**	**38.50**	**0.93**		**14.33**	**0.00**	**18.54**	**53.99**	**34.81**	**7.51**
21	Mankachar	Dhubri	38.42	22.55	22.60		4.18	12.21		25.42	34.79	39.82
22	Salmara South		52.62	50.51	31.70		0.75	7.45		2.25	14.92	39.79
23	Dhubri		51.20	49.65	21.82		13.70	40.84		3.86	13.29	5.65
24	Gauripur		42.99	44.17	42.16		6.17	46.18		2.34	8.68	7.30
25	Golakganj		44.65	35.01	9.72		30.53	53.31		9.35	15.10	2.34
26	Bilasipara(West)		52.45	32.97	22.90		3.19	24.65		7.07	21.46	35.31
27	Bilasipara(East)		47.90	29.54	38.38		7.45	41.16		8.80	6.27	20.51
37	Goalpara(East)		45.10	35.00	20.06		20.20	44.52		4.63	14.64	15.85
38	Goalpara(West)		24.36	15.87	43.33		10.43	27.99		1.64	21.87	54.50
39	Jaleswar		33.52	23.48	54.34		4.93	15.38		1.74	7.22	59.40
		Total Votes	43.61	34.17	30.10		10.45	32.77		7.05	15.84	26.01
28	Gossaingaon	Kokrajhar	3.33	9.90							96.67	90.10
29	Kokrajhar(West)		2.20	5.31							97.80	94.69
30	Kokrajhar(East)		0.79	4.74							99.21	95.26
31	Sidli(ST)		4.60	9.25							95.40	90.75
33	Bijni		5.97	6.02							94.03	93.98
40	Sorbhog		19.49	11.71							80.51	88.29
41	Bhabanipur		18.22	6.35							81.78	93.65
58	Tamulpur		4.59	7.38							95.41	92.62
62	Barama		10.17	9.13							89.83	90.87
63	Chapaguri(ST)		2.12	1.72							97.88	98.28
		Total Votes	**6.35**	**7.24**							**93.65**	**92.76**

(Contd...)

			2004	1999	2004	1999	2004	1999	2004	1999	2004	1999
32	Bongaigaon	Barpeta	18.49	12.37	47.17		23.82	47.25	5.59	37.30	4.93	3.07
34	Abhayapuri(North)		35.61	38.38	35.92		10.50	14.28	6.37	41.95	11.60	5.39
35	Abhayapuri(South)		34.37	38.17	30.18		20.91	33.04	1.85	20.60	12.69	8.20
42	Patacharkuchi		12.61	11.05	27.37		38.08	69.94	9.32	15.88	12.63	3.12
43	Barpeta		36.31	42.18	22.98		13.27	44.57	3.11	4.17	24.32	9.09
44	Jania		45.47	78.05	6.94		3.20	6.24	11.33	7.64	33.06	8.06
45	Baghbor		57.68	73.67	11.78		1.87	3.32	5.03	5.22	23.65	17.78
46	Sarukhetri		27.49	46.77	9.85		13.66	35.16	12.91	13.89	36.08	4.18
47	Chenga		45.78	60.14	26.11		10.26	23.61	5.76	9.27	12.09	6.97
61	Dharmapur		39.56	31.02	43.45		11.34	33.52	2.65	34.14	3.00	1.32
		Total Votes	**35.01**	**43.20**	**26.07**		**14.56**	**31.34**	**6.37**	**18.73**	**17.99**	**6.73**
56	Kamalpur	Mangaldoi	30.98	31.69	17.30	10.46	48.33	54.64			3.39	3.21
57	Pangiya		30.12	29.33	19.91	14.80	46.10	39.57			3.86	16.29
59	Nalbari		31.51	27.32	25.31	20.77	39.08	49.13			4.11	2.78
64	Paneri		29.64	25.20	7.84	6.67	56.61	24.70			5.91	43.43
65	Kalaigaon		31.96	28.76	22.28	17.26	40.20	32.40			5.56	21.59
66	Sipajhar		39.28	36.54	29.78	41.08	26.91	21.35			4.03	1.03
67	Mangaldoi(ST)		44.50	42.12	22.69	23.67	27.73	30.19			5.08	4.02
68	Dalgaon		63.75	40.20	7.02	31.07	24.78	18.31			4.45	10.42
69	Udalguri(ST)		24.67	37.40	6.89	2.96	63.80	21.63			4.64	38.01
70	Majbat		38.16	40.51	11.62	8.96	42.49	30.76			7.73	19.78
		Total Votes	**37.22**	**34.09**	**17.21**	**18.58**	**40.74**	**32.11**			**4.83**	**15.21**
36	Dudhnoi(ST)	Gauhati	41.79	34.31	7.21	9.25	37.19	44.73			13.80	11.71
48	Boko(SC)		50.35	53.79	23.12	21.96	18.19	19.43			8.35	4.83
49	Chaygaon		47.01	51.45	41.54	33.34	6.98	12.64			4.46	2.56
50	Palasbari		34.05	28.77	36.66	34.38	23.44	35.67			5.85	1.18
51	Jalukbari		51.28	31.66	17.35	4.39	28.51	62.74			2.86	1.21

(Contd...)

			2004	1999	2004	1999	2004	1999	2004	1999	2004	1999
52	Dispur		29.42	25.83	12.94	7.75	48.43	64.36			9.21	2.06
53	Gauhati(East)		25.25	21.61	14.22	5.75	56.62	71.22			3.91	1.42
54	Gauhati(West)		26.94	23.97	20.30	12.05	48.34	62.66			4.42	1.32
55	Hajo		33.20	40.69	30.38	17.25	32.48	41.18			3.94	0.88
60	Barkhetri		61.81	58.42	9.04	2.83	24.10	37.58			5.05	1.16
		Total Votes	**40.06**	**36.97**	**20.51**	**14.22**	**33.12**	**45.93**			**6.30**	**2.88**
79	Jagiroad	Nowgong	37.20	30.24	15.32	16.70	43.87	48.43			3.60	4.63
80	Morigaon		36.56	32.02	5.98	11.50	54.28	46.44			3.18	10.05
81	Laharighat		55.65	57.12	5.90	8.66	35.19	30.91			3.25	3.32
86	Nowgong		37.01	39.06	15.61	13.62	44.29	44.64			3.09	2.68
87	Barhampur		30.86	29.17	16.50	21.84	48.88	46.37			3.76	2.62
90	Jamunamukh		49.32	48.76	29.45	30.17	17.56	16.70			3.67	4.37
91	Hojai		36.10	34.75	7.96	9.23	51.62	53.59			4.32	2.43
92	Lumding		36.51	40.15	11.79	4.48	48.39	47.63			3.31	7.74
		Total Votes	**39.57**	**38.35**	**13.34**	**14.37**	**43.53**	**42.63**			**3.55**	**4.65**
71	Dhekiajuli	Tezpur	35.27	35.33	27.24	19.88	31.48	36.10	2.32		3.69	8.69
72	Barchalla		40.94	31.06	27.42	20.35	26.96	43.60	2.10		2.58	4.99
73	Tezpur		36.04	30.63	35.00	14.95	25.78	51.14	1.60		1.59	3.29
74	Rangapara		41.96	42.95	21.14	20.83	29.51	29.98	3.73		3.66	6.25
75	Sootea		44.95	28.70	43.93	55.05	6.47	13.64	2.24		2.41	2.61
76	Biswanath		42.99	34.98	36.80	43.44	14.39	18.05	2.43		3.39	3.53
77	Behali		32.48	31.72	12.12	22.81	36.09	29.15	13.74		5.57	16.33
78	Gohpur		47.30	41.69	30.98	34.40	15.91	19.02	3.17		2.65	4.89
109	Bihpuria		35.93	26.68	34.17	30.08	26.96	41.10	1.41		1.52	2.14
		Total Votes	**40.27**	**34.10**	**30.48**	**30.00**	**22.88**	**30.29**	**3.42**		**2.95**	**5.61**

(Contd...)

			2004	1999	2004	1999	2004	1999	2004	1999	2004	1999
83	Dhing	Kaliabor	45.15	79.85	12.25	11.85	0.00	5.79			42.60	2.51
84	Batadroba		38.24	54.03	22.15	15.59	0.00	28.77			39.61	1.61
85	Rupohihat		34.80	63.16	14.44	23.38	0.00	11.41			50.77	2.05
88	Samaguri		47.47	45.27	29.38	23.84	0.00	29.92			23.15	0.97
89	Kaliabor		26.81	30.26	55.18	40.94	0.00	27.32			18.01	1.47
93	Bokakhat		40.55	47.80	22.87	31.14	0.00	19.75			36.58	1.31
94	Sarupathar		32.61	39.34	40.92	33.88	0.00	25.54			26.46	1.24
95	Golaghat		49.76	42.61	33.52	32.02	0.00	24.50			16.72	0.86
96	Khumtai		40.23	43.00	36.89	29.77	0.00	25.35			22.88	1.88
97	Dergaon		40.81	41.32	44.63	31.20	0.00	25.99			14.56	1.49
		Total Votes	**39.56**	**49.23**	**30.75**	**27.17**	**0.00**	**22.05**			**29.69**	**1.54**
99	Majuli	Lakhimpur	38.88	26.95	48.27	29.07	10.22	22.78			2.63	21.21
110	Naoboicha		36.36	50.09	30.69	20.03	25.94	25.63			7.00	4.26
111	Lakhimpur		31.19	30.44	41.32	27.94	21.58	29.10			5.91	12.52
112	Dhakuakhana(ST)		43.48	27.96	30.73	24.68	20.54	22.87			5.24	24.48
113	Dhemaji(ST)		30.38	24.83	43.18	33.70	18.97	26.93			7.47	14.54
114	Jonai(ST)		44.56	18.03	40.03	28.80	11.38	25.51			4.04	27.66
121	Chabua		21.17	45.66	36.30	34.45	32.54	17.90			9.99	1.98
125	Doomdooma		23.72	59.72	21.60	10.80	39.23	27.44			15.45	2.04
126	Sadiya		26.69	38.24	43.77	32.26	19.09	23.36			10.46	6.14
		Total Votes	**34.09**	**34.38**	**37.60**	**27.15**	**21.14**	**24.78**			**7.16**	**13.70**
115	Moran	Dibrugarh	31.73	55.45	43.99	21.15	19.80	22.67	0.82	0.56	3.67	0.17
116	Dibrugarh		22.32	35.62	28.90	6.65	45.39	56.84	0.88	0.64	2.51	0.25
117	Lahowal		19.43	62.03	41.77	10.25	29.34	26.80	3.38	0.56	6.07	0.35
118	Duliajan		23.83	46.72	38.95	11.54	31.93	40.61	1.06	0.37	4.22	0.76
119	Tingkhong		25.06	47.90	51.21	19.28	18.17	30.94	1.50	1.68	4.05	0.20

(Contd...)

			2004	1999	2004	1999	2004	1999	2004	1999	2004	1999
120	Naharkatia		26.89	45.85	42.91	19.74	24.88	33.29	1.36	0.77	3.96	0.35
122	Tinsukia		26.63	41.18	21.00	10.59	45.58	46.67	2.21	1.09	4.59	0.47
123	Digboi		31.93	49.88	24.09	8.30	37.09	39.88	1.66	1.54	5.23	0.40
124	Margherita		34.04	52.93	23.01	14.50	36.92	31.26	1.26	0.88	4.77	0.42
		Total Votes	**27.03**	**48.57**	**35.00**	**13.62**	**32.06**	**36.53**	**1.56**	**0.90**	**4.35**	**0.38**
98	Jorhat	Jorhat	32.51	26.66	28.01	20.18	22.93	52.42	14.69		1.86	0.74
100	Titabor		35.69	40.70	21.02	38.29	13.96	20.76	24.39		4.94	0.26
101	Mariani		24.85	47.11	10.46	16.00	29.34	36.48	28.57		6.78	0.41
102	Teok		37.61	43.79	13.85	19.27	21.62	36.62	23.26		3.65	0.32
103	Amguri		37.24	50.71	29.66	28.80	10.64	20.31	19.21		3.25	0.19
104	Nazira		26.18	61.85	2.69	11.90	13.39	25.74	53.85		3.89	0.51
105	Mahmara		31.67	55.35	13.26	14.75	25.94	29.61	24.65		4.46	0.29
106	Sonari		40.20	61.23	4.04	6.07	36.31	32.41	13.06		6.39	0.29
107	Thowra		28.75	51.69	10.04	21.77	32.38	26.21	24.56		4.28	0.34
108	Sibsagar		37.63	43.34	5.79	14.31	17.09	41.71	37.56		1.94	0.64
		Total Votes	**33.54**	**48.32**	**14.00**	**18.74**	**22.47**	**32.53**	**25.84**		**4.16**	**0.40**

Appendix 7

Number of votes in favour of Contesting Candidates AC wise, 14th Lok Sabha poll, 2004

Name of the AC	Party	Candidate	Votes in Favour
	Autonomous District (ST) Parliamentary Constituency		
Halflong (ST)			
	CPI (ML) (L)	Dr. Jayanta Rongpi	8005
	INC	Biren Singh Engti	25063
	BJP	Ratan Teron	14888
	AGP	Sailendra Hasnu	582
	ASDC	Elwin Teron	14691
	SAP	Harsing Teron	437
	IND	Chember G. Momin	471
	IND	Sanmoni Kemprai	9550
Bokajan (ST)			
	CPI (ML) (L)	Dr. Jayanta Rongpi	19409
	INC	Biren Singh Engti	19772
	BJP	Ratan Teron	6893
	AGP	Sailendra Hasnu	733
	ASDC	Elwin Teron	15292
	SAP	Harsing Teron	523
	IND	Chember G. Momin	2456
	IND	Sanmoni Kemprai	2292

(Contd...)

Name of the AC	Party	Candidate	Votes in Favour
Howraghat (ST)	CPI (ML) (L)	Dr. Jayanta Rongpi	15766
	INC	Biren Singh Engti	23547
	BJP	Ratan Teron	8808
	AGP	Sailendra Hasnu	508
	ASDC	Elwin Teron	16858
	SAP	Harsing Teron	493
	IND	Chember G. Momin	771
	IND	Sanmoni Kemprai	2004
Diphu (ST)	CPI (ML) (L)	Dr. Jayanta Rongpi	20932
	INC	Biren Singh Engti	28527
	BJP	Ratan Teron	12688
	AGP	Sailendra Hasnu	903
	ASDC	Elwin Teron	19934
	SAP	Harsing Teron	626
	IND	Chember G. Momin	696
	IND	Sanmoni Kemprai	8132
Baithalangsho (ST)	CPI (ML) (L)	Dr. Jayanta Rongpi	10253
	INC	Biren Singh Engti	28963
	BJP	Ratan Teron	14168
	AGP	Sailendra Hasnu	1020

(Contd...)

Name of the AC	Party	Candidate	Votes in Favour
	ASDC	Elwin Teron	34976
	SAP	Harsing Teron	1098
	IND	Chember G. Momin	3608
	IND	Sanmoni Kemprai	4674
		Barpeta Parliamentary Constituency	
Bongaigaon	AGP	Kumar Deepak Das	40759
	INC	A.F.Golam Osmani	15975
	CPM	Manoranjan Talukdar	4833
	BJP	Ranjit Thakuria	20586
	UMFA	Abdus Samad Ahmed	1209
	LJNSP	Abdus Salam	342
	SP	Syed Nurur Rohman	299
	IND	Jilane Hoque Laskar	357
	IND	Dr.Tara Prasad Das	2055
Abhayapuri (North)	AGP	Kumar Deepak Das	28315
	INC	A.F.Golam Osmani	28075
	CPM	Manoranjan Talukdar	5018
	BJP	Ranjit Thakuria	8274
	UMFA	Abdus Samad Ahmed	6938
	LJNSP	Abdus Salam	287

(Contd...)

Name of the AC	Party	Candidate	Votes in Favour
	SP	Syed Nurur Rohman	217
	IND	Jilane Hoque Laskar	234
	IND	Dr.Tara Prasad Das	1472
Abhayapuri (South)	AGP	Kumar Deepak Das	26790
	INC	A.F.Golam Osmani	30511
	CPM	Manoranjan Talukdar	1641
	BJP	Ranjit Thakuria	18564
	UMFA	Abdus Samad Ahmed	8173
	LJNSP	Abdus Salam	428
	SP	Syed Nurur Rohman	303
	IND	Jilane Hoque Laskar	308
	IND	Dr.Tara Prasad Das	2055
Patacharkuchi	AGP	Kumar Deepak Das	15939
	INC	A.F.Golam Osmani	7343
	CPM	Manoranjan Talukdar	5427
	BJP	Ranjit Thakuria	22180
	UMFA	Abdus Samad Ahmed	845
	LJNSP	Abdus Salam	489
	SP	Syed Nurur Rohman	230
	IND	Jilane Hoque Laskar	218
	IND	Dr.Tara Prasad Das	5574

(Contd...)

Name of the AC	Party	Candidate	Votes in Favour
Barpeta	AGP	Kumar Deepak Das	21384
	INC	A.F.Golam Osmani	33783
	CPM	Manoranjan Talukdar	2898
	BJP	Ranjit Thakuria	12348
	UMFA	Abdus Samad Ahmed	6671
	LJNSP	Abdus Salam	629
	SP	Syed Nurur Rohman	302
	IND	Jilane Hoque Laskar	359
	IND	Dr.Tara Prasad Das	14662
Jania	AGP	Kumar Deepak Das	5689
	INC	A.F.Golam Osmani	37250
	CPM	Manoranjan Talukdar	9283
	BJP	Ranjit Thakuria	2618
	UMFA	Abdus Samad Ahmed	17276
	LJNSP	Abdus Salam	773
	SP	Syed Nurur Rohman	377
	IND	Jilane Hoque Laskar	294
	IND	Dr.Tara Prasad Das	8361
Baghbor	AGP	Kumar Deepak Das	7619
	INC	A.F.Golam Osmani	37290
	CPM	Manoranjan Talukdar	3251

(Contd...)

Name of the AC	Party	Candidate	Votes in Favour
	BJP	Ranjit Thakuria	1206
	UMFA	Abdus Samad Ahmed	8137
	LJNSP	Abdus Salam	763
	SP	Syed Nurur Rohman	406
	IND	Jilane Hoque Laskar	323
	IND	Dr.Tara Prasad Das	5659
Sarukhetri	AGP	Kumar Deepak Das	8456
	INC	A.F.Golam Osmani	23607
	CPM	Manoranjan Talukdar	11088
	BJP	Ranjit Thakuria	11732
	UMFA	Abdus Samad Ahmed	2733
	LJNSP	Abdus Salam	1296
	SP	Syed Nurur Rohman	482
	IND	Jilane Hoque Laskar	438
	IND	Dr.Tara Prasad Das	26029
Chenga	AGP	Kumar Deepak Das	15618
	INC	A.F.Golam Osmani	27386
	CPM	Manoranjan Talukdar	3443
	BJP	Ranjit Thakuria	6139
	UMFA	Abdus Samad Ahmed	727
	LJNSP	Abdus Salam	408

(Contd...)

Name of the AC	Party	Candidate	Votes in Favour
	SP	Syed Nurur Rohman	266
	IND	Jilane Hoque Laskar	226
	IND	Dr.Tara Prasad Das	5605
Dharmapur	AGP	Kumar Deepak Das	28266
	INC	A.F.Golam Osmani	25740
	CPM	Manoranjan Talukdar	1723
	BJP	Ranjit Thakuria	7381
	UMFA	Abdus Samad Ahmed	361
	LJNSP	Abdus Salam	168
	SP	Syed Nurur Rohman	137
	IND	Jilane Hoque Laskar	181
	IND	Dr.Tara Prasad Das	1104
Dhubri Parliamentary Constituency			
Mankachar			
	INC	Anwar Hussain	37847
	AGP	Afzalur Rahman	22261
	BJP	Jabeen Borbhuyan	4122
	MUL	Mohor Uddin Mondal	285
	IND	Gandhi Nath	617
	IND	Dr. Jayashree Goswami Mahanta	3145

(Contd...)

Name of the AC	Party	Candidate	Votes in Favour
	IND	Dr.Motiur Rahman Mondal	24768
	IND	Minhar Ali Mandal	15094
	IND	Radhaballav Adhikary	391
	IND	Listi Rabha	403
	IND	Shajahan Sheikh	3064
South Salmara	INC	Anwar Hussain	43386
	AGP	Afzalur Rahman	26139
	BJP	Jabeen Borbhuyan	618
	MUL	Mohor Uddin Mondal	238
	IND	Gandhi Nath	477
	IND	Dr. Jayashree Goswami Mahanta	1095
	IND	Dr.Motiur Rahman Mondal	6698
	IND	Minhar Ali Mandal	1906
	IND	Radhaballav Adhikary	276
	IND	Listi Rabha	305
	IND	Shajahan Sheikh	1307
Dhubri	INC	Anwar Hussain	44679
	AGP	Afzalur Rahman	19040
	BJP	Jabeen Borbhuyan	11952
	MUL	Mohor Uddin Mondal	344
	IND	Gandhi Nath	648

(Contd...)

Name of the AC	Party	Candidate	Votes in Favour
	IND	Dr. Jayashree Goswami Mahanta	1529
	IND	Dr.Motiur Rahman Mondal	6183
	IND	Minhar Ali Mandal	354
	IND	Radhaballav Adhikary	568
	IND	Listi Rabha	377
	IND	Shajahan Sheikh	1596
Gauripur	INC	Anwar Hussain	41634
	AGP	Afzalur Rahman	40829
	BJP	Jabeen Borbhuyan	5975
	MUL	Mohor Uddin Mondal	272
	IND	Gandhi Nath	326
	IND	Dr. Jayashree Goswami Mahanta	876
	IND	Dr.Motiur Rahman Mondal	1866
	IND	Minhar Ali Mandal	275
	IND	Radhaballav Adhikary	1707
	IND	Listi Rabha	1840
	IND	Shajahan Sheikh	1249
Golakganj	INC	Anwar Hussain	41785
	AGP	Afzalur Rahman	9098
	BJP	Jabeen Borbhuyan	28572
	MUL	Mohor Uddin Mondal	700

(Contd...)

Name of the AC	Party	Candidate	Votes in Favour
	IND	Gandhi Nath	519
	IND	Dr. Jayashree Goswami Mahanta	1654
	IND	Dr.Motiur Rahman Mondal	1425
	IND	Minhar Ali Mandal	449
	IND	Radhaballav Adhikary	7295
	IND	Listi Rabha	516
	IND	Shajahan Sheikh	1578
Bilasipara (West)	INC	Anwar Hussain	37821
	AGP	Afzalur Rahman	16515
	BJP	Jabeen Borbhuyan	2301
	MUL	Mohor Uddin Mondal	370
	IND	Gandhi Nath	485
	IND	Dr. Jayashree Goswami Mahanta	8794
	IND	Dr.Motiur Rahman Mondal	3369
	IND	Minhar Ali Mandal	315
	IND	Radhaballav Adhikary	368
	IND	Listi Rabha	383
	IND	Shajahan Sheikh	1393
Bilasipara (East)	INC	Anwar Hussain	47735
	AGP	Afzalur Rahman	38250
	BJP	Jabeen Borbhuyan	7427

(Contd...)

Name of the AC	Party	Candidate	Votes in Favour
	MUL	Mohor Uddin Mondal	371
	IND	Gandhi Nath	491
	IND	Dr. Jayashree Goswami Mahanta	1047
	IND	Dr. Motiur Rahman Mondal	1064
	IND	Minhar Ali Mandal	314
	IND	Radhaballav Adhikary	644
	IND	Listi Rabha	662
	IND	Shajahan Sheikh	1656
Goalpara (East)	INC	Anwar Hussain	40319
	AGP	Afzalur Rahman	17939
	BJP	Jabeen Borbhuyan	18059
	MUL	Mohor Uddin Mondal	412
	IND	Gandhi Nath	446
	IND	Dr. Jayashree Goswami Mahanta	2426
	IND	Dr.Motiur Rahman Mondal	689
	IND	Minhar Ali Mandal	491
	IND	Radhaballav Adhikary	592
	IND	Listi Rabha	6560
	IND	Shajahan Sheikh	1476
Goalpara (West)	INC	Anwar Hussain	18108
	AGP	Afzalur Rahman	32210

(Contd...)

Name of the AC	Party	Candidate	Votes in Favour
	BJP	Jabeen Borbhuyan	7756
	MUL	Mohor Uddin Mondal	297
	IND	Gandhi Nath	354
	IND	Dr. Jayashree Goswami Mahanta	1206
	IND	Dr.Motiur Rahman Mondal	615
	IND	Minhar Ali Mandal	1442
	IND	Radhaballav Adhikary	451
	IND	Listi Rabha	10848
	IND	Shajahan Sheikh	1044
Jaleswar	INC	Anwar Hussain	23229
	AGP	Afzalur Rahman	37653
	BJP	Jabeen Borbhuyan	3414
	MUL	Mohor Uddin Mondal	244
	IND	Gandhi Nath	322
	IND	Dr. Jayashree Goswami Mahanta	536
	IND	Dr.Motiur Rahman Mondal	537
	IND	Minhar Ali Mandal	418
	IND	Radhaballav Adhikary	278
	IND	Listi Rabha	1934
	IND	Shajahan Sheikh	731

(Contd...)

Name of the AC	Party	Candidate	Votes in Favour
Dibrugarh Parliamentary Constituency			
Moran	BJP	Kamakhya Tasa	13256
	INC	Paban Singh Ghatowar	21241
	AGP	Sarbananda Sonowal	29449
	CPI (ML) (L)	Subhas Sen	549
	SAP	Titus Bhengra	487
	IND	Amrit Borgohain	637
	IND	Badhram Rajgarh	1333
Dibrugarh	BJP	Kamakhya Tasa	28757
	INC	Paban Singh Ghatowar	14141
	AGP	Sarbananda Sonowal	18308
	CPI (ML) (L)	Subhas Sen	556
	SAP	Titus Bhengra	306
	IND	Amrit Borgohain	416
	IND	Badhram Rajgarh	868
Lahowal	BJP	Kamakhya Tasa	19391
	INC	Paban Singh Ghatowar	12838
	AGP	Sarbananda Sonowal	27605
	CPI (ML) (L)	Subhas Sen	2235

(Contd...)

Name of the AC	Party	Candidate	Votes in Favour
	SAP	Titus Bhengra	781
	IND	Amrit Borgohain	800
	IND	Badhram Rajgarh	2433
Duliajan	BJP	Kamakhya Tasa	23367
	INC	Paban Singh Ghatowar	17441
	AGP	Sarbananda Sonowal	28500
	CPI (ML) (L)	Subhas Sen	778
	SAP	Titus Bhengra	550
	IND	Amrit Borgohain	663
	IND	Badhram Rajgarh	1876
Tingkhong	BJP	Kamakhya Tasa	13645
	INC	Paban Singh Ghatowar	18823
	AGP	Sarbananda Sonowal	38455
	CPI (ML) (L)	Subhas Sen	1129
	SAP	Titus Bhengra	714
	IND	Amrit Borgohain	679
	IND	Badhram Rajgarh	1652
Naharkatia	BJP	Kamakhya Tasa	16790
	INC	Paban Singh Ghatowar	18147
	AGP	Sarbananda Sonowal	28955
	CPI (ML) (L)	Subhas Sen	917

(Contd...)

Name of the AC	Party	Candidate	Votes in Favour
	SAP	Titus Bhengra	576
	IND	Amrit Borgohain	615
	IND	Badhram Rajgarh	1483
Tinsukia	BJP	Kamakhya Tasa	32637
	INC	Paban Singh Ghatowar	19067
	AGP	Sarbananda Sonowal	15036
	CPI (ML) (L)	Subhas Sen	1581
	SAP	Titus Bhengra	654
	IND	Amrit Borgohain	720
	IND	Badhram Rajgarh	1914
Digboi	BJP	Kamakhya Tasa	22637
	INC	Paban Singh Ghatowar	19489
	AGP	Sarbananda Sonowal	14700
	CPI (ML) (L)	Subhas Sen	1011
	SAP	Titus Bhengra	579
	IND	Amrit Borgohain	788
	IND	Badhram Rajgarh	1826
Margherita	BJP	Kamakhya Tasa	31881
	INC	Paban Singh Ghatowar	29394
	AGP	Sarbananda Sonowal	19870
	CPI (ML) (L)	Subhas Sen	1086

(Contd...)

Name of the AC	Party	Candidate	Votes in Favour
	SAP	Titus Bhengra	682
	IND	Amrit Borgohain	932
	IND	Badhram Rajgarh	2509
		Gauhati Parliamentary Constituency	
Dudhnoi (ST)	INC	Kirip Chaliha	36287
	BJP	Bhupen Hazarika	32291
	AGP	Bhrigu Kumar Phukan	6262
	TNGP	Deven Dutta	475
	SAP	Nipon Dholua	299
	SP	Bhubaneswar Barman	296
	IND	Umesh Chandra Das	268
	IND	Kazi Nekib Ahmed	527
	IND	Dhwajen Brahma	361
	IND	Bhabani Boro	400
	IND	Rajat Chandra Rabha	7850
	IND	Sumitra Das	1510
Boko (SC)	INC	Kirip Chaliha	48105
	BJP	Bhupen Hazarika	17377
	AGP	Bhrigu Kumar Phukan	22085
	TNGP	Deven Dutta	722

(Contd...)

Name of the AC	Party	Candidate	Votes in Favour
	SAP	Nipon Dholua	335
	SP	Bhubaneswar Barman	410
	IND	Umesh Chandra Das	279
	IND	Kazi Nekib Ahmed	500
	IND	Dhwajen Brahma	439
	IND	Bhabani Boro	423
	IND	Rajat Chandra Rabha	2966
	IND	Sumitra Das	1903
Chaygaon	INC	Kirip Chaliha	39068
	BJP	Bhupen Hazarika	5805
	AGP	Bhrigu Kumar Phukan	34525
	TNGP	Deven Dutta	676
	SAP	Nipon Dholua	211
	SP	Bhubaneswar Barman	187
	IND	Umesh Chandra Das	148
	IND	Kazi Nekib Ahmed	265
	IND	Dhwajen Brahma	213
	IND	Bhabani Boro	263
	IND	Rajat Chandra Rabha	549
	IND	Sumitra Das	1197
Palasbari	INC	Kirip Chaliha	23698

(Contd...)

Name of the AC	Party	Candidate	Votes in Favour
	BJP	Bhupen Hazarika	16315
	AGP	Bhrigu Kumar Phukan	25515
	TNGP	Deven Dutta	796
	SAP	Nipon Dholua	187
	SP	Bhubaneswar Barman	210
	IND	Umesh Chandra Das	178
	IND	Kazi Nekib Ahmed	215
	IND	Rajat Chandra Rabha	1004
	IND	Dhwajen Brahma	206
	IND	Bhabani Boro	257
	IND	Sumitra Das	1020
Jalukbari	INC	Kirip Chaliha	46107
	BJP	Bhupen Hazarika	25637
	AGP	Bhrigu Kumar Phukan	15596
	TNGP	Deven Dutta	434
	SAP	Nipon Dholua	137
	SP	Bhubaneswar Barman	144
	IND	Umesh Chandra Das	122
	IND	Kazi Nekib Ahmed	186
	IND	Dhwajen Brahma	142
	IND	Bhabani Boro	165

(Contd...)

Name of the AC	Party	Candidate	Votes in Favour
	IND	Rajat Chandra Rabha	243
	IND	Sumitra Das	997
Dispur	INC	Kirip Chaliha	32603
	BJP	Bhupen Hazarika	53657
	AGP	Bhrigu Kumar Phukan	14338
	TNGP	Deven Dutta	5668
	SAP	Nipon Dholua	458
	SP	Bhubaneswar Barman	424
	IND	Umesh Chandra Das	359
	IND	Kazi Nekib Ahmed	445
	IND	Dhwajen Brahma	429
	IND	Bhabani Boro	360
	IND	Rajat Chandra Rabha	545
	IND	Sumitra Das	1517
Gauhati (East)	INC	Kirip Chaliha	21771
	BJP	Bhupen Hazarika	48815
	AGP	Bhrigu Kumar Phukan	12257
	TNGP	Deven Dutta	1703
	SAP	Nipon Dholua	142
	SP	Bhubaneswar Barman	216
	IND	Umesh Chandra Das	109

(Contd...)

Name of the AC	Party	Candidate	Votes in Favour
	IND	Kazi Nekib Ahmed	229
	IND	Dhwajen Brahma	167
	IND	Bhabani Boro	140
	IND	Rajat Chandra Rabha	175
	IND	Sumitra Das	491
Gauhati (West)	INC	Kirip Chaliha	25883
	BJP	Bhupen Hazarika	46447
	AGP	Bhrigu Kumar Phukan	19503
	TNGP	Deven Dutta	989
	SAP	Nipon Dholua	192
	SP	Bhubaneswar Barman	248
	IND	Umesh Chandra Das	190
	IND	Kazi Nekib Ahmed	258
	IND	Dhwajen Brahma	274
	IND	Bhabani Boro	265
	IND	Rajat Chandra Rabha	739
	IND	Sumitra Das	1089
Hajo	INC	Kirip Chaliha	24851
	BJP	Bhupen Hazarika	24316
	AGP	Bhrigu Kumar Phukan	22741
	TNGP	Deven Dutta	741

(Contd...)

Name of the AC	Party	Candidate	Votes in Favour
	SAP	Nipon Dholua	183
	SP	Bhubaneswar Barman	148
	IND	Umesh Chandra Das	136
	IND	Kazi Nekib Ahmed	273
	IND	Dhwajen Brahma	190
	IND	Bhabani Boro	166
	IND	Rajat Chandra Rabha	245
	IND	Sumitra Das	864
Barkhetri	INC	Kirip Chaliha	54859
	BJP	Bhupen Hazarika	21391
	AGP	Bhrigu Kumar Phukan	8025
	TNGP	Deven Dutta	2728
	SAP	Nipon Dholua	155
	SP	Bhubaneswar Barman	182
	IND	Umesh Chandra Das	125
	IND	Kazi Nekib Ahmed	191
	IND	Dhwajen Brahma	165
	IND	Bhabani Boro	114
	IND	Rajat Chandra Rabha	172
	IND	Sumitra Das	652

(Contd...)

Name of the AC	Party	Candidate	Votes in Favour
		Jorhat Parliamentary Constituency	
Jorhat	BJP	Dayananda Borgohain	17482
	AGP	Dulal Chandra Baruah	21355
	CPI	Dhrupad Borgohain	11199
	INC	Bijoy Krishna Handique	24780
	SAP	Joyram Mout	584
	RCPI(R)	Raj Kumar Dowara	832
Titabor	BJP	Dayananda Borgohain	9384
	AGP	Dulal Chandra Baruah	14124
	CPI	Dhrupad Borgohain	16390
	INC	Bijoy Krishna Handique	23982
	SAP	Joyram Mout	1182
	RCPI(R)	Raj Kumar Dowara	2139
Mariani	BJP	Dayananda Borgohain	18284
	AGP	Dulal Chandra Baruah	6520
	CPI	Dhrupad Borgohain	17801
	INC	Bijoy Krishna Handique	15481
	SAP	Joyram Mout	2198
	RCPI(R)	Raj Kumar Dowara	2026
Teok	BJP	Dayananda Borgohain	12915

(Contd...)

Name of the AC	Party	Candidate	Votes in Favour
	AGP	Dulal Chandra Baruah	8275
	CPI	Dhrupad Borgohain	13896
	INC	Bijoy Krishna Handique	22462
	SAP	Joyram Mout	838
	RCPI(R)	Raj Kumar Dowara	1345
Amguri	BJP	Dayananda Borgohain	7267
	AGP	Dulal Chandra Baruah	20266
	CPI	Dhrupad Borgohain	13123
	INC	Bijoy Krishna Handique	25442
	SAP	Joyram Mout	948
	RCPI(R)	Raj Kumar Dowara	1272
Nazira	BJP	Dayananda Borgohain	8763
	AGP	Dulal Chandra Baruah	1758
	CPI	Dhrupad Borgohain	35245
	INC	Bijoy Krishna Handique	17134
	SAP	Joyram Mout	873
	RCPI(R)	Raj Kumar Dowara	1676
Mahmara	BJP	Dayananda Borgohain	16591
	AGP	Dulal Chandra Baruah	8482
	CPI	Dhrupad Borgohain	15766
	INC	Bijoy Krishna Handique	20255

(Contd...)

Name of the AC	Party	Candidate	Votes in Favour
	SAP	Joyram Mout	975
	RCPI(R)	Raj Kumar Dowara	1879
Sonari	BJP	Dayananda Borgohain	30695
	AGP	Dulal Chandra Baruah	3412
	CPI	Dhrupad Borgohain	11040
	INC	Bijoy Krishna Handique	33978
	SAP	Joyram Mout	1840
	RCPI(R)	Raj Kumar Dowara	3560
Thowra	BJP	Dayananda Borgohain	17086
	AGP	Dulal Chandra Baruah	5296
	CPI	Dhrupad Borgohain	12960
	INC	Bijoy Krishna Handique	15169
	SAP	Joyram Mout	964
	RCPI(R)	Raj Kumar Dowara	1292
Sibsagar	BJP	Dayananda Borgohain	11315
	AGP	Dulal Chandra Baruah	3834
	CPI	Dhrupad Borgohain	24873
	INC	Bijoy Krishna Handique	24917
	SAP	Joyram Mout	613
	RCPI(R)	Raj Kumar Dowara	670

(Contd...)

Name of the AC	Party	Candidate	Votes in Favour
		Kaliabor Parliamentary Constituency	
Dhing	AGP	Keshab Mahanta	11026
	INC	Dip Gogoi	40632
	LJNSP	Anil Choudhury	2649
	SAP	Ataur Rahman	1055
	SP	Dimbeswar Bora	544
	JD(U)	Rashidul Haque	30198
	IND	Jitu Sarmah	550
	IND	Jiten Gogoi	595
	IND	Juren Rajkhowa	524
	IND	Bikash Tanti	1060
	IND	Binod Gogoi	1156
Batadroba	AGP	Keshab Mahanta	16163
	INC	Dip Gogoi	27912
	LJNSP	Anil Choudhury	1679
	SAP	Ataur Rahman	1065
	SP	Dimbeswar Bora	682
	JD(U)	Rashidul Haque	21965
	IND	Jitu Sarmah	379

(Contd...)

Name of the AC	Party	Candidate	Votes in Favour
	IND	Jiten Gogoi	826
	IND	Juren Rajkhowa	414
	IND	Bikash Tanti	910
	IND	Binod Gogoi	992
Rupohihat	AGP	Keshab Mahanta	12235
	INC	Dip Gogoi	29494
	LJNSP	Anil Choudhury	1835
	SAP	Ataur Rahman	1181
	SP	Dimbeswar Bora	506
	JD(U)	Rashidul Haque	35704
	IND	Jitu Sarmah	559
	IND	Jiten Gogoi	573
	IND	Juren Rajkhowa	468
	IND	Bikash Tanti	1088
	IND	Binod Gogoi	1112
Samaguri	AGP	Keshab Mahanta	22893
	INC	Dip Gogoi	36986
	LJNSP	Anil Choudhury	1816
	SAP	Ataur Rahman	797
	SP	Dimbeswar Bora	254
	JD(U)	Rashidul Haque	12150

(Contd...)

Name of the AC	Party	Candidate	Votes in Favour
	IND	Jitu Sarmah	213
	IND	Jiten Gogoi	325
	IND	Juren Rajkhowa	327
	IND	Bikash Tanti	822
	IND	Binod Gogoi	1335
Kaliabor	AGP	Keshab Mahanta	37100
	INC	Dip Gogoi	18026
	LJNSP	Anil Choudhury	1235
	SAP	Ataur Rahman	517
	SP	Dimbeswar Bora	249
	JD(U)	Rashidul Haque	5571
	IND	Jitu Sarmah	255
	IND	Jiten Gogoi	949
	IND	Juren Rajkhowa	359
	INC	Dip Gogoi	25212
	LJNSP	Anil Choudhury	2010
	SAP	Ataur Rahman	460
	SP	Dimbeswar Bora	264
	JD(U)	Rashidul Haque	2556
	IND	Jitu Sarmah	479
	IND	Jiten Gogoi	10899

(Contd...)

Name of the AC	Party	Candidate	Votes in Favour
	IND	Juren Rajkhowa	824
	IND	Bikash Tanti	780
	IND	Binod Gogoi	2192
Bokakhat	AGP	Keshab Mahanta	14215
	INC	Dip Gogoi	25212
	LJNSP	Anil Choudhury	2010
	SAP	Ataur Rahman	460
	SP	Dimbeswar Bora	264
	JD(U)	Rashidul Haque	2556
	IND	Jitu Sarmah	479
	IND	Jiten Gogoi	10899
	IND	Juren Rajkhowa	824
	IND	Bikash Tanti	1445
	IND	Binod Gogoi	3805
Sarupathar	AGP	Keshab Mahanta	43071
	INC	Dip Gogoi	34325
	LJNSP	Anil Choudhury	2914
	SAP	Ataur Rahman	1009
	SP	Dimbeswar Bora	509
	JD(U)	Rashidul Haque	10784
	IND	Jitu Sarmah	542

(Contd...)

Name of the AC	Party	Candidate	Votes in Favour
	IND	Jiten Gogoi	5930
	IND	Juren Rajkhowa	758
	IND	Bikash Tanti	1506
	IND	Binod Gcgoi	3901
Golaghat	AGP	Keshab Mahanta	25650
	INC	Dip Gogoi	38080
	LJNSP	Anil Choudhury	1934
	SAP	Ataur Rahman	600
	SP	Dimbeswar Bora	288
	JD(U)	Rashidul Haque	3580
	IND	Jitu Sarmah	549
	IND	Jiten Gogoi	2708
	IND	Juren Rajkhowa	454
	IND	Bikash Tanti	850
	IND	Binod Gogoi	1835
Khumtai	AGP	Keshab Mahanta	19104
	INC	Dip Gogoi	20833
	LJNSP	Anil Choudhury	1522
	SAP	Ataur Rahman	389
	SP	Dimbeswar Bora	243
	JD(U)	Rashidul Haque	1311

(Contd...)

Name of the AC	Party	Candidate	Votes in Favour
	IND	Jitu Sarmah	352
	IND	Jiten Gogoi	5298
	IND	Juren Rajkhowa	377
	IND	Bikash Tanti	718
	IND	Binod Gogoi	1636
Dergaon	AGP	Keshab Mahanta	33166
	INC	Dip Gogoi	30331
	LJNSP	Anil Choudhury	1371
	SAP	Ataur Rahman	518
	SP	Dimbeswar Bora	242
	JD(U)	Rashidul Haque	2139
	IND	Jitu Sarmah	263
	IND	Jiten Gogoi	2699
	IND	Juren Rajkhowa	442
	IND	Bikash Tanti	833
	IND	Binod Gogoi	2316
	Karimganj(SC) Parliamentary Constituency		
Ratabari (SC)	AGP	Nepal Chandra Das	3976
	BJP	Parimal Suklabaidya	36568

(Contd...)

Name of the AC	Party	Candidate	Votes in Favour
	INC	Lalit Mohan Suklabaidya	25087
	IND	Babul Ram Das	510
	IND	Babul Roy	297
	IND	Radha Kanta Tanty	407
	IND	Kulendra Roy	399
	IND	Sushil Kumar Das	690
Patharkandi	AGP	Nepal Chandra Das	4900
	BJP	Parimal Suklabaidya	37898
	INC	Lalit Mohan Suklabaidya	43155
	IND	Babul Ram Das	794
	IND	Babul Roy	442
	IND	Radha Kanta Tanty	509
	IND	Kulendra Roy	626
	IND	Sushil Kumar Das	913
Karimganj (North)	AGP	Nepal Chandra Das	7856
	BJP	Parimal Suklabaidya	36974
	INC	Lalit Mohan Suklabaidya	39662
	IND	Babul Ram Das	552
	IND	Babul Roy	260
	IND	Radha Kanta Tanty	590
	IND	Kulendra Roy	265

(Contd...)

Name of the AC	Party	Candidate	Votes in Favour
	IND	Sushil Kumar Das	448
Karimganj (South)	AGP	Nepal Chandra Das	19920
	BJP	Parimal Suklabaidya	33815
	INC	Lalit Mohan Suklabaidya	25878
	IND	Babul Ram Das	398
	IND	Babul Roy	195
	IND	Radha Kanta Tanty	234
	IND	Kulendra Roy	177
	IND	Sushil Kumar Das	249
Badarpur	AGP	Nepal Chandra Das	10347
	BJP	Parimal Suklabaidya	24983
	INC	Lalit Mohan Suklabaidya	34921
	IND	Babul Ram Das	362
	IND	Babul Roy	176
	IND	Radha Kanta Tanty	266
	IND	Kulendra Roy	207
	IND	Sushil Kumar Das	274
Hailakandi	AGP	Nepal Chandra Das	22993
	BJP	Parimal Suklabaidya	18804
	INC	Lalit Mohan Suklabaidya	45782
	IND	Babul Ram Das	307

(Contd...)

Name of the AC	Party	Candidate	Votes in Favour
	IND	Babul Roy	161
	IND	Radha Kanta Tanty	266
	IND	Kulendra Roy	148
	IND	Sushil Kumar Das	230
Katlicherra	AGP	Nepal Chandra Das	8393
	BJP	Parimal Suklabaidya	18317
	INC	Lalit Mohan Suklabaidya	78052
	IND	Babul Ram Das	518
	IND	Babul Roy	206
	IND	Radha Kanta Tanty	258
	IND	Kulendra Roy	247
	IND	Sushil Kumar Das	375
Algapur	AGP	Nepal Chandra Das	28089
	BJP	Parimal Suklabaidya	21451
	INC	Lalit Mohan Suklabaidya	28308
	IND	Babul Ram Das	484
	IND	Babul Roy	222
	IND	Radha Kanta Tanty	330
	IND	Kulendra Roy	316
	IND	Sushil Kumar Das	462

(Contd...)

Name of the AC	Party	Candidate	Votes in Favour
Kokrajhar (ST) Parliamentary Constituency			
Gossaingaon	INC	Derhagra Mochahary	3812
	IND	Rajendra Mushahary	1413
	IND	Sabda Ram Rabha	56446
	IND	Sansuma Khunggur Bwiswmuthiary	52684
Kokrajhar (West)	INC	Derhagra Mochahary	2432
	IND	Rajendra Mushahary	876
	IND	Sabda Ram Rabha	16704
	IND	Sansuma Khunggur Bwiswmuthiary	90295
Kokrajhar (East)	INC	Derhagra Mochahary	926
	IND	Rajendra Mushahary	359
	IND	Sabda Ram Rabha	5687
	IND	Sansuma Khunggur Bwiswmuthiary	110237
Sidli (ST)	INC	Derhagra Mochahary	5411
	IND	Rajendra Mushahary	946
	IND	Sabda Ram Rabha	10752
	IND	Sansuma Khunggur Bwiswmuthiary	100474
Bijni	INC	Derhagra Mochahary	4621
	IND	Rajendra Mushahary	1299
	IND	Sabda Ram Rabha	18699

(Contd...)

Name of the AC	Party	Candidate	Votes in Favour
	IND	Sansuma Khunggur Bwiswmuthiary	52844
Sorbhog	INC	Derhagra Mochahary	17442
	IND	Rajendra Mushahary	1995
	IND	Sabda Ram Rabha	32727
	IND	Sansuma Khunggur Bwiswmuthiary	37334
Bhabanipur	INC	Derhagra Mochahary	12213
	IND	Rajendra Mushahary	1082
	IND	Sabda Ram Rabha	23354
	IND	Sansuma Khunggur Bwiswmuthiary	30385
Tamulpur	INC	Derhagra Mochahary	4746
	IND	Rajendra Mushahary	1026
	IND	Sabda Ram Rabha	11187
	IND	Sansuma Khunggur Bwiswmuthiary	86392
Barama (ST)	INC	Derhagra Mochahary	7824
	IND	Rajendra Mushahary	931
	IND	Sabda Ram Rabha	12124
	IND	Sansuma Khunggur Bwiswmuthiary	56066
Chapaguri (ST)	INC	Derhagra Mochahary	1971
	IND	Rajendra Mushahary	519
	IND	Sabda Ram Rabha	17794
	IND	Sansuma Khunggur Bwiswmuthiary	72886

(Contd...)

Name of the AC	Party	Candidate	Votes in Favour
		Lakhimpur Parliamentary Constituency	
Majuli	AGP	Arun Kumar Sarma	33914
	BJP	Uday Shankar Hazarika	7178
	INC	Ranee Narah	27311
	SAP	Padmeswar Phukan	497
	RSP	Puspa Gogoi	147
	LJNSP	Sunmoni Das	123
	IND	Isak Korkoria	82
	IND	Ghanashyam Bhattarai	82
	IND	Biju Narah	160
	IND	Rabin Deka	141
	IND	Hekjal Wood	618
Naoboicha	AGP	Arun Kumar Sarma	28934
	BJP	Uday Shankar Hazarika	24452
	INC	Ranee Narah	34277
	SAP	Padmeswar Phukan	1347
	RSP	Puspa Gogoi	978
	LJNSP	Sunmoni Das	405
	IND	Isak Korkoria	367
	IND	Ghanashyam Bhattarai	328

(Contd...)

Name of the AC	Party	Candidate	Votes in Favour
	IND	Biju Narah	510
	IND	Rabin Deka	584
	IND	Hekjal Wood	2082
Lakhimpur	AGP	Arun Kumar Sarma	34366
	BJP	Uday Shankar Hazarika	17952
	INC	Ranee Narah	25940
	SAP	Padmeswar Phukan	662
	RSP	Puspa Gogoi	1129
	LJNSP	Sunmoni Das	487
	IND	Isak Korkoria	206
	IND	Ghanashyam Bhattarai	177
	IND	Biju Narah	363
	IND	Rabin Deka	353
	IND	Hekjal Wood	1542
Dhakuakhana (ST)	AGP	Arun Kumar Sarma	30637
	BJP	Uday Shankar Hazarika	20480
	INC	Ranee Narah	43342
	SAP	Padmeswar Phukan	969
	RSP	Puspa Gogoi	1258
	LJNSP	Sunmoni Das	268
	IND	Isak Korkoria	206

(Contd...)

Name of the AC	Party	Candidate	Votes in Favour
	IND	Ghanashyam Bhattarai	230
	IND	Biju Narah	495
	IND	Rabin Deka	401
	IND	Hekjal Wood	1399
Dhemaji (ST)	AGP	Arun Kumar Sarma	47767
	BJP	Uday Shankar Hazarika	20990
	INC	Ranee Narah	33610
	SAP	Padmeswar Phukan	823
	RSP	Puspa Gogoi	4143
	LJNSP	Sunmoni Das	276
	IND	Isak Korkoria	225
	IND	Ghanashyam Bhattarai	219
	IND	Biju Narah	454
	IND	Rabin Deka	379
	IND	Hekjal Wood	1746
Jonai (ST)	AGP	Arun Kumar Sarma	51117
	BJP	Uday Shankar Hazarika	14529
	INC	Ranee Narah	56897
	SAP	Padmeswar Phukan	957
	RSP	Puspa Gogoi	1007
	LJNSP	Sunmoni Das	281

(Contd...)

Name of the AC	Party	Candidate	Votes in Favour
	IND	Isak Korkoria	214
	IND	Ghanashyam Bhattarai	254
	IND	Biju Narah	432
	IND	Rabin Deka	355
	IND	Hekjal Wood	1653
Chabua	AGP	Arun Kumar Sarma	25898
	BJP	Uday Shankar Hazarika	23219
	INC	Ranee Narah	15104
	SAP	Padmeswar Phukan	850
	RSP	Puspa Gogoi	608
	LJNSP	Sunmoni Das	355
	IND	Isak Korkoria	422
	IND	Ghanashyam Bhattarai	387
	IND	Biju Narah	694
	IND	Rabin Deka	878
	IND	Hekjal Wood	2935
Doomdooma	AGP	Arun Kumar Sarma	13975
	BJP	Uday Shankar Hazarika	25383
	INC	Ranee Narah	15349
	SAP	Padmeswar Phukan	1063
	RSP	Puspa Gogoi	546

(Contd...)

Name of the AC	Party	Candidate	Votes in Favour
	LJNSP	Sunmoni Das	487
	IND	Isak Korkoria	718
	IND	Ghanashyam Bhattarai	543
	IND	Biju Narah	819
	IND	Rabin Deka	1187
	IND	Hekjal Wood	4637
Sadiya	AGP	Arun Kumar Sarma	34119
	BJP	Uday Shankar Hazarika	14879
	INC	Ranee Narah	20804
	SAP	Padmeswar Phukan	720
	RSP	Puspa Gogoi	1922
	LJNSP	Sunmoni Das	266
	IND	Isak Korkoria	325
	IND	Ghanashyam Bhattarai	665
	IND	Biju Narah	529
	IND	Rabin Deka	627
	IND	Hekjal Wood	3096
	Mangaldoi Parliamentary Constituency		
Kamalpur	AGP	Apurba Bhattacharjee	13254

(Contd...)

Name of the AC	Party	Candidate	Votes in Favour
	BJP	Narayan Chandra Borkataky	37032
	INC	Madhab Rajbangshi	23740
	SAP	Shaheda Begum	655
	IND	Aroon Baruah	574
	IND	Tridip Pati Singha	453
	IND	Bhupendra Nath Kakati	915
Rangiya	AGP	Apurba Bhattacharjee	17396
	BJP	Narayan Chandra Borkataky	40270
	INC	Madhab Rajbangshi	26312
	SAP	Shaheda Begum	833
	IND	Aroon Baruah	755
	IND	Tridip Pati Singha	650
	IND	Bhupendra Nath Kakati	1136
Nalbari	AGP	Apurba Bhattacharjee	21427
	BJP	Narayan Chandra Borkataky	33087
	INC	Madhab Rajbangshi	26677
	SAP	Shaheda Begum	824
	IND	Aroon Baruah	716
	IND	Tridip Pati Singha	790
	IND	Bhupendra Nath Kakati	1150
Paneri	AGP	Apurba Bhattacharjee	5866

(Contd...)

Name of the AC	Party	Candidate	Votes in Favour
	BJP	Narayan Chandra Borkataky	42368
	INC	Madhab Rajbangshi	22179
	SAP	Shaheda Begum	1084
	IND	Aroon Baruah	831
	IND	Tridip Pati Singha	1005
	IND	Bhupendra Nath Kakati	1505
Kalaigaon	AGP	Apurba Bhattacharjee	19053
	BJP	Narayan Chandra Borkataky	34372
	INC	Madhab Rajbangshi	27330
	SAP	Shaheda Begum	1080
	IND	Aroon Baruah	913
	IND	Tridip Pati Singha	862
	IND	Bhupendra Nath Kakati	1897
Sipajhar	AGP	Apurba Bhattacharjee	24203
	BJP	Narayan Chandra Borkataky	21870
	INC	Madhab Rajbangshi	31925
	SAP	Shaheda Begum	762
	IND	Aroon Baruah	612
	IND	Tridip Pati Singha	410
	IND	Bhupendra Nath Kakati	1493
Mangaldoi(ST)	AGP	Apurba Bhattacharjee	24017

(Contd...)

Name of the AC	Party	Candidate	Votes in Favour
	BJP	Narayan Chandra Borkataky	29353
	INC	Madhab Rajbangshi	47111
	SAP	Shaheda Begum	1626
	IND	Aroon Baruah	1096
	IND	Tridip Pati Singha	642
	IND	Bhupendra Nath Kakati	2015
Dalgaon	AGP	Apurba Bhattacharjee	6988
	BJP	Narayan Chandra Borkataky	24669
	INC	Madhab Rajbangshi	63474
	SAP	Shaheda Begum	1671
	IND	Aroon Baruah	843
	IND	Tridip Pati Singha	587
	IND	Bhupendra Nath Kakati	1328
Udalguri (ST)	AGP	Apurba Bhattacharjee	5737
	BJP	Narayan Chandra Borkataky	53091
	INC	Madhab Rajbangshi	20527
	SAP	Shaheda Begum	985
	IND	Aroon Baruah	795
	IND	Tridip Pati Singha	594
	IND	Bhupendra Nath Kakati	1484
Majbat	AGP	Apurba Bhattacharjee	8113

(Contd...)

Name of the AC	Party	Candidate	Votes in Favour
	BJP	Narayan Chandra Borkataky	29677
	INC	Madhab Rajbangshi	26652
	SAP	Shaheda Begum	1340
	IND	Aroon Baruah	1071
	IND	Tridip Pati Singha	866
	IND	Bhupendra Nath Kakati	2123
		Nowgong Parliamentary Constituency	
Jagiroad	AGP	Dhruba Kumar Saikia	15139
	INC	Bisnu Prasad	36754
	BJP	Rajen Gohain	43344
	UMFA	Haji Abdur Rouf	1114
	SAP	Biren Chandra Das	856
	RPI	Bhupen Chandra Mudoi	1583
Morigaon	AGP	Dhruba Kumar Saikia	4943
	INC	Bisnu Prasad	30225
	BJP	Rajen Gohain	44869
	UMFA	Haji Abdur Rouf	920
	SAP	Biren Chandra Das	539
	RPI	Bhupen Chandra Mudoi	1170

(Contd...)

Name of the AC	Party	Candidate	Votes in Favour
Laharighat	AGP	Dhruba Kumar Saikia	4554
	INC	Bisnu Prasad	42955
	BJP	Rajen Gohain	27164
	UMFA	Haji Abdur Rouf	940
	SAP	Biren Chandra Das	588
	RPI	Bhupen Chandra Mudoi	982
Nowgong	AGP	Dhruba Kumar Saikia	12997
	INC	Bisnu Prasad	30805
	BJP	Rajen Gohain	36869
	UMFA	Haji Abdur Rouf	1033
	SAP	Biren Chandra Das	594
	RPI	Bhupen Chandra Mudoi	946
Barhampur	AGP	Dhruba Kumar Saikia	12904
	INC	Bisnu Prasad	24140
	BJP	Rajen Gohain	38235
	UMFA	Haji Abdur Rouf	840
	SAP	Biren Chandra Das	696
	RPI	Bhupen Chandra Mudoi	1403
Jamunamukh	AGP	Dhruba Kumar Saikia	23030
	INC	Bisnu Prasad	38564
	BJP	Rajen Gohain	13729

(Contd...)

Name of the AC	Party	Candidate	Votes in Favour
	UMFA	Haji Abdur Rouf	1295
	SAP	Biren Chandra Das	502
	RPI	Bhupen Chandra Mudoi	1075
Hojai	AGP	Dhruba Kumar Saikia	8577
	INC	Bisnu Prasad	38903
	BJP	Rajen Gohain	55638
	UMFA	Haji Abdur Rouf	2966
	SAP	Biren Chandra Das	611
	RPI	Bhupen Chandra Mudoi	1080
Lumding	AGP	Dhruba Kumar Saikia	9673
	INC	Bisnu Prasad	29968
	BJP	Rajen Gohain	39712
	UMFA	Haji Abdur Rouf	1114
	SAP	Biren Chandra Das	553
	RPI	Bhupen Chandra Mudoi	1053
Silchar Parliamentary Constituency			
Silchar	BJP	Kabindra Purkayastha	49032
	CPM	Noorul Huda	2855
	INC	Sontosh Mohan Dev	35112

(Contd...)

Name of the AC	Party	Candidate	Votes in Favour
	SAP	Alok Sen	438
	SP	Anwar Hussain Laskar	13648
	IND	Ashutosh Das	186
	IND	Kantimoy Deb	225
	IND	Kshitindra Sarkar	147
	IND	Benu Bhuson Nath	162
	IND	Manoranjan Das	130
	IND	Samarendra Ghosh	503
Sonai	BJP	Kabindra Purkayastha	25449
	CPM	Noorul Huda	2072
	INC	Sontosh Mohan Dev	36713
	SAP	Alok Sen	507
	SP	Anwar Hussain Laskar	25668
	IND	Ashutosh Das	225
	IND	Kantimoy Deb	160
	IND	Kshitindra Sarkar	137
	IND	Benu Bhuson Nath	115
	IND	Manoranjan Das	98
	IND	Samarendra Ghosh	454
Dholai	BJP	Kabindra Purkayastha	38011
	CPM	Noorul Huda	3086

(Contd...)

Name of the AC	Party	Candidate	Votes in Favour
	INC	Sontosh Mohan Dev	28083
	SAP	Alok Sen	749
	SP	Anwar Hussain Laskar	14544
	IND	Ashutosh Das	340
	IND	Kantimoy Deb	531
	IND	Kshitindra Sarkar	292
	IND	Benu Bhuson Nath	302
	IND	Manoranjan Das	262
	IND	Samarendra Ghosh	967
Udharbond	BJP	Kabindra Purkayastha	28884
	CPM	Noorul Huda	2299
	INC	Sontosh Mohan Dev	30204
	SAP	Alok Sen	761
	SP	Anwar Hussain Laskar	13063
	IND	Ashutosh Das	284
	IND	Kantimoy Deb	172
	IND	Kshitindra Sarkar	251
	IND	Benu Bhuson Nath	363
	IND	Manoranjan Das	299
	IND	Samarendra Ghosh	1040

(Contd...)

Name of the AC	Party	Candidate	Votes in Favour
Lakhipur	BJP	Kabindra Purkayastha	26042
	CPM	Noorul Huda	3831
	INC	Sontosh Mohan Dev	41481
	SAP	Alok Sen	779
	SP	Anwar Hussain Laskar	10748
	IND	Ashutosh Das	240
	IND	Kantimoy Deb	165
	IND	Kshitindra Sarkar	236
	IND	Benu Bhuson Nath	388
	IND	Manoranjan Das	258
	IND	Samarendra Ghosh	835
Barkhola	BJP	Kabindra Purkayastha	25429
	CPM	Noorul Huda	3277
	INC	Sontosh Mohan Dev	32447
	SAP	Alok Sen	557
	SP	Anwar Hussain Laskar	12405
	IND	Ashutosh Das	184
	IND	Kantimoy Deb	135
	IND	Kshitindra Sarkar	181
	IND	Benu Bhuson Nath	157
	IND	Manoranjan Das	218

(Contd...)

Name of the AC	Party	Candidate	Vctes in Favour
	IND	Samarendra Ghosh	648
Katigora	BJP	Kabindra Purkayastha	31862
	CPM	Noorul Huda	2583
	INC	Sontosh Mohan Dev	42045
	SAP	Alok Sen	726
	SP	Anwar Hussain Laskar	9729
	IND	Ashutosh Das	213
	IND	Kantimoy Deb	142
	IND	Kshitindra Sarkar	190
	IND	Benu Bhuson Nath	233
	IND	Manoranjan Das	154
	IND	Samarendra Ghosh	543
		Tezpur Parliamentary Constituency	
Dhekiajuli	BJP	Ghisa Lal Agarwal	24866
	AGP	Padma Hazarika	21517
	INC	Moni Kumar Subba	27856
	CPI (ML) (L)	Rubul Sarma	1836
	IND	Dipen Tanti	2912
Barchalla	BJP	Ghisa Lal Agarwal	20317

(Contd...)

Name of the AC	Party	Candidate	Votes in Favour
	AGP	Padma Hazarika	20667
	INC	Moni Kumar Subba	30851
	CPI (ML) (L)	Rubul Sarma	1579
	IND	Dipen Tanti	1946
Tezpur	BJP	Ghisa Lal Agarwal	20332
	AGP	Padma Hazarika	27607
	INC	Moni Kumar Subba	28427
	CPI (ML) (L)	Rubul Sarma	1261
	IND	Dipen Tanti	1253
Rangapara	BJP	Ghisa Lal Agarwal	23269
	AGP	Padma Hazarika	16666
	INC	Moni Kumar Subba	33083
	CPI (ML) (L)	Rubul Sarma	2938
	IND	Dipen Tanti	2884
Sootea	BJP	Ghisa Lal Agarwal	5798
	AGP	Padma Hazarika	39350
	INC	Moni Kumar Subba	40263
	CPI (ML) (L)	Rubul Sarma	2006
	IND	Dipen Tanti	2159
Biswanath	BJP	Ghisa Lal Agarwal	11851
	AGP	Padma Hazarika	30317

(Contd...)

Name of the AC	Party	Candidate	Votes in Favour
	INC	Moni Kumar Subba	35414
	CPI (ML) (L)	Rubul Sarma	2003
	IND	Dipen Tanti	2792
Behali	BJP	Ghisa Lal Agarwal	23047
	AGP	Padma Hazarika	7742
	INC	Moni Kumar Subba	20740
	CPI (ML) (L)	Rubul Sarma	8777
	IND	Dipen Tanti	3558
Gohpur	BJP	Ghisa Lal Agarwal	16041
	AGP	Padma Hazarika	31230
	INC	Moni Kumar Subba	47681
	CPI (ML) (L)	Rubul Sarma	3192
	IND	Dipen Tanti	2671
Bihpuria	BJP	Ghisa Lal Agarwal	19091
	AGP	Padma Hazarika	24194
	INC	Moni Kumar Subba	25444
	CPI (ML) (L)	Rubul Sarma	1001
	IND	Dipen Tanti	1077

(Contd...)

Appendix 8.A

Fig. Assembly elections in Assam: Performance of AGP, Congress & BJP

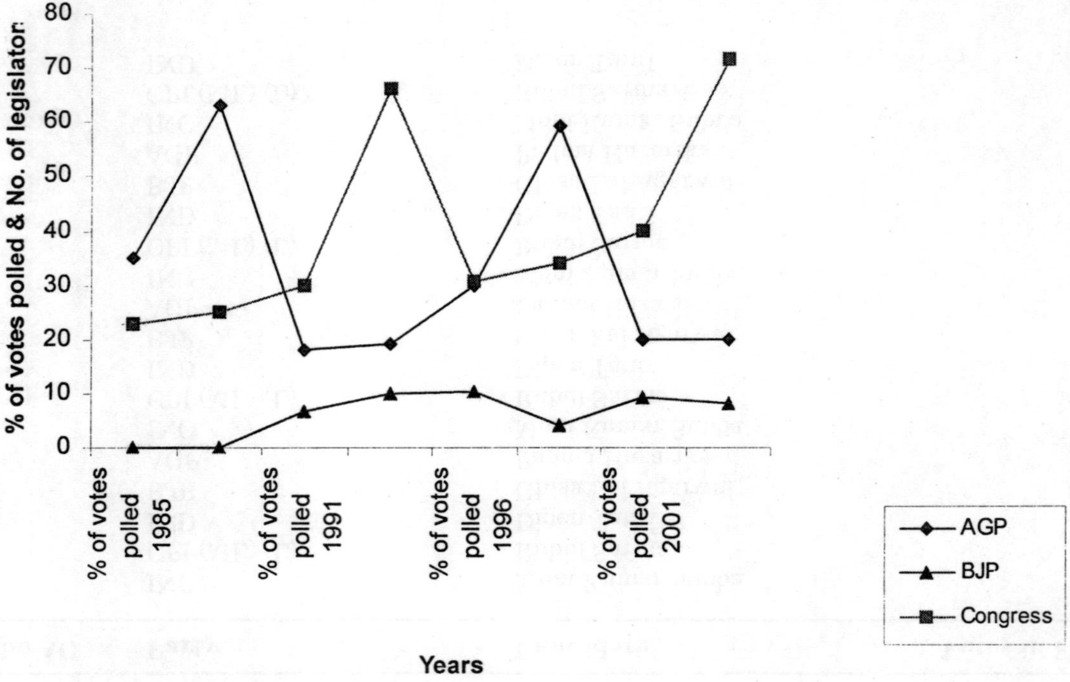

Appendix 8.B

Fig. Percentage of voters turnout in Assembly polls, Assam

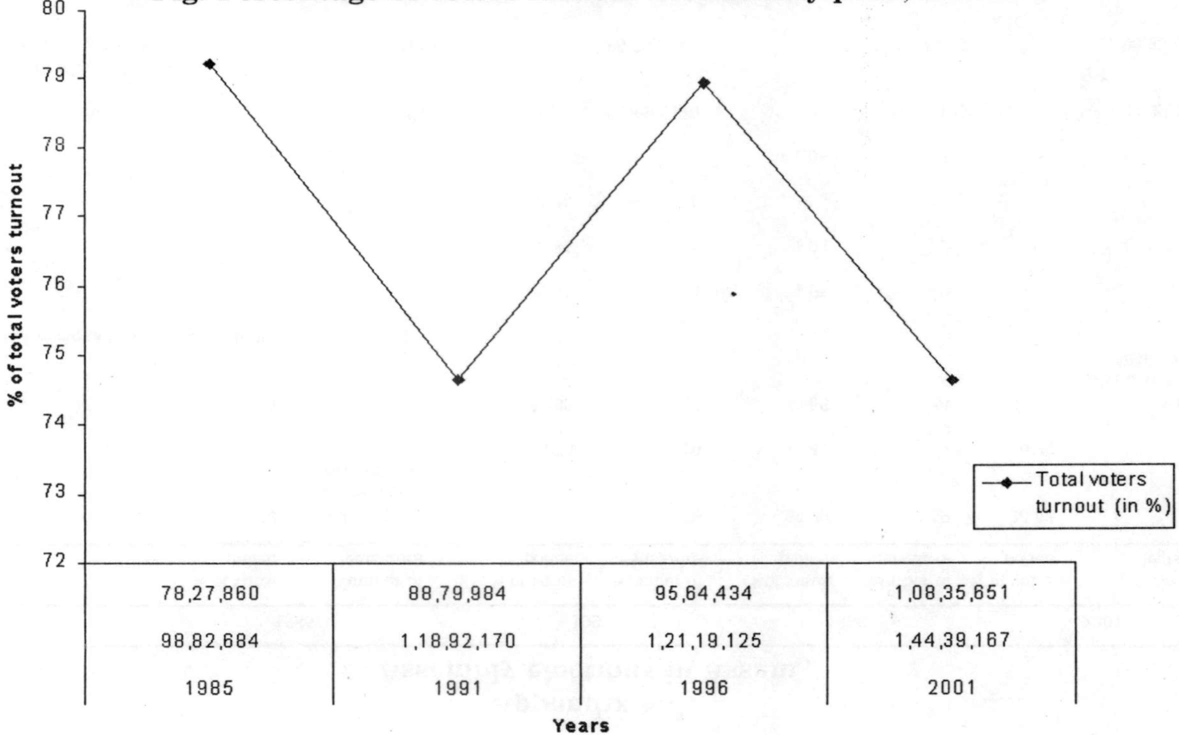

Appendix 8.C
Assembly elections in Assam

Parties	1985		1991		1996		2001	
	% of votes polled	Number of legislators	% of votes polled	Number of legislators	% of votes polled	Number of legislators	% of votes polled	Number of legislators
AGP	34.84	63 (+ three independent candidates)	17.93	19	29.70	59	20.02	20
BJP	-	-	6.55	10	10.41	4	9.35	8
Congress	23.00	25	29.93	66	30.56	34	39.75	71 (+ seven MLAs including NCP's three)
United Minorities Front	10.85	17	-	-	-	-	-	-
CPI	-	-	2.47	4	1.95	3	-	-
CPI (M)	4.48	2	3.85	2	1.94	2	-	-
NAGP	-	-	5.45	5	-	-	-	-
ASDC	-	-		-	1.98	5	-	-
Total voters (in numbers)		98,82,684		1,18,92,170		1,21,19,125		1,44,39,167
Total voters who caste their votes (in numbers)		78,27,860		88,79,984		95,64,434		1,08,35,651
Total voters turnout (in %)		79.21		74.67		78.92		74.63

Bibliography

Ahmed, Abu Nasar Saied (2006) (ed.), *Nationality Question in Assam: The EPW 1980-81 Debate*. New Delhi: Akansha. Introduction.

_________. (Forthcoming). "Participation of Muslims in Governance: A Case of the Muslims of Assam" in K.N. Jahangir and M.A. Jawaid (eds) *Minorities in India in the New Millennium*. New Delhi: Manas.

An Educational Study on Voting Behaviour of Electorate and Development Works done in Constituencies of Assam (2001). Guwahati: National Education Foundation.

Apter, David (1964). *Ideology and Discontent*. New York: Free Press.

Asom Pradesh Congress Committeer Karma Khushi (2004). The Manifesto of the Assam Pradesh Congress.

Assam Development Report. (2002). Planning Commission, Government of India.

Assam: The Pre- Poll Panorama (2001). A Freelance Peace. Vedanti: Burning Assam, Back Issues, http// www.vedanti.com.

Barpujari, Indrani (Forthcoming). "Illegal Migrants (Determination by Tribunals) Act and Assam–Promulgation and Repeal: A Contextual Analysis". New Delhi: Akansha.

Baruah, Apurba Kumar (1998). "Assam Elections 1996: The Congress Debacle" in Girin Phukon and Adil-ul-Yasin (eds), *Working of Parliamentary Democracy and Electoral*

Politics in North East India. New Delhi: South Asian Publishers.

Bete´ille, Andre (2005). *Social Class*. Guwahati: Foundation Day Lecture, OKDISCD.

Bharator Communist Party (Marxbadi). Asom Raizik Committee. Nirbashani Gushona Patra. Chaturdaksh Loka Sabha Nirbashan, 2004.

Bharator Communist Partyr Asom Raizik Parishad, Nirbashani Istahaar. Chaturdaksh Loka Sabha. 2004.

Bhaumik, Anirban (2004). "BJP Silent on ULFA Crackdown in Bhutan for Poll Reasons". *Deccan Herald*.

Bhushan, Chandra (2004). *Terrorism and Separation in North-East India*. Delhi: Kalpaz.

Brass, Paul R. (1991), *Ethnicity and Nationalism: Theory and Comparison*. New Delhi: Sage Publication.

Brindaban Goswami (2004). *India News On Line*, North East Scenario. http://www.indiamart.news.com.

Campbell, Angus *et.al* (1968). *Elections and the Political Order*. New York: John Wiley and Sons.

Chandhoke, N (2000). *State and Civil Society- Explorations in Political Theory*. New Delhi: Sage Publications. p. 163.

_________. (2003). *The Conceits of Civil Society*. New Delhi: Oxford University Press. p. 206.

Charge Sheet against Congress Government (2004). Bharatiya Janata Party Assam Pradesh.

Chaubey, S. K. (1985). *Electoral Politics in North East India*. Madras: Universities Press. Chapter II, p.63.

Chowdhury, Jyoti Lal (2004). "Assam: Why is Jamiat Ulema Sore with Congress?". *Statescan*, Organiser. April 11. http://www.organiser.org.

CMIE, Public Finance 2002.

Community Information Centre (CIC) Gabharu. District Profile. http://www.cic.nic.in.

Community Information Centre (CIC) Pub Chayduar. Sonitpur District. Assam. www.sonitpur.nic.in.

Das, Samir Kumar (1998). "An Interpretation of the Assam Elections of 1996" in Girin Phukon and Adil-ul-Yasin (eds), *Working of Parliamentary Democracy and Electoral Politics in North East India*. New Delhi: South Asian Publishers.

Das, Samir K. (2004). *ULFA (United Liberation Front of Assam): A Political Analysis*. Delhi: Ajanta Publications.

Das Gupta, Barun (1998). Assam. *Frontline*. Volume 15, No. 06. March 21 – April 3.

De, Bimal J. and Dilip K. Lahiri (1985). *Assam Muslims: Politics and Cohesion*. New Delhi: Mittal.

Deccan Herald (2004). April 9.

Devraj, Ranjit (2003). "Tribal autonomy a step for peace". *Manushi: A Journal about Women and Society*. February. http://www.indiatogether.org.

Duverger, Maurice (1971). "The Influence of the Electoral System on Political Life". *International Social Science Bulletin* II. Summer. p. 314.

Economic Survey, Assam 2001.

________. Assam 2002-2003.

Election Analysis: Assam (2001). "On Predictable Lines". *Frontline*. Vol.18, Issue 11, May 26-June 8.

Election Commission of India. Various years, http://www.eci.gov.in.

ElectionNext, www.electionnext.com, 2004.

Gohain, Hiren (1980). "Cudgel of Chauvinism", *Economic and Political Weekly*, February 23, pp.418-20.

Goswami, Kanaka (1999). "Election Politics in Assam: A Study of Elections held in 1983 and 1985". Unpublished PhD Dissertation, Dibrugarh University.

Goswami, Sandhya (1998). "Assam Lok Sabha Election, 1996: An Analysis" in Girin Phukon and Adil-ul-Yasin (eds), *Working of Parliamentary Democracy and Electoral Politics in North East India*. New Delhi: South Asian Publishers.

_________. (2004). "Mixed Verdict", *Economic and Political Weekly*, Vol XXXIX No, 51. December 18-24.

Guruswamy, Mohan (2005). *Left Behind: A Case Study of Assam*. Centre for Policy Alternatives (CPA), New Delhi.

Hussain, Wasbir (2001). "Elections under the Shadow of the Gun". *Economic and Political Weekly*. Vol XXXVI, No 5 & 6. February 3-10.

_________. (2004). "Political Marriages, Divorce and Patch-ups". *The Sentinel*, March 6.

_________. (2005). *"Assam: Truce before the Storm?" South Asia Intelligence Review, Weekly Assessments & Briefings. Volume 3, No. 46. May 30.*

Indian Express. www.indianexpress.com, 2001.

Indian Printer Publisher. http:/ www.indianprinterpublisher.com/aug/archive-i.../ newspaper%20readership%20in%20indian.htm.

Institute of Regional Studies (2005). "Coalition Politics in India: Dynamics of a Winning Combination". Focus on Regional Issues. Vol XXIV, No. 1. Islamabad. www.irs.org.pk.

Jakubowicz, Karl (2002). "Media in Transition: The Case of Poland" *in* M E Price, B Rozumilowicz and S G Verhulst (eds.) *Media Reform: Democratizing the Media, Democratizing the State*. London: Routledge.

Kar, M. (1990). *Muslims in Assam Politics*. New Delhi: Omson. p.161.

Katyal K K (2004). "Issues and Trends in Indian Elections". *South Asian Journal*. Vol. July-September, No. 5.

Kothari, Rajni (1970). "Social Infrastructure" in *Politics in India*. Boston: Little, Brown and Co. Chapter VI.

________. (1970) "Caste in Indian Politics" in *Caste in Indian Politics*. New Delhi: Orient and Longman

Leuthold, David A. (1968). *Electioneering in a Democracy: Campaign for Congress*. New York: John Wiley. Chapter I. Introduction.

McClosky, Herbert and Harold Dahlgren (1959). "Primary Group Influence on Party Loyalty". *American Political Science* Review: 53. pp. 757-76.

McConnell Patrick J and Becker Lee B (2002). "The Role of Media in Democratization". A paper presented at the Political Communication Section of the International Association for Media and Communication Research at the Barcelona Conference, July. Accessed at the website: http://www.portalcomunicacion.com/bcn2002/n_eng/programme/prod_id/asp4.asp?id_pro=1461

Mill, John Stuart (1962). *Considerations on Representative Government*. Chicago: Henry Regnery Company. p. 170.

Mishra, Kirti (2005). "Growing Discontent of Adivasis in Assam". April 12. http://www.countercurrents.org.

Myron Weiner (1978). *India at the Polls: The Parliamentary Elections of 1977*. Washington: American Enterprise Institute.

Nirbashani Istahaar, Asom Gana Parishad. (2004). *Chatur Daksh Loka Sabha Nirbashan*. Election Manifesto, Asom Gana Parishad, 14th Lok Sabha Polls.

North East News Agency (2005). "BJP eyeing for Assam". Special Report. Vol. 3, Issue No. 29. June 7-21. http://www.nenanews.com.

Pai, Sudha (2002). "Parliamentary Elections in Contemporary India –Breakdown of Dominant Party System and Ascendancy of Regional Parties" in Arun K Jana & Bhupen Sarmah (eds.) *Class, Ideology and*

Political Parties in India. New Delhi: South Asian Publishers Pvt. Ltd. p. 68.

Pakem, B. (1997). *Insurgency in Northeast India.* New Delhi: Omson Publication.

Palmer, Norman D. (1976). *Election and Political Development: The South Asian Experience.* New Delhi: Vikas. P.1.

Pathak, Geetartha. "Tea Garden Labour Neglected in Assam". http://www.dayafterindia.com.

"Polarisation and Consensus"(1999). *Economic and Political Weekly,* Vol. XXXIV, No. 34-35. August 21– 27/28, September 3.

Police Records, Government of Assam.

Prabhakar, M.S. (2002). "The Bodo Question", *Frontline.* Volume 19, Issue 15. July 20 - August 02.

_________. (2003). "Promises and Problems". *Frontline.* Volume 20, Issue 05. March 01 – 14.

_________. (2004). "From Agitation to Governance". www.flonnet.com, Vol 21, Issue 08.

_________. (2004). "Northeastern Challenges". www.flonnet.com, Vol 21, Issue 08.

Profiles of some Constituencies (2004). http://www.cpiml.org.

Rogus, Benjamin O. (2001). "Ethnic Parties and Centre-State Relations: The Case of Assam in Northeast India". San Francisco State University. http://www.bss.sfsu.edu.

Rongphar, Borsing (2005). *Karbi Anglongor Rajnaitik Itihas.* Diphu: Fu Fu Publication. Karbi Anglong.

Rosenau, James N. (1973). *The Dramas of Politics.* Boston: Little, Brown. p. 171.

Sahni, Ajai (2002). "Survey of Conflicts & Resolution in India's Northeast". *Faultlines–Writings on conflict and resolution.* Volume 12. New Delhi. Bulwark Books. May.

Sarangi, Prakash (2001). "The Party System in India".

Teaching South Asia: An Internet Journal of Pedagogy. Volume I, No. 1. Winter. http://www.mssu.edu

Schumpeter, Joseph A. (1962). *Capitalism, Socialism and Democracy*. New York: Harper. Third edition. p. 269.

Statistical Handbook of Assam (1999). Government of Assam.

_________. (2000). Government of Assam.

_________. (2004). Government of Assam.

Tea workers' movement is gaining momentum in Assam (2002). June. http://www.cpiml.org

Three Member Experts Committee Report (1991). Government of India: Ministry of Home Affairs. Vol. IV, 25th February.

Tribune India. http://www.tribuneindia.com.

USAID (1999). "The Role of Media in Democracy: A Strategic Approach", *Centre for Democracy and Governance, Bureau of Global Programs, Field Support, and Research*, Washington, D.C., June.

_________. (2002). n. 2, p. 3.

_________. (2002). n. 3, p. 1.

Vedanti: Burning Assam (Earlier Issues). Various Issues. http://www.vedanti.com.

Vinayak, G. (2004). *Rediff Special*, September 24.

Vision Document (2004). Bharatiya Janata Party.

Weiner, Myran and John Osgood Field (1975). "How Tribal Constituencies Vote" in *Studies in Electoral Politics in Indian States*. New Delhi: Manohar. Vol. II. Chapter II.

Yadav Y (2004). "Elusive Mandate of 2004". *Economic and Political Weekly*. Vol. 39. No. 51, December 18, p. 5394.

Newspapers consulted

Amar Asom, Dainik Janambhumi, Pratidin, The Assam Tribune, The Sentinel & The Telegraph

Index

O

P